A Leaven of Ladies

A History of
The Calgary Local Council of Women

Marjorie Norris

Detselig Enterprises Ltd.

Calgary, Alberta, Canada

© 1995 Marjorie Norris

Canadian Cataloguing in Publication Data

Norris, Marjorie, date
  A leaven of ladies

Includes bibliographical references.
ISBN 1-55059-123-1

  1. Local Council of Women of Calgary—History.   I. Title.
HQ1910.C35N67   1995   305.42′06′0712338   C95-910473-9

Detselig Enterprises Ltd. appreciates the financial assistance received
for its 1995 publishing program from the Department of Canadian Heritage, the Canada Council and the Alberta Foundation for the Arts, a
beneficiary of the Lottery Fund of the Government of Alberta.

Detselig Enterprises Ltd.
210, 1220 Kensington Rd. N.W.
Calgary, Alberta, Canada
T2N 3P5

Cover Design by Dean MacDonald.

Printed in Canada   ISBN 1-55059-123-1   SAN 115-0324

Contents

ᑲᑐ ᑲᑐ ᑲᑐ ᑲᑐ

Preface v

PART I   HISTORY

Chapter 1   The Council, the Countess and Calgary 13
*Introduction, American Roots, Canada's Council Founded –
Countess Accepts Presidency, The Mothering Mission, Their
Excellencies – The Divinity Which Doth Hedge a King, Lady
Aberdeen's British Credentials, The Young City, Twelve Hours
of Calgary Hospitality, A Command Performance at the Opera
House, The Founding Meeting, The Charity Ball*

Chapter 2   The Mothering Endeavor 29
*Lady Lougheed Made Alberta's First National Vice-President,
Calgary Local Council's First Annual Meeting, A Curfew Bell
– The First Petition, The Calgary Relief Committee – Suffering
Alleviated, Civic Finances – The Velvet Glove Lay Undis-
turbed, Indian Famine Fund – An ICW Charitable Cause,
Victorian Society's Ways and Means, In Hospital Aid Service,
Local Council's Waning and Suspension, The Aberdeen's De-
parture, Post Script*

Chapter 3   A Canadian Organization Better Suited 43
*A New Presence, Social Conscience Raising, Civic Indifference
and Voter Reaction, Timing the Women's Civic League/Local
Council Option, Local Council Launched, Maude Riley to the
Fore, Voter Canvass Leavened by Frost, The Women's Forum
– A Tactical Triumph*

Chapter 4   Positioning for Power 59
*The Club Scene, Local Council Mounts Broad Membership
Campaign, WCTU Claims Honor of Being First to Join, The
YWCA Holds the Balance of Power, First Annual Meeting
Reconvened, Procedural Wrangles Not Uncommon, Forty-
Seven Societies Provide a Broad Base, Local Council's Hand-
maiden Role, Frank Opinions Were the Mode of the Times, How
La Crème Rose to the Top*

Chapter 5   Out with Moral Stave and Shovel 81
*The Agenda Furore, Recycling – The Curfew Bell, The Virtue
of Thrift – Copper Coinage, The Ruthenian Problem, Equal
Franchise – Theirs for the Asking, The Woman's Platform*

Chapter 6   Weaving Golden Threads of Thought 101
             Rising to the Occasion, Actual Progress and Aspirations, Tensions – The Old Guard Versus the New, Want Women in the Senate Forthwith, Banquet Closes in Stately Style, Epilogue

Chapter 7   Silver Threads Among the Gold 117
             A Standing Ovation and a Surprise Osculation

             Epilogue 121

PART II   **HIGHLIGHTS**
Chapter 8   Annie Foote and Gender Balance 131
             Calgary's First Woman School Trustee

Chapter 9   Canada's First Woman Alderman 143
             Calgary's Annie Gale

Chapter 10   This Highest Office Yet Achieved
             by Woman 163
             Alice Jamieson, First Woman Juvenile Court Judge

Chapter 11   Wanted? A Woman Policeman 175
             Local Council Versus Chief Cuddy

Chapter 12   Marketing – The Woman's Toy 187
             How Georgina Newhall's Consumers' League Revitalized the City Market

Chapter 13   Railroading Laid Bare 197
             CPR - City Redevelopment Plan Exposed

Chapter 14   Justice Should be Seen to be Done 213
             Local Council's Irene Murdoch Fund

PART III   **LIFE MEMBER AUTOBIOGRAPHIES**
Chapter 15   Eleven Ladies Plus One 231
             Ruth Gorman, Grace Stonewall, Flo Frawley, Frances Roessingh, Beth Hoar, Millie Luft, Marjorie Norris, Margaret R. Buckmaster, Dorothy Helen Groves, Gwen Thorssen, Mary Guichon, Donalda Vine,

             Local Council Presidents 1895-1994 263
             Background Readings 265
             Notes 266

Preface

ඏ ඏ ඏ ඏ

In her introduction to *The Splendid Vision, Centennial History of the National Council of Women of Canada 1893-1993*, eminent Canadian historian Dr. Naomi Griffiths states, "The history of this body reflects the history of the country itself, its tensions and its angers, its visions and its dreams. It is the story of women who worked because they felt they must, within the communities that were, indeed, theirs to build."

A Leaven of Ladies records how Calgary's own Local Council of Women "worked because they felt they must" to better their community. The title is drawn from a June 1913 *Calgary News-Telegram* editorial which gave qualified support to the Calgary Local Council of Women's petition for a City Charter amendment that would make women eligible for election to the office of school trustee. That long ago writer believed "a leaven of ladies" – not a majority – would be of benefit to the Public School Board, and proposed that their number of seats be restricted to a minority, lest unintended consequences result. "It might transpire," the writer said, "that the ladies could carry the whole of the seats in a contested election, and this would not be satisfactory to the citizens at large."

A Leaven of Ladies is a project long delayed. Twenty-one years ago, during my presidency, the Calgary Local Council of Women endorsed a resolution inspired by Mary Winspear and a grant negotiated by Joni Chorny to prepare the Council's history as a commemorative gift to Century Calgary 1975. Instead, fate willed 1994, the city's centennial year.

While researching the 85-year history of Calgary's once-dominant forum and lobby for women's societies, I have emphasized the personal aspect – how prominent members interacted with each other to exert their influence within the Local Council and beyond, how city officials treated them. The focus is on the triumphs, the trials and the defeats of the Women's Council. Look not for a chapter on each decade. Instead I have been arbitrarily selective. The formative years and early achievements for which official records are missing are resurrected in intimate detail from 1895 until the early 1920s. This lost history begins with the auspicious launching of the original 1895 Calgary Local Council of Women by Lady Ishbel Aberdeen, President of the National Council of Women of Canada and wife of Canada's then Governor-General, and Lady Lougheed, wife of Calgary's Senator James Lougheed. After tracing the operation of this short-lived Council under the presidency of Madame Elvina Rouleau, a prominent leader in Calgary's French community and wife of Justice

Charles Rouleau, the acccount moves to the strategy engineered by Maude Riley and Emily Kerby to establish the second and enduring Local Council in 1912. The intimate history of these radiant early years culminates in the 1920s, after Calgary had hosted the 28th Annual Meeting of the National Council of Women of Canada in June of 1921. By then the presidency of the Calgary Local Council of Women was the highest position an aspiring clubwoman could attain. Calgary Local Council last hosted a National Council conference in the spring of 1978 at Banff. By then contemporary feminism had challenged the venerable mothering movement. One reporter captioned, "Senator says Council of Women irrelevant."

Special chapters are devoted to the Council's role in electing Calgary's first woman school trustee, Annie Foote, and Canada's first city alderwoman, Annie Gale, and in appointing the first woman magistrate of a Juvenile Court in the British Empire, Local Council's own president, Alice Jamieson. The stories are told here, as well, of the struggle to have women appointed as police officers and of the war Georgina Newhall and her Consumers' League waged on Calgary's high cost of living. Beyond these early years, only two noteworthy undertakings are highlighted in detail. Ruth Gorman's leadership of Local Council's strong opposition to the CPR's effort to relocate its rail line along the south bank of the Bow River embroiled the women's federation in an acrimonious civic power struggle in the early 1960s. A decade later, in 1974, urged on by activists Patricia Krasinski, Joni Chorny and Dorothy Groves, the establishment of the Irene Murdoch Trust Fund generated publicity and contributions far beyond Alberta's borders.

A Leaven of Ladies closes with the autobiographies of "Eleven Plus One" of Local Council's Honorary Life Members, beginning with that of Dr. Ruth Gorman, the Council's long-time Convenor of Laws, who was honored as Alberta's Woman of the Century in Canada's Centennial Year. Their stories form the living history component – each of them is a rare, personal gift to Calgary's centennial memoirs.

Essential source materials for this history came from newspaper accounts beginning in 1894 and the comprehensive records of Local Council's years since 1920, now in the Glenbow Archives, and from the archival holdings of the University of Calgary's MacKimmie Library. I am very grateful for the interest shown by their respective staff. Fortunately, in the early decades of this century, strong-minded women spoke their piece and literate reporters sketched the scenarios. Selected excerpts from these long ago accounts provided a wealth of restorative color.

Lilian MacLennan's Local Council of Women history, painstakingly organized into a decade by decade time frame, oriented me. Dr. Ruth Gorman launched me in 1991 by sharing her store of information, and Professor Donald B. Black negotiated my faltering steps along the road to computer literacy. Dr. Naomi Griffiths, FRSC, who read my early work, encouraged me and stayed on as an editor, guiding me, when necessary, to make sure I had "got it right." Through Nancy Millar I was directed to editor Beth Duthie and through her to Denise Withnell. Linda Berry handled editing and typesetting for Detselig Enterprise Ltd. in the final publication. These three rare perfectionists edited my elongated manuscript to camera-ready stage. All of their assistance notwithstanding, I accept full responsibility for the content and for any errors therein. Throughout the endeavor Grace Stonewall, Gwen Thorssen, Frances Roessingh, Norma Bicknell and other staunch Local Council former presences stood by me whilst I crafted the tribute which must be paid. Above all others I dedicate this history to them.

If *A Leaven of Ladies* provides a nourishing read leavened with humor for former Local Council members and history buffs, then its purpose will have been achieved.

Marjorie Norris

COMMITTED TO THE DEVELOPMENT OF CULTURE AND THE ARTS

Part One

History

Lady Ishbel Aberdeen
National President 1893-1898
(courtesy of Glenbow Archives)

Lady Isabella Lougheed
National Vice-President,
District of Alberta, 1896-1898
(courtesy of Glenbow Archives)

Madame Elvina Rouleau
Calgary Local Council President
1895-1898
(courtesy of Glenbow Archives)

Chapter One

The Council, the Countess and Calgary

∽ ∽ ∽ ∽

Introduction

Calgary's very first Local Council of Women began under auspicious circumstances, launched by the young city's great and near-great who gathered in the Hull Opera House in the late evening of November 26, 1895. One hundred years ago, a standing room only audience of men and women listened and applauded while the first President of the National Council, Lady Ishbel Aberdeen, wife of Canada's Governor-General, spoke for 45 minutes on the organization's purpose. Anointing messages poured forth from the lips of Church leaders, the Governor-General himself and Senator James Lougheed. In this atmosphere of general approbation, the Senator's wife, Lady Isabella Lougheed, moved that a branch of the National Council of Women be formed in Calgary. The resolution passed unanimously. In closing, people bowed their heads in silent prayer then sang *God Save the Queen*. The Queen was Victoria.

With Lady Aberdeen in the chair, the next morning's founding meeting chose as its first president Madame Elvina Rouleau, leader of Calgary's French community and the wife of Justice Charles Rouleau. Those women who espoused this new federation movement were neither of the "fashion plate" nor "pink tea" variety. Their interests were more philanthropic, more attuned to needs of others, more responsive to National Council's lofty purpose – the application of the Golden Rule to society, custom and law.

Under this new banner, Calgary's women aligned themselves with a federated movement American in origin; a National Council led by a British aristocrat; a Local Council headed by a French-Canadian Catholic. The guiding beacon for all was the Christian admonition, "Do Unto Others As Ye Would That They Should Do Unto You."

In those days, members of philanthropic societies were sometimes called "women workers." They shared a common conviction that maternal instincts especially qualified women to work for social reform, but they differed in how to go about achieving their goals. The more conventional held that women should continue in a symbiotic, complementary relationship with the existing male establishment if they wanted to change society for the better; however, a more activist component wanted to elevate the status of women to equality with men. These suffragists believed that only when women voted and held elected office would they wield the political power necessary to effect social reform. The two ideologies, the mothering and the feminist, would diverge and converge throughout the history of the National Council of Women movement as well as within the Calgary Local Council itself. First launched as a short-lived mothering organization in Calgary in 1895, then resurrected permanently in the momentum of the women's franchise movement in 1912, this city's Local Council of Women now resembles the original mothering society. It may have come full circle.

American Roots

The Council of Women movement originated in Washington, D.C., at the close of the 1888 International Women's Congress, a conference of women's philanthropic organizations. Forty-nine delegations came from the United States and eight other countries, including Canada, England, France, Denmark, Norway, Sweden, Finland, and India. The six-member Canadian contingent included Emily Howard Stowe of the Dominion Women's Enfranchisement Association (DWEA) and Bessie Starr Keefer of the Women's Christian Temperance Union (WCTU). Ideas exchanged on organized philanthropy, legal and political injustice, industrial conditions, temperance, missionary and hospital work convinced the assembly of the need for a permanent international co-ordinating body. Before the Congress closed, delegates launched the International Council of Women. It was to be a democratic, neutral forum where women of different nations representing volunteer societies shared their special philanthropic knowledge, then worked towards consensus on common humanitarian issues.

Although the federated concept promised the power of consensus, there were other fundamental guarantees: autonomy and equality. If prospective affiliates were judged to have aims in harmony with the movement, they were accepted. A member organization was guaranteed its own autonomy, its freedom to pursue independently its own special goals. The principle of equality also prevailed. Regardless of size, all federates within each council – international, national and local – were to carry the same number of votes and pay the same dues. Mrs. May Wright Sewall, the American founding president of the International Council, explained why the peer principle must pervade the organization: "This basic principle prevents rivalry among the constituent parts of a Council, fosters mutual respect based on inherent quality and makes for true democracy of feeling and attitude."[1] They knew the work ahead of them included "plans for action to secure for women greater access to higher education and professional training, with equal wages for equal work, and with the respect for identical social standards of 'personal purity and morality for men and women.'"[2] The attainment of women's suffrage was only one of the early goals, despite the fact that the 1888 Congress marked the 40th anniversary of the first women's rights meeting held in Seneca Falls, N.Y., in 1848.

At first the International Council of Women movement seemed stalemated, U.S.-centred. During the next five years, the American National Council was the only one firmly established. Nevertheless, the first quinquennial was held at the Palmer House hotel in Chicago during the May 1893 World Exposition. There delegates from women's societies and individual attendees firmed the still nebulous vision into reality. The International Council became more formally structured; delegates were advised on how to set up their own national councils beginning with a provisional founding executive.

Those founders envisioned a three-tiered umbrella federation of women's volunteer societies built from the top down. National councils were to form next, because they were the essence of the international body. Nationally organized societies and local councils in turn comprised the membership of each country's own national council. At the base of the tier was the local council itself, comprising member societies within a particular town or city.

At a time when women were not enfranchised and when there was no social security net, councils of women at every level were to be neutral, democratic forums which identified how the lot of the politically, educationally, economically and socially disadvantaged should be bettered. Under the umbrella of the council, a range of member societies informed and motivated each other, but the council itself acted only when a majority approved a proposed petition or resolution. This slow screening process winnowed out controversial and radical proposals likely to erode the organization's credibility and alienate membership. But it also predetermined a conservative approach to measures intended to better the welfare of the family and the nation. Ideas before their time had to bide their time.

Five Canadian organizations – the Dominion Order of King's Daughters, the Missionary Society of Canada, the Women's Christian Temperance Union (WCTU), the Dominion Women's Enfranchisement Association (DWEA) and the Young Women's Christian Association (YWCA) – sent three delegates each to that 1893 International Council of Women Quinquennial. Now very aware that their disparate kind of representation lacked the authority of one official binding national federation, the Canadian women took a first step towards founding their own National Council modelled on the American one. Mrs. Richard MacDonnell became the provisional vice-president and Mrs. Emily Willoughby Cummings, the secretary. Both were from Toronto. In anticipation that the second quinquennial would be held in London, England, Lady Aberdeen, a delegate from the National Union of Women Workers (the British equivalent of the National Council), accepted the International Council Presidency. Her election was of particular relevance to Canada because her husband, the seventh Earl of Aberdeen, had just been appointed the new Governor-General.

Canada's Council Founded – Countess Accepts Presidency

Four months after the Washington Congress, the Canadian delegation reconvened in September in Toronto to plan a late October public meeting, which Lady Aberdeen had graciously consented to chair. Time constraints excluded contacts with the presidents and executive officials of large societies beyond the central core of Canada, so the Toronto committee limited its 200 special invitations to Ottawa, Kingston, London, Hamilton, Quebec City and Montreal. The presence of the International Council President attracted a capacity audience of 1500 women from every type of organization to Toronto's Allan Gardens Pavilion on October 26, 1893. The organizing committee's inspired decision to ask the 37-year-old Governor-General's wife to head Canada's National Council was the other crucial factor which enhanced the movement's prestige from its outset. Her Excellency was the one dedicated eminent leader strategically able to travel the breadth of the Dominion. When approached by Mrs. Adelaide Hoodless, the provisional treasurer, the Countess at first declined because she felt the presidency should be held by a Canadian. It was not to be: the committee wanted her, and the meeting endorsed her nomination unanimously. Her personal thoughts on this new presidency reveal a sense of anticipation rather than apprehension:

> It is wonderful to feel & see the intense desire & readiness of the women for some such movement as this & it is awe-inspiring to find this work just prepared all ready to my hand – a work to which no one can take exception, as it is intended to combine all sections of thought & work, secular, philanthropic & religious.[3]

The Countess believed passionately that women's organized zeal could awaken a nation's conscience and better the society therein. At this time, Canada provided that challenge. The historian John Saywell described the economic and social disparity so evident then in the new Dominion:

> the nation's social conscience had not kept pace with its economic growth, however slow the latter might have been. Railway interests, financial houses, and land speculators gave little thought to the human cost of western settlement, nor did the government. Industrial development and urbanization created new problems of human exploitation of which only a few people were beginning to be aware.[4]

By the end of April, 1894, all of the cities represented at the founding national meeting had their own local councils in place, each launched in the presence of Lady Aberdeen. As the National Council President, the energetic Countess soon seeded new councils while accompanying her husband on his viceregal duties. In her shared viceregal role, this highly intelligent, persuasive mother of four also sought advice from the couple's politically influential friends during their frequent rail travels by private coach across the Dominion. Early local councils formed in towns as well as cities and sometimes during the same viceregal tour.[5]

When the First Annual Meeting was held on the 11th and 12th of April in Ottawa, the cities of Quebec, Montreal, Winnipeg, London, Toronto and Hamilton sent delegates from their local councils, as did three nationally organized societies. Two of the latter group, The Woman's Art Association of Canada and The Girls' Friendly Society of Canada, had aims quite in harmony with the National Council. The third did not. Women's Suffrage was a movement which Lady Aberdeen felt was too controversial to be incorporated in the aims of the Canadian National Council at that time. In spite of this early disappointment, the DWEA joined. By 1893, federation with the National Council of Women seemed a timely option because the DWEA was in a holding pattern after having little success with franchise bills in the Ontario Legislature.[6] But the largest and most powerful nationally organized society in Canada at that time, the WCTU, did not join. Although she was sympathetic to the promotion of temperance, Lady Aberdeen considered their methods extreme, and her judgment prevailed; however, the alienation was not total. Some local branches of the WCTU – Toronto, Hamilton, Ottawa, Winnipeg – affiliated at the municipal level.

Despite earlier pre-conference anxieties, Lady Aberdeen was more than impressed with that First Annual Meeting. Her journal entry dated April 14, 1894, reads:

> *I have never presided over an assembly of women where such attention has been paid to points of order & business-like proceedings & the whole tone has been very high throughout. In fact, the high level has been a revelation to the women themselves – they could not repress their astonishment at being themselves.*

This early preoccupation with points of order and business-like proceedings would in subsequent years prove both a blessing and a curse. It would justly earn the National Council the alternate designation "The Women's Parliament," but it would frustrate and delay decisive action on major issues. Lady Aberdeen also commended the calibre of papers as "remarkably good – very much better than could reasonably have been expected for a first start-off, & the attitude . . . most womanly throughout."

Those first conference papers addressed co-operation in and among volunteer societies, the benefits of women's clubs, and parental responsibilities. Nothing groundbreaking, but rather a practical look at the value and challenges of organized volunteer work and maternal responsibility.

Specific plans for co-ordinated action, in the form of resolutions, were debated before the conference closed. Two of them, one requesting provincial governments to appoint police matrons and another calling for the appointment of female inspectors to factories and workshops employing women, passed unanimously. The resolution urging the National Council to work for the introduction of manual (housekeeping) training for girls into the public schools passed after considerable discussion. These first two resolutions evidenced a common concern for the protection of women afoul of the law and for the exploitive industrial conditions under which women worked, while the third acknowledged that women needed training different from men to fill their role in society. More importantly, with these resolutions the Parliament of Women had embarked upon its political lobbying course.

Lady Aberdeen's greatest anxiety was whether the women's council concept had attracted broad-minded leaders, "the really nice and influential women." This new movement ran counter to the convention that each women's society had a specific goal "to promote either directly religious or missionary work, or women's suffrage work, & so the idea of an organization simply to bind together all workers, to get them to know and appreciate one another & to unite for common purposes was difficult to inoculate." Reassured that the old narrow mold was now broken, she wrote, "it has been done and we have got capital women together & we are thankful to see from whose hands the movement has been delivered."[7]

High calibre women workers had responded, had accepted the federation's Confession of Faith which remains relatively unchanged to this day:

> We, Women of Canada, sincerely believing that the best good of our homes and nation will be advanced by our own greater unity of thought, sympathy and purpose, and that an organized movement of women will best conserve the highest good of the Family and State, do hereby band ourselves together to further the application of the Golden Rule to society, custom and law.[8]

The Mothering Mission

Lady Aberdeen made it clear from the outset that she wanted the members' overriding mission to be mothering. "We are not all called upon to be mothers of little children, but every woman is called upon to 'mother' in some way or another," she said, "and it is impossible to be in this country, even for a little while, and not be impressed with a sense of what a great work of 'mothering' is in a special sense committed to the women of Canada."[9]

By mothering, Lady Aberdeen meant women extending their maternal commitment beyond their homes to better conditions in their own community and across the nation. In truth, not all could spare the time and money required to mother in this wider sphere. Within ladies' societies it was often the elite, whose husbands could afford to hire domestic help, who were more free to undertake good deeds in their chosen organization. As well, ladies from the few prominent families added welcome prestige to the groups and worthy causes they headed. A noteworthy, supportive husband's initials after "Mrs." provided an additional credential, especially if the husband was politically influential or served on the men's board of the church, hospital or some other volunteer organization rendering social service to the community.

Their Excellencies – The Divinity Which Doth Hedge a King

Lady Aberdeen enjoyed the full support of her devoted husband in this pioneer Canadian effort to co-ordinate women's energies for the betterment of society in general. Born and bred Presbyterians, their Excellencies were probably the most reform-minded, devout couple ever to serve as the Queen's representative in Canada. On his mother's side, Oxford-educated Lord Aberdeen was a descendant of John Knox, the 16th century Scottish Reformation leader. Lady Aberdeen, née Ishbel Maria Majoribanks, daughter of Lord Tweedmouth, was molded as a young child by a devout mother whose "deeply religious character and ardent faith" made "things eternal a great reality" in her own life.

Throughout their marriage, the Aberdeens remained close friends of the British reformer Prime Minister William Gladstone and his wife. Philosophically, the couple also shared Gladstone's idealism – a total commitment to the social gospel of the Liberal party. They likened Liberalism to "the Christianity of politics" and believed "those who take service under its banner must apply its principles to all relations of life, both public and private."[10] It was Lord Aberdeen's strong Liberal and personal ties with Gladstone which resulted in his being appointed Lord Lieutenant of Ireland in 1886. To the couple's disappointment, however, this term of office terminated a brief five months later with the defeat of the Gladstone government. When the Liberals returned to power in Britain, the Aberdeens hoped to be returned to Ireland. Instead, Gladstone offered them a different choice: India or Canada. Based upon favorable impressions gained during two previous trips to the young Dominion, the Aberdeens chose the latter. In accepting viceregal office, the Aberdeens were expected to eschew politics, but their unwavering dedication to Liberalism and its social reform movements caused tensions during Conservative rule and within the rather rigid Canadian social establishment itself.

Lady Aberdeen's British Credentials

The Countess was a charismatic woman of strong social conscience, indomitably devoted to causes which bettered the lot of the underclass. Without doubt she was an over-achiever, schooled from childhood to excel. Throughout her life this deep sense of personal commitment sometimes undermined her own health. In trying to meet all her family, social and philanthropic obligations, she suffered a major collapse in mid-1889.[11] Thereafter she endured recurring blinding headaches and periods of depression.

To Katherine Tynan, who worked with her for many years and knew her well, we owe this vivid verbal portrait:

> She was a big, handsome woman, with a warm, soft personality that seemed to reach out and envelop her friends and associates. Inwardly reserved and shy, outwardly she possessed a compelling frankness and an infectious, somewhat boyish, gaiety; secretly often depressed and fearful, she maintained a front of unshakeable optimism. She was that peculiar combination of a democrat-aristocrat. She could work with people of all kinds, ignoring distinctions of birth and occupation, airing views that bordered on socialism, and supporting trade unions and co-operatives. . . . in appearance and manner Lady Aberdeen was every inch a grande dame of the aristocracy who could when she chose mount the pedestal of her position and gaze coldly upon those who had presumed upon her democratic spirit.[12]

The Countess's volunteer background fitted well with the young Council of Women movement in Canada. Her most viable asset was practical knowledge acquired during years of leadership in British mothering societies and women's suffrage organizations.[13]

To some, Lady Aberdeen's participation in particular causes seemed inappropriate for a woman of her political and aristocratic status. A case in point, the Strand Rescue Mission offered a personal opportunity for Lady Aberdeen to salvage life's unfortunates in London's famous theatre district. This mothering effort centred on the young street girls who loitered in the evening outside theatres after the plays had started. A rescue team of two mission members would invite the girls to come along with them for a nice warm cup of tea, words of sympathy and a "saving" chat. Lady Aberdeen felt her own efforts bore fruit, but not without a certain blemish being cast upon her status. "My people did not much like my undertaking this, even though A. approved. So they went to Mr. Gladstone and asked him to dissuade me. But he stood by me, too. 'If she hears a call to do this, she should go,' he said."[14]

In the Aberdeen memoirs she likened her Women's Liberal Federation experiences to a "a wonderful school of training, the gateway to endless opportunities," even though a fractious 1892 English Federation resolution calling for the adoption of women's suffrage as a goal did cause her great stress and difficulty. As recounted by Lady Aberdeen, the proposed policy change also compromised Prime Minister Gladstone and his wife.

When it was known that the English Federation was going to make women's suffrage one of its goals, two strong parliamentary opponents, Sir William Harcourt and the chief whip, Mr. Arnold Morley, were so upset that they suggested the Prime Minister's wife should resign her presidency of the Federation. But Lady Aberdeen, who believed it to be "manifestly absurd for an organization of women professing Liberal principles not to demand definitely and work for the opportunity of doing their full duty as citizens," convinced Mrs. Gladstone that it was the will of the federation that she stay to maintain morale. Although the suffrage resolution ultimately passed, 26 associations seceded to join a new organization, the Women's National Liberal Organization. Women's enfranchisement had proven a very contentious issue. In that spring of 1892, the Countess wrote to the aging William Gladstone, now in his fourth and final term of office, apologizing for causing her loyal friend extra worry at a time of great anxiety. His reply indicated more concern for the stress she had suffered:

> *My Dear Lady Aberdeen, – Undoubtedly the addition of Woman Suffrage to my cares in connection with the masculine part of creation has been a little less than convenient, but I feel and think more of the real and urgent weight which you have had to carry, in your intermediate position.*[15]

In reality, this new prime ministerial care was not at this time a burdensome one. Although an enfranchisement petition had been presented to Parliament as early as 1867, that effort and subsequent bills failed. The opposition was just too widespread, for in Britain, the women greatly outnumbered the men. Powerful politicians such as Harcourt and Morley considered equal suffrage an intolerable prospect which threatened to overwhelm the existing male-dominated political system. More than 20 years would elapse before the women of Britain were granted even limited suffrage. In early 1914, the House of Lords passed a women's enfranchising bill restricting the vote to those 30 years of age and older, to householders and wives of householders. These requirements served to "reduce the number of women voters, so that they should not be in a majority."[16] In those times, "the powers that be" hedged their bets.

Meanwhile, beyond the sceptred Isle, in a loyal territorial outpost of empire such as Calgary, where Queen Victoria provided the model of exemplary womanhood, local churchwomen identified much more with the Countess of Aberdeen's conventional Victorian commitment.

The Young City

In the late 1890s, Calgary was still in its formative years, having attained city status in 1894, the year before the Local Council of Women formed. Its heritage was British through and through. The Royal Northwest Mounted Police, the old country ranching gentry and the Canadian Pacific Railway brought British blood, British law and order and British money to Calgary.[17] But in those frontier years of the late 19th century there was an emerging presence which grew as land-hungry farmers and ranchers trekked across the border to settle on free land in Alberta. Lady Aberdeen, ever the journalist-commentator, noted that American component. While journeying north from Calgary in early August of 1895, the

Countess identified the threat of U.S. values eroding British ones and urged that no quarter be given.

A large number of immigrants from the U.S.A. are arriving, many of them originally Eastern Canadians, who have by no means realized their golden dreams of the Western States. It is to be hoped that they will leave all U.S.A. ideas behind them & realize that they have returned to a country where freedom & liberty exists for all & not for some, where law and order are respected, & where treaties with Indians are respected. A great number of these new immigrants are doing well & heartily glad to be British citizens, but there is a remnant who would like to introduce American ideas as to what conduct "in the West" should be. These must be dealt with ruthlessly, & the magistrates and N.W. Mounted Police are determined that this shall be the case . . . , if they can manage it. Our desire for the country to be filled up must not lead to any undue leniency towards these newcomers.[18]

She need not have feared. Calgary historian Max Foran has evaluated the British element as being so dominant that, immigration from other European countries and the United States notwithstanding, the original British values would endure for decades up to World War II.

Twelve Hours of Calgary Hospitality

In October of 1894, the Governor-General and his wife paid an official visit to Calgary. Fortunately for historians, during these years Lady Aberdeen kept a superbly detailed journal which later provided the definitive account of Canadian politics and society of that period. In her journal she recorded personal impressions of that October 12th visit, the events planned in honor of the viceregal couple, and the people they met. During that fully scheduled day, Lady Aberdeen explored the possibility of forming an Aberdeen Society and consulted with a few prominent leaders interested in founding a Local Council of Women.

Lady Aberdeen's impressions of that day – not all of them complimentary – began with their train's arrival at eight o'clock in the morning:

It is a real relief to get here with the tips of the rockies showing over the edge of the horizon like little painted toy hills – but convincing one that the dreary prairies are left behind. This little prosperous looking town with its stone buildings has enlarged itself a good deal since we were here & remembers that it means to be an important place someday as the capital of Alberta. Meanwhile it is feeling the depression a good deal.[19]

The Countess then described how their Excellencies coped with an exhausting 12-hour program of events which began at 10:45 a.m., when they were met by Mayor Wesley Orr, Senator James Lougheed and a Mounted Police escort. The entourage conveyed by two four-in-hands proceeded directly to the Hull Opera House, where civic officials, school trustees and school children awaited, each group prepared to present a formal address of welcome. The Governor-General responded to civic officials first, then to the trustees and school children together. Lady Aberdeen did not accompany her husband on his tour of the YMCA, but they both visited the Roman Catholic convent and school run by the Sisters of the Faithful Companions of Jesus to hear the musical program prepared in their honor. The Countess describes these children as being "prettily shy, an attitude not often seen amongst Canadian children." During the tour of the Holy Cross Hospital operated by the Grey Nuns (Sisters of Charity), Lady Aberdeen noted the presence of private wards where "ranch people & others come in their need." There was no official visit to the General Hospital that day because it had not yet been disinfected after a summer outbreak of diphtheria. Better to err on the side of caution.

At the close of a noon luncheon, Lady Aberdeen contacted Mrs. Barwis, a Calgary lady who Mrs. Wilfred Laurier suggested might undertake the formation of a local Aberdeen Society. Her effort bore fruit, for the Calgary branch formed that month. Named in honor of the Countess, the Aberdeen Society was a kind of literary charity, apolitical and non-denominational. It addressed the problem of the scarcity of good reading material in outlying areas by distributing literature to settlers upon request. The volunteer members appealed for donations of wholesome books and periodicals that were related to travel, biography, natural science and religion and illustrated magazines appropriate for children. Literacy efforts notwithstanding, there was a certain wariness of novels; only "good novels, guaranteed by the name of the author" were acceptable.[20]

Two Indian tribes provided the afternoon's outdoor entertainment. Lady Aberdeen judged the Blackfoot and Sarcee Indian tribe's sports events and sham fight only moderately successful because "the Blackfeet were only warned yesterday, & had to ride in for 100 miles & then ride their wretched steeds for races & assaults." Her further observations reveal a perceptive pessimism regarding their "sad state" and bleak future. The day's outdoor events closed with a mock demonstration of the "tremendous speed" at which the Calgary brigade responded to a call. Following that, Lord Aberdeen returned to their private coach while the Countess attended a social gathering at the home of Senator and Mrs. Lougheed. It evolved into a discussion on the possibility of forming a Local Council in Calgary, a prospect much favored by Mrs. Pinkham, wife of the Anglican Bishop of Calgary. The outcome was a decision to meet with Lady Aberdeen on her return journey.

Calgary's afternoon events were not over. Lady Aberdeen returned to the special viceregal coach to interview a Mrs. McDonnell, who wished to devote herself to good works for the blind, in memory of her deceased blind husband. After sending off a few telegrams, the Aberdeens were again whisked off in a carriage to the Opera House. There "addresses were presented by the Scottish, English, French & Irish Societies & which were responded to in one by H.E. – music in between – a reception of all & sundry & returned to our car escorted by the St. Andrew's men, very sleepy & very ready for an 11 p.m. supper."[21]

The following day, the Aberdeens proceeded to Edmonton, where the Countess founded that city's local council.[22] In her president's report to the Second Annual National Council Conference, she described how the women organized there:

> *His Excellency and I . . . found on the platform at Edmonton a deputation of ladies, who said that they had arranged a public meeting, that they had nominated officers and had everything all ready to start a Local Council; and when I ventured to ask whether they thought that they were quite ripe for taking up this movement, they said, "It is just because we are so far away, we feel that we need to have something that will keep us in touch with the centres of the country, and which will help us to carry on our work here."[23]*

Background readings about Calgary around 1895 suggest a disparate population of around 5000, divided both economically and socially. Besides the emerging establishment whose members belonged in quite a sophisticated social, cultural, fraternal and church milieu, there were many others far removed from such Victorian values and lifestyles. Men outnumbered women four to one. Moreover, many of the men were single, rootless, separated from their families by the search for work. The situation for single women, especially young girls, was not dissimilar. This less fortunate populace who lived and worked in unhealthy crowded conditions created an ever-present social and moral concern, as did the distressing plight of the abandoned married woman with children. Even the more fortunate women with provident husbands worked long hours to raise their comparatively large families. The reality was that more were in need of assistance than were able to give it.

At this same time, the women's church groups were in their early years, having emerged within the last decade. Volunteer service on their behalf was a churchwoman's duty. Five ladies' aid groups formed between 1885 and 1890, the first two being Central Methodist and Knox Presbyterian. The Ladies of St. Mary's Church was formed in 1890, as were the Ladies' Guild of the Anglican Church of the Redeemer and the First Baptist Church Women's Auxiliary. The Central Methodist Women's Missionary Society came into being two years later.

A Command Performance at the Opera House

In late November of 1895, Lady Aberdeen returned to Calgary at the invitation of a committee representing the officers of the various Ladies' Aid Societies who were aware that Winnipeg, Regina, Victoria, Vancouver and Edmonton already had branches of the National Council of Women. On this occasion, the Governor-General's wife also consented to be patroness of the General Hospital Ladies' Aid Society charity ball to be held on November 28th, thus confirming this annual event as the highlight of the social season.

On Calgary's social scale, the November 26th meeting ranked as a command performance, "called at Her Excellency's request with a view to explaining the objects and work of the National Council of Women of Canada." In an era when Christian values and loyalty to Queen and Empire were the accepted beliefs of the social and political elite, this was a prestigious occasion eagerly anticipated by advance notices in the paper and carefully planned by a special committee of officers from Ladies' Aid Societies of Calgary's churches. Notices prepared by the Committee Secretary, Lady Lougheed, clarified that "Gentlemen are at liberty to attend as well as ladies." When the auspicious day arrived, a capacity crowd dressed in their best flocked to the Hull Opera House, cattle baron and meat magnate William Roper Hull's new $10 000 two-storey sandstone edifice to culture. The chandeliered and richly furnished interior was arrayed in patriotic theme: red, white and blue bunting with Union Jacks unfurled from on high. The stage resembled a regally furnished drawing room highlighted by two magnificent candelabra. A profusion of flowers belied the winter season. Gentlemen took the liberty of attending in numbers equal to that of the ladies.

All rose as the viceregal party – His Excellency the Governor-General and Lady Aberdeen accompanied by Honorable Senator and Mrs. Lougheed – proceeded through the cheering crowd to stage. Among those chosen to grace the stage were Calgary's prominent women: Madame Rouleau, wife of Honorable Justice Charles Rouleau, Judge of the Supreme Court of the North West Territories; Mrs. J.D. Lafferty, wife of Dr. Lafferty, a former mayor and co-founder of Lafferty and Smith Banks; and Mrs. Rowe, wife of Amos Rowe, the Dominion lands agent. The eminent gentlemen who later commended the ideals of the Council of Women included the Governor-General himself, the Anglican Bishop of Saskatchewan and Calgary, the leading clergy from Presbyterian and Baptist churches, and Senator Lougheed. At a less luminous level, the Calgary Fire Department band played a scrambled version of the national anthem. Applause was spontaneous and frequent; both newspapers, *The Alberta Tribune* and *The Daily Herald*, printed the full text of the Countess's address.

The meeting opened in formal style, with Madame Rouleau reading the Committee's address of welcome from a beautifully illuminated scroll. Following Lady Aberdeen's cordial acknowledgement, Miss Symons, elegantly dressed in white, presented a glorious bouquet to her Excellency.

Lady Aberdeen's opening disclaimers elicited audience approval. She explained that Council was not a (women's) political organization formed to support a particular party; rather, it was apolitical. Nonetheless, if and when Canadian women formed political associations, these organizations could join. She discounted women's franchise as being the organization's goal but clarified that some suffrage groups were already members of a few local councils, participating on the same basis as other members. These two apprehensions – party politics and suffrage – were laid to rest at the outset.

She then elaborated on the Council of Women's *raison d'être*, one more in tune with local aspirations. It was a federation where all aspects of women's work and interests converged, and the wishes of the majority determined its work. The audience cheered when Lady Aberdeen assured them that although woman's first priority was the home, she must carry the same strength of commitment into her wider mission – mothering. Her call to care for the orphans, the poor, the sick, the tempted and the erring, and to elevate social life through literature and education evoked applause, and still more followed after her reassurance that "this wider life" would not conflict with a woman's home duties. To enhance Canada's future, Lady Aberdeen stressed overcoming divisive ethnic and religious differences through love and understanding. Her eloquent parting entreated the women of Canada:

> to carry that spirit of love, which they already recognize as the principle
> governing home life, into this higher life, and thus from one end of Canada to
> the other we shall find ourselves bound in a golden link of sisterhood, "to love,
> to understand and serve one another."[24]

The men then took the floor, adding impressive, cordial endorsements in more than one instance elevated by patriotic reference to Canada's exemplary Queen. Lord Aberdeen pointed out that as the Council of Women worked in the best interests of the home and society, rather than feign indifference, men should wish their women well in their endeavors. Speaking for the Anglican Church, His Lordship Bishop Cyprian Pinkham pronounced that a women's organization with such high ideals would influence the young city for the better. Reverend J.C. Herdman of the Presbyterian Church echoed Lady Aberdeen's view which attributed the rapid development of womanhood to the example set by Queen Victoria and, in the oratorical fashion of the time, concluded his benedictions with an inspirational quote on women's sisterhood by Victorian poet Elizabeth Barrett Browning: "Might the women of the world become one confederate sisterhood ever onward." Reverend Gold of the Baptist Church also referred to the Queen's lasting influence on womanhood. After speaking briefly on behalf of Reverend Buchanan, the Methodist leader who was called away untimely, Honorable James Lougheed shrewdly noted, "It would be a very impolitic thing for any man to face this audience and decry the movement just started." He astutely assessed Lady Aberdeen as the skillful co-ordinator now able to unify women of diverse commitments into a moral and political power. The active sympathies of Calgary's husbands and brothers, he predicted, would exceed those in any other town and cities where local branches might be formed. Masculine support was thus avowed.

The vote to form a Local Council on a motion by Lady Isabella Lougheed was unanimous. In closing, Lady Aberdeen asked the audience to bow their heads in a silent prayer "for the blessing of God on the work which they were about to undertake." The meeting closed with *God Save the Queen.*

The Founding Meeting

Their mothering mission thus blessed, the ladies convened at the Opera House the next morning to found a Calgary Local Council of Women. With Lady Aberdeen in the chair, the constitution was explained further and officers elected as follows: president, Madame Rouleau; first vice-president, Mrs. J.A. Lougheed; second vice-president, Mrs. J.D. Lafferty; third vice-president, Mrs. Amos Rowe; fourth vice-president, Mrs. J.R. Costigan; corresponding secretary, Mrs. George MacDonald; recording secretary, Mrs. Horace Harvey; and treasurer, Mrs. D.W. Marsh. These and the presidents of all affiliating societies, who automatically became ex-officio vice-presidents, comprised the executive committee. Meetings were to be held monthly in the post office, but in fact, they were judiciously elevated to a higher locale, the court house. Women's societies would be invited to join for a fee of two dollars.

After wishing the new Calgary Local Council of Women success, Lady Aberdeen warned the novices against becoming discouraged. When the Countess left Calgary she was able to write on November 26th in her notebook: "Calgary Council formed . . . Mdme. Rouleau President . . . good meeting."

The Charity Ball

Although the Countess and her husband were unable to remain for the charity ball, their patronage added such prestige that the event was described as "The best ball Calgary has had for years." Mesdames Pearce, Lafferty, Lougheed, Symons, Douglas, Rowe, Lindsay, Perley and Allan co-ordinated the event so that the elegant drawing room furnishings used for the November 26th meeting were retained for the evening of November 28th to provide a gathering area where chaperones could, "meet and admire the fleeting visions of beauty which passed before them."[25] In its account the *Alberta Tribune* rated the 200 dancers who crowded the ballroom floor (viewed by an equal number of onlookers) as being possibly the best dressed ever seen in Calgary. An impressive compliment given that Calgarians followed British custom, requiring formal dress for many occasions. The reviewer playfully justified the expensive fashion of large puff-sleeved dresses then in vogue: "In the dreadful crush of the early dances, it was found that those much abused 'superfluities' formed excellent pneumatic buffers; which, by lessening the shock of inevitable collisions, doubtless saved many lives."[26] The gala evening raised $402; ticket sales amounted to $308.65 and the remainder came from donations.

The visit of the viceregal couple was a triumph. Both Lord and Lady Aberdeen had cultivated the ability to recall previous acquaintance so well that they had enshrined themselves in local memory. At the close of their short sojourn, a literate reporter for the *Alberta Tribune* tendered a regal compliment, "The 'divinity' which 'doth hedge a king' manifests itself in their Excellencies' case by general affability."[27]

Chapter Two

The Mothering Endeavor

~ ~ ~ ~

Lady Lougheed Made Alberta's First National Vice-President

Calgary Local Council's links with National were soon forged. Upon her return to Ottawa, Lady Aberdeen sponsored Calgary's affiliation, and when National held its annual meeting in May of 1896, Lady Lougheed was elected the vice-president for the district of Alberta. National Council's Third Annual Meeting memorandum revealed the diplomacy involved in this innovative move:

> In the case of the North-West Territories, where no Vice-President had been elected before, two ladies were nominated for the post – Mrs. Lougheed, by Calgary, and Madame Forget, by Regina. In consideration of the great distances which have to be travelled in the North-West, it was decided that a Vice-President should be appointed for each Territory and thus Mrs. Lougheed has been elected Vice-President for Alberta, and Madame Forget for Assiniboia.[1]

Lady Lougheed continued to hold that prestigious office after the Calgary Local Council had ceased to function.

Calgary Local Council's First Annual Meeting

Rarely does an organization's finest hour occur at its founding, but this seemed to be the case with Calgary's first Council of Women. Two innovative proposals – the institution of a city curfew and the introduction of sewing and knitting classes in Calgary's public schools – remained pending matters under consideration by City Council. Moreover, its more successful commitments – service on the Calgary Relief Committee and raising monies for the International Council of Women's Indian Famine Fund – were not exactly innovative undertakings.

Calgary's First Annual Meeting was held within a few weeks of its founding on January 10, 1896, with Madame Rouleau presiding and the original executive unchanged except for the addition of a fifth vice-president, Mrs. Freeze. Madame Rouleau, who held the presidency until the Women's Council disbanded, had come to Calgary with her husband, the district's stipendiary magistrate. (One obituary notice refers to her having arrived in the city in the spring of 1885 after fleeing Battleford, Saskatchewan, "in a most wonderful escape from the Indians" during the Riel Rebellion.)

At that first annual meeting, nine local groups affiliated, others were pending and most of the remaining women's societies were represented. Although these nine were not identified in contemporary newspaper accounts, 11 federated societies were named three months later when the Calgary Local Council of Women submitted its first annual report to the National Council. Church societies predominated, and the mix was inter-denominational: the Catholic St. Mary's Church Ladies' Aid Society; the Methodist Church Ladies' Aid Society; the (Anglican) Church of the Redeemer Women's Guild and its Women's Missionary Society; Knox (Presbyterian) Church Women's Aid Society and its Christian Endeavour Society. The Baptist Church Women's Auxiliary did not join. There were also four philanthropic affiliates – the Calgary General Hospital, the Women's Christian Temperance Union (WCTU), the Women's Christian Union and the Aberdeen Society. The (Catholic) Convent of the Sacred Heart, an educational institution, belonged as well.[2]

The Women's Christian Union, an early charity, early on became the cornerstone of the Calgary Relief Committee. With the support of local merchants and City Council, WCU members Mrs. Amos Rowe, Mrs. Alexander Allan, Madame Rouleau and others worked to "relieve distress in its many forms." The Aberdeen Society began with a founding membership of eight ladies and joined the Local Council of Women for one year only. Among those receiving literature in the first year (1884-85) were families and bachelors living in the Fort Saskatchewan, Olds, High River and Calgary environs. When the Postmaster General exempted Aberdeen Society mailings from postal charges in 1895 – a gesture in deference to its national importance – this cost-saving measure enabled the struggling young branch in Calgary to send materials to more distant, deprived areas.

At the January 10th meeting, Calgary's fledgling Local Council looked first to its parent for guidance. The National Council executive committee minutes were read, thus directing the novice organization to appropriate municipal projects. Council women discussed the merits of a curfew bell and deputized Mrs. Pinkham, Mrs. Lafferty and Mrs. Rowe to petition city fathers for its implementation. As well, no less than a nine-member committee composed of Mrs. Rowe, Mrs. Shore, Mrs. Robertson, Mrs. Lafferty, Madame Rouleau, Mrs. McHugh, Mrs. Freeze, Mrs. Ward and Mrs. I.S. Freeze was struck to offer Local Council's services to the Calgary Relief Committee.

A Curfew Bell – The First Petition

The idea of a curfew surfaced as early as December 13, 1895, when the following news item appeared in the *Daily Herald*,

The matter of a curfew bell in Calgary is receiving a good deal of attention just now and it is said that the local branch of the National Council of Women intended to take the matter up and get a bylaw passed for a bell to be rung each evening warning all boys and girls under 16 years of age to get home or be subject to arrest by the police.[3]

The notice closed on an encouraging note; such a bylaw would receive the community's "approbation."

Hopes were high for this initial sortie into the field of local government. The community was receptive, and the policy had its blessing from on high, where National Council felt that a curfew was one way of returning to parental control those children who roamed freely in the streets. The simple, hand-written petition dated January 26, 1896, signed by Jean A. Pinkham, C. Rowe and Jessie P. Lafferty on behalf of the Women's Council read:

At a meeting of the Women's Council, held on Jan. 7th., it was decided to petition the City Council to institute a Curfew bell in this city.

The Women's Council feel, and feel very deeply that some such measure is urgently required in this town, and would be of great service to the rising generation.

They therefore humbly petition your honourable body to give the matter your earnest consideration.

The city fathers denied the petition because they had no authority in the matter. Permission lay with the Territorial Legislature.

The curfew was not totally forgotten, for when Lady Aberdeen revisited Calgary Local the following December, she encouraged the group to persevere because the Legislative Assembly of the Northwest Territories had since passed legislation giving town councils authority in the matter. The Council in Calgary did consider the proposal but took no action. In March of 1900, some two years after the Council of Women disbanded, the WCTU, an organization of long standing in the community, successfully circulated a curfew bell petition signed by 428 ratepayers. R.B. Bennett, the lawyer who three decades later would become Prime Minister, presented the petition to the City Council on February ninth, 1900, and on March 22nd aldermen voted three in favor, two opposed, with three abstentions. Mayor Cushing declared the vote carried. Unsupervised children under 15 years of age were to be in their homes by 8:00 p.m. from November to April inclusive and by 9:30 during the other six months of the year. Those parents indifferent to warnings could be fined in magistrate's court and if in default of payment, imprisoned. That curfew bell did not last, but the idea did. Over a decade later, the 1912 Local Council of Women would petition for reinstatement but to no avail. Then, almost a decade later, Local Council would try again.

In 1896, following through on another National Council recommendation, Calgary's Council of Women approached civic authorities with a proposal that plain sewing and knitting be introduced into the city's public schools. Alderman agreed to discuss the advisability of such a move, but by the spring of 1897 the matter was still pending.

The Calgary Relief Committee – Suffering Alleviated

Local Council's second municipal involvement, membership on the Calgary Relief Committee, proved very successful: the timing was right. By early January of 1896, the Relief Committee's allocation from city funds was depleted and the charitable energies of the Christian Women's Union were overtaxed by the distribution of necessities to the city's poverty-stricken. Volunteer help from "The National Council of Women" (as it was mistakenly referred to) was welcomed. Mrs. Rowe and Madame Rouleau, and later Mrs. Lafferty, joined Alderman Parslow, clerical representatives and the Christian Women's Union on the Executive Committee. The women's role was to identify needy cases and authorize the distribution of food. Under a new policy, the undeserving would be culled from the deserving like chaff from wheat. The chaff included those "who can go to every ball and concert that comes along, and have their keg of beer in the house." The policy warned that they "will not get free coal in future unless they work for it."[4] Demonstrating true entrepreneurial spirit, the Relief Committee provided a wood yard, ready-to-hand work for the willing and able. Unemployable indigents were housed in a rented shelter.

It was soon evident that amalgamating the city charities saved money, time and labor, with the further result that more of the deserving poor benefitted. The year's work in 1896 was rated "probably the most satisfactory year in the city's history for charitable work." The Calgary Relief Committee procured work for the unemployed; instructed the poor in household economies; encouraged unemployed men and girls to seek work; arranged for shelter of the homeless and for burial of the penniless. Donations of cast-off clothing, food and fuel were solicited.

When Lady Aberdeen congratulated Local Council's Relief Committee members on their efforts during her December 1896 return visit, she cautioned them of "the importance of inquiring into cases, of giving in such a manner as not to pauperize and of organization to prevent the overlapping of charity."[5]

Later, when Corresponding Secretary Mary Macdonald sent Calgary's 1897 report to the National, she commented upon the sense of mission engendered among the Council women who worked on the Committee:

> The members of this organization became deeply interested in this branch of work. Great credit is due them for the efficient manner in which the deserving poor were looked up and provided for. No work is nobler; none can take a higher place in woman's sphere; suffering is the deepest part of human nature; its alleviation must be the purest and most refining outcome of Christianity.[6]

This was the mothering mission eulogized.

Civic Finances – The Velvet Glove Lay Undisturbed

One very early and probably premature temptation to enlighten City Hall, and one that the Local Council novices did not yield to, suggests that the women were hesitant to duel on the civic scene. Within three days of Lady Aberdeen's founding visit, the members were invited to critique civic finances (the major local issue in those days) at a public meeting prior to the impending annual election. Those reading the Friday, November 29th edition of the *Daily Herald* learned the mayor had tossed a velvet glove:

> *The significance of the establishment of a branch of the national council of women at Calgary is already being felt. Mayor Orr has given a cordial invitation to the ladies to take part in the public meeting tonight to consider the city's financial condition, and may probably hear something about civic housekeeping not altogether to his liking. If the ladies take part it is doubtful who will have the last word. The proceedings should prove highly interesting.[7]*

They didn't. The velvet glove lay undisturbed. Follow-up reports indicate the men – and aldermen at that – did the talking. In fact, very few of the fair sex attended, even though in deference to the ladies the meeting was moved to the Opera House and the dress circle designated for them. The 50 ratepayers present were chided for being "dumb as an oyster."

By contrast, in the fall of 1912, the new Women's Council would prove anything but silent observers of civic matters. They would challenge candidates publicly, then ably chair a pre-election civic soul-searching forum.

Indian Famine Fund – An ICW Charitable Cause

The interests of the International Council of Women, over which Lady Aberdeen also presided, drew the new Local Council into raising monies for ICW's relief projects, causes quite in accord with local interdenominational interests. Calgarians were already aware of the terrible sufferings of the women and children of Armenia, where Christians were being massacred by the Muslim Turks. In early June of 1896, a special canvass by Local Council's Armenian Relief committee raised $64. A later, more successful venture was the sponsoring of a charity ball at the Hull Opera House on February 18, 1897, to raise monies for the Indian Famine Fund.

Early that year His Excellency, Lord Aberdeen, with full press coverage, called upon Canadians to come to the aid of another part of the empire – India – where large populations were being ravaged by drought, plague and famine. Generous contributions poured in first from the settled provinces of central and eastern Canada, and it was hoped that prairie people, although less prosperous, would not be "behindhand."

The proclamation issued by Honorable C.H. Mackintosh, Lieutenant-Governor of the Northwest Territories read, in part:

> I . . . appeal to all classes throughout the Canadian Northwest Territories to assist in this noble work. The heart-rending details of want and suffering throughout vast areas of Her Majesty's Indian Empire are too harrowing to dwell upon, and death by starvation should be unknown where civilization is vouchsafed the opportunity of preventing it.[8]

The Lieutenant-Governor requested that all subscribers submit their names along with the amount subscribed so that recognition could be given.

By February 13th the *Tribune* notified its readers that the Calgary Branch of the National Council of Women would give a charity ball in aid of the Indian Famine Fund on February 18th in the Hull Opera House. Tickets at one dollar for gentlemen and 50 cents for ladies were available from Madame Rouleau, Mrs. Lougheed, Mrs. Lafferty, Mrs. Rowe, Mrs. Costello and Mrs. Allan. Proceeds from the ball, $251.25, were forwarded from Molson's Bank, Calgary. Although the sum seemed smaller than that usually raised for local hospital support, Indian Famine Fund donations were also solicited by the *Tribune* and Calgary's banks.[9] The Council of Women's effort was acknowledged in a March third telegram signed Ishbel Aberdeen.

Calgary's Local Council of Women may have overestimated city support for fund-raising projects suggested by National. Its locally federated societies were hard pressed to spare the time for fund-raising outside their own organization. Far removed projects may have seemed less of a priority when the young city's social and entertainment milieu was counted upon as a prime source for fund-raising at home.

Victorian Society's Ways and Means

Charitable organizations depended very much on volunteers to host, plan, sell tickets, and attend balls, dances, carnivals, plays, lectures, and musical and literary evenings. In deference to the rules of Victorian etiquette, a sense of what events were most popular in a certain season and sponsorship by prominent people mattered. In-depth press coverage of important events named the hosts and the guests, described the most fashionable gowns worn by the ladies, the theme for decorations, and identified soloists and performers. In reports of charitable events and causes, individuals were publicly acknowledged for the tickets they sold, and the money, gifts or facilities donated.

Ladies who followed etiquette of the time entertained personal friends at garden parties, afternoon teas, "at homes," five o'clocks and soirees. Being included on certain guest lists was a confirmation of one's social status, particularly if one's name appeared in the papers. When Calgary's single men wished to repay the hospitality extended to them by friends and their families, several would give a Bachelors' Ball honoring previous hosts with the designation of steward and lady patroness. An early January 1896 *Alberta Tribune* notice of one such ball to which 200 people were invited named the patronesses: Mesdames Lougheed, Scott, Rouleau, Rogers, McCulloch, Symons and Howe. The year 1896 being a leap year, the program included two lady's choice dances. Calgary's elite also prided themselves on entertaining visitors from eastern Canada, the United States and Britain, and probably the most frequently mentioned mansion was Lougheed's, Beaulieu, built in 1891. Its prestige was established at the outset. When the Senator and his wife held their housewarming in February of 1892, a local paper listed all of the 150 invited guests – the elite of Calgary and its environs, Edmonton, Banff and Macleod. Thereafter, the Lougheeds generously made their home available for official, charitable and social functions.

Some entertainments which attracted popular support in Calgary are now quite out of fashion. Euchre, a card game where all cards below seven are excluded and where the aim of each player is to take three tricks, was all the rage, played as avidly as bridge in its heyday. Local clergy sometimes chastised their female congregation for expending energies on euchre parties instead of church work, but the game was popular during fund-raising events, where it followed short musical or dramatic programs or provided a timely diversion for *terpsichoreans* who tired of dancing.[10]

The names given to social and charitable events were not necessarily English. The use of French or Italian terms, *musicale* and *conversazione*, for example, lent an air of sophistication to musical and literary occasions. Special events sometimes bore intriguing names. Organizers of a "Conundrum Social" held in Methodist Church in the spring of 1896 prepared a menu with items in riddle form. On this occasion, according to the *Herald* reporter, the conundrums were so difficult that the bill of fare "took longer to interpret than to enjoy." Being a Methodist group, it is not surprising that the titillating libation named "comfort" was a glass of water. Cold, no doubt. "Old maids" were hard ginger cookies, suitably contoured. A cutting revelation for sensitive spinsters. "After the inner man had been satisfied," according to the report, three solos, one recitation, one reading and two quartettes gratified the cultural appetite.

The designation "Panopticon" identified a major fund-raising event. In mid-September of 1895, Mrs. J.D. Lafferty convened a highly successful Panopticon, or Carnival of Nations, sponsored by the Ladies' Aid Society of Knox Presbyterian Church:

> As a spectacle it delighted everybody, and as a means of raising money it surpassed expectations. Willing hands directed by tasteful ingenuity had completely transformed the appearance of the Opera House. Beneath the galleries were erected booths of all the principal nations of the world; and,

*entering, the visitor found himself in a regular Midway Plaisance in minia-
ture.*[11]

Winter carnivals were also very popular major events, possibly looked
forward to with too much anticipation, if one editorial comment is any
indicator. In this instance the *Alberta Tribune* writer referred to the time
consumed by members of the Ladies' Guild of the Church of the Redeemer in making costumes and questioned the appropriateness of this
method of fund-raising for a church:

> There has, of course, been considerable discussion as to the ethics of raising
> money for the Church by an entertainment the name of which is a synonym
> for "The World, the Flesh and the Devil," and as to the propriety of its being
> held on Friday, one of the Church's Fast Days; but whether the masquers be
> inspired by sentiments of devotion or desire of gaiety, there is no doubt that the
> Carnival will be a great success.[12]

Such a chastisement, albeit gentle, does seem unwarranted when one
recognizes that the Anglican Guild was one of Calgary's most active,
hardworking church groups.

In Hospital Aid Service

Very probably, though, it was the hospital aid societies which required
the greatest continuous commitment. The Women's Hospital Auxiliary
owed its origin to a dying Chinese laborer who entrusted his life savings
of $100 to the Reverend Cyprian Pinkham to build a hospital. Soon after
her arrival, the Anglican Bishop's wife, Jean, undertook that obligation,
persevering beyond a discouraging first meeting which attracted only
two Calgary women to a second one at which 47 gathered. Beginning in
1888, she and her first executive – Mrs. Pearce, Mrs. MacKid, Mrs. Marsh,
Mrs. Perley and Miss Myer – joined others to lobby the Mayor and
Council to establish a general hospital in Calgary. Two years later, the
first patients were received in a rented eight-bed cottage. For their part,
the women promised to furnish and support it with gifts and donations.
These members who gave of their own time to sew linens also canvassed,
and sponsored dances, dinners and bridge parties to raise funds for staff
salaries, hospital equipment and supplies.[13] At the time of Lady
Aberdeen's November 1895 founding visit, Mrs. Jean Pinkham was still
president of the Women's Hospital Aid Society, and her executive included Mesdames Lougheed, Symons, MacKid, Lindsay and Allan. By
1895 Calgary's general hospital had moved from its original cottage to
the new sandstone structure on the present site of Rundle Lodge.

Madame Elvina Rouleau was one of the founders of the Holy Cross
Hospital operated by the Sisters of Charity. For its first year and a half
the Catholic hospital was housed in a wooden building, then, in November of 1892, it was moved to a new brick building. Auxiliary support was
given by the Ladies of St. Mary's, of which Madame Rouleau was president. An announcement of one charity ball in aid of the Holy Cross

Hospital named Madame Rouleau, Mrs. J.J. McHugh, Mrs. Costigan, Mrs. P.J. Nolan and Mrs. Costello as members of the committee. In the *Alberta Tribune* of January fourth, 1896, the Sisters of Charity acknowledged their gifts, which included $55 from Madame Rouleau, which came from the Hospital's share of the Christmas sale proceeds, and gifts in kind – a load of kindling wood, turkeys, a ham, a sack of flour, pillow slips, and oranges – complete with the donors' names.

Regular, detailed newspaper accounts of private, social, church and hospital functions recycle the names of early Local Council executive members: Mrs. J.A. Lougheed, Madame Rouleau, Mrs. J.D. Lafferty, Mrs. Allan, Mrs. J.R. Costigan, Mrs. Amos Rowe, Mrs. Cyprian Pinkham, Mrs. Marsh. In those early days, the obligations of these noteworthy community leaders dedicated to Lady Aberdeen's vision of woman's "wider mission" now seem overwhelming. Calgary's volunteer organizations were in their infancy, local charitable needs were great, and the number of women able to work for them few.

The eloquent tributes to Madame Elvina Rouleau, who died in 1901 at 53 years of age, testify to one of those lives dedicated to application of the Golden Rule. The following is a front page excerpt from *The Albertan* and *Alberta Tribune* of May 29, 1901:

> *The deceased lady was one of the first residents of Calgary and we are safe in saying that to all high, low, rich and poor, she was always a true friend to help those in wants, trouble or need of any kind and was in consequence held in the highest esteem and in fact beloved by all who knew her. Her sad demise will leave a blank impossible to fill as no one knows half the charitable and kindly work done by her. It was chiefly owing to her exertions that the noble institution in which she died (The Holy Cross Hospital) was founded and her name was constantly associated with worthy deeds. Her memory will ever live in the recollection of those with whom she came in contact.*

Local Council's Waning and Suspension

Two years after its formation, there are indications that the Local Council's enthusiasm and energies had waned. Regular newspaper notices of quarterly meetings at the courthouse and the annual meeting cease at the end of 1897. Beyond that year there are no accounts of Council work. Because Calgary did not send a delegate to National in 1896 or 1897, it is quite possible this lack of personal contact with the core of the movement further weakened bonds made tenuous by distance.

Some of National's projects which worked successfully in the older, more urbanized areas of Canada could not be replicated in the expanses of sparsely settled North West Territories. When Lady Aberdeen visited the Calgary Local Council in December of 1896, she urged members to raise funds and press for nursing aid to settlers in outlying districts, where women and children were particularly vulnerable to illness and disease. This special service, known as the Victorian Order of Home

Helpers, would consist of uniformed young women wearing a distinctive "VR" badge and trained and tested for competency in midwifery, first aid and home care. Proposals to meet the costs of the service included a one million dollar funding campaign and contributions from the districts employing home helpers.

A committee of the Local Council of Women considered the proposal at its meeting on February 24, 1897. Although members agreed that the million dollars could be raised, the feasibility of extending nursing services in sparsely settled areas was questioned. Instead, the Calgary members favored a more limited popular approach – the establishment of cottage hospitals at larger centres along the railway with nurses and trained workers to offer patient care both in and out of the hospital. At that time there were only six hospitals in the North West Territories.[14]

By the spring of 1897 there were nine Local Council affiliates, two fewer than the previous year. Evidently the organization was not growing. The constitution designated the presidents of affiliated societies as vice-presidents of the Local Council executive. This dual executive role placed a heavy obligation on those women already managing their own organization. By April of its first year, 1896, the Local Council had held six executive and two public meetings, with National's correspondence claiming most of the agenda at three of them. The quarterly meeting, for example, spent so much time on discussions of national resolutions by the executive members that input from federated societies was postponed until the next meeting, when affiliate presidents were to return with the opinions of their own groups. What must have been a rather frustrating agenda imbalance did not cause dissension, for Calgary's first annual report to the NCWC contains the comment "utmost harmony has prevailed throughout."

During that summer the Local Council set up an impure literature committee. "The gratifying report was brought in that only one prohibited magazine was found, while the aid of the postmaster was secured in suppressing any impure literature that might find its way into the district." Not much of a challenge there. The plan to raise funds for a public library for "young men and women of small means . . . often practically alone, strangers among strangers" did not materialize because no viable fund-raising proposal could be devised. When Lady Aberdeen visited in December she encouraged the Local Council members to carry on.

There is only a terse reference to Calgary in the 1898 Fifth Annual NCWC conference proceedings, which should have included at least a report of the work undertaken since the spring of 1897. Instead, it reads, "Local circumstances having led to suspension of work, no Report was submitted by the Calgary Local Council."[15] "Local circumstances" may have been that the Council of Women movement which Lady Aberdeen described with the inspirational word "mothering" was not a new notion to Calgary's women of good works. It was simply an elaboration on what they were already doing.

The Aberdeens' Departure

In early May of 1898, the Aberdeens notified Liberal Prime Minister Sir Wilfrid Laurier that, for private and family reasons, they wished to return to Britain before their six-year appointment came to an end. Their memoirs do reveal that the burdensome cost of carrying out official duties was one reason. Besides living in Ottawa and Quebec City's official residences, the Aberdeens also resided periodically in Toronto, Montreal, Halifax and Victoria. This determination to meet and entertain in other Canadian centres proved very expensive, well beyond their personal resources. Their 1889 purchase of a 480-acre farm on the shores of Lake Okanagan in British Columbia intended for a retreat and a source of income proved a financial disappointment.

The Aberdeens' tenure had not been free of political and social disappointments either. This viceregal couple just could not serve in the traditional politically neutral mold, masking their personal convictions behind the puppetry of protocol. Of the two, the Countess was the dominant one. Admirable as her philanthropic leadership was, her influence in viceregal matters earned her the designation "Governor-Generaless." Nor did the Aberdeens' unwavering political commitment to Liberalism go unnoticed in an era of Conservative government. Their mutual determination to establish the Victorian Order of Nurses (VON), against the wishes of a strong medical lobby and despite warnings that their perseverance was inappropriate to their viceregal role, exacted a personal toll. The historian Saywell also identified the opposition of "the anti-feminists to her well-meaning attempts to increase the influence of women in public life" and noted other dissatisfactions. "Some were offended by their [the Aberdeens'] piety, while others, perhaps equally pious, found their Presbyterianism too exacting. Even more confirmed non-conformists disliked their tolerance of Roman Catholics, Jews, and Unitarians. Temperance leaders were annoyed because they drank; socialites because they were temperate."[16] However, the reason most directly related to the Canada's National Council was Lady Aberdeen's decision that as President of the International Council of Women, she should return to Britain to prepare for the 1899 meeting to be held in London.

Rideau Hall's *châtelaine* had been such an energizing force in the National Council (19 of the 21 Local Councils had been launched by her) that there was serious concern the organization might wane. This did not happen. By the turn of the century, the National Council consisted of 21 Local Councils strung across the Dominion from Prince Edward Island to Vancouver Island. Nine nationally organized societies belonged. The NCWC could count among its accomplishments at the provincial level the introduction of manual training in Ontario schools; the appointment of women factory inspectors in Ontario and Quebec; the appointment of women on school trustee boards in New Brunswick and eligibility for election to that office in British Columbia. On a national scale, Local Councils investigated and identified examples of impure literature. National Council's most ambitious achievement was a national summary of provincial Laws for the Protection of Women and Children, complete with proposed amendments, submitted to the Minister of Justice for consideration in 1899. This seminal project was headed by NCWC's Convenor of Laws, Henrietta Muir Edwards, who in the autumn of 1912 would mentor the formation of Calgary's second Local Council of Women.

By 1900 the National Council of Women had already exerted considerable political influence acquired through deference to prominent politicians and churchmen of the time. The rapport proved mutually beneficial because male leaders assessed the Council of Women movement as a unifying patriotic and moral force in Canada.[17] Lady Aberdeen acknowledged this symbiotic relationship in a 1900 retrospective on the purpose and achievements of Canada's National Council of Women, written from abroad in February of 1900 at Haddo House, the family seat in Scotland:

> the Canadian Women's Council has had the great advantage of working from the outset with the sympathy of many of the men of most weight in the country, who have treated the representations made to them by the Council with that consideration which has given an added sense of responsibility to our members. When people feel they possess a real influence in affairs, they have little temptation to be aggressive, and the policy and fixed principle of our Council have been to trust the men, and to endeavour ever to work in co-operation with them toward the aims we have in view; we have found this policy to be the truest, and we have found our confidence rewarded.[18]

In fact, male interest and support was so valued by the movement in its early years that the National Council considered including men other than as patrons. During Calgary's first year as a Local Council, Lady Aberdeen referred to the prospect in her Presidential Address to the NCWC conference in Montreal.

> There are many of us who think that "the best good of our homes and nation" would be yet further advanced if both men and women could be federated together in this movement which is intended to bring about greater unity of thought, sympathy and purpose, by a mutual endeavour to further the application of the Golden Rule to all departments and relations of life. . . .
>
> The time for this may not be ripe, . . . but let us all remember to keep this evolution in view, and in the meantime to endeavour to secure and retain the interest of our men friends by persuading them to join us as patrons, and by ever welcoming their counsel and their help.[19]

Lady Aberdeen remained as president *in absentia* until she returned from Britain to attend NCWC's Sixth Annual Meeting in Hamilton in October, 1899. Canada's new president was not the wife of the Governor-General, the Earl of Minto, but the wife of Sir Thomas Taylor, the Chief Justice of Manitoba. Lady Taylor, as head of Winnipeg's Local Council, had served as one of National's vice-presidents. This leadership change was in keeping with the Countess's earnest wish that the new National President be a Canadian woman living in Canada and experienced in Council work. In special recognition of her inspiring, indomitable nurturing, Lady Aberdeen was elected Advisory President for Life. Thus the bonds were not totally severed with one of the truly great leaders of her time.

With the exception of two brief periods, Lady Aberdeen presided over the International Council of Women until 1936. Her lifetime of dauntless leadership was acknowledged by Irish Nobel Laureate, William Butler Yeats.

> *To tread the walks of life she stood prepared,*
> *And what she greatly thought she nobly dared,*
> *For she has journeyed far in wisdom's ways,*
> *Has scorned delights and lived laborious days,*
> *And life gives naught without a world of toil,*
> *They still must sow who wish to reap the spoil.*
> W. B. Yeats on Lady Aberdeen

Post Script

When the Calgary Local Council of Women disbanded, it ceased for 14 years. Even when the Calgary newspapers regularly reported the proceedings of the International Council of Women Quinquennial held in Ottawa in June of 1909, there was no reference to Calgary having had a Local Council nor any suggestion that one should be formed. If there was any recollection of the achievements of the first short-lived Women's Council, it may have been that their initial efforts bore little if any new fruit: more was seeded than reaped.

When a post-conference touring party of some 50 ICW delegates representing 22 nationalities and colonies arrived in Calgary by special train on July seventh, 1909, for a very brief visit, there was no indication that the original Local Council leaders met with them. These distinguished ladies were greeted and accompanied by civic officials: Mayor Jamieson, Alderman Mitchell and Alderman Hornby.

> *On arrival of the train, the delegates were conveyed in carriages about the city and afterwards out to the fair grounds, where they spent a most enjoyable time visiting the arts building and other sights to be seen there. Perhaps the greatest treat they enjoyed was witnessing the squaw race at the fairgrounds. This was one decidedly western experience and they were all pleased with it.*[20]

By historic coincidence, Mayor Reuben Jamieson was the husband of
Alice Jamieson, the woman destined to become the first president of a
new Local Council which organized on October 26, 1912. Alice Jamieson
was also destined to become the first woman magistrate in the British
Empire.

Chapter Three

A Canadian Organization Better Suited

∽ ∽ ∽ ∽

A New Presence

When Calgary's original Local Council of Women came into being in late 1895, it was uncontested, anointed by the authority and presence of Lady Aberdeen. When the Council re-emerged in 1912, it did so under less auspicious circumstances and amidst strong competition from Civic League proponents. This time its role had to be more activist – the co-ordination of contemporary social and political reform movements within the community and beyond. And, in the West, women's suffrage was in the offing.

Fortunately for Local Council advocates, their mentor was Henrietta Muir Edwards, one of the eminent authorities on the work of National Council. Vice-president for Alberta, responsible for organizing its Local Councils, her work with NCWC began in 1893 during Lady Aberdeen's presidency. From the outset she was chosen the national convenor of the Standing Committee on Laws, a position she held throughout her lifetime because of her special knowledge of family legislation. By 1908 she had compiled her first summary of all the laws in the Dominion of Canada which pertained to women and children – a comprehensive pioneer undertaking.

Mrs. O.C. Edwards was a leader well-suited to the times, for she had earned credentials in other women's organizations over a period that spanned almost two decades. Much earlier on, in 1893, Edwards had espoused the suffrage movement as a member of the Dominion Women's Enfranchisement Association (DWEA), which later became the Canadian Suffrage Association (CSA). By 1910 she was instrumental in persuading the National Council of Women to endorse the CSA's women's suffrage resolution. Obtaining the endorsement of the conservative NCW was a strategic victory. She was a founding member of the Alberta and Saskatchewan WCTU, which formed in 1905, as well as its Superintendent of Equal Franchise and Citizenship. The WCTU believed that if women voted, moral and civic reform would follow; however, their conviction was not widely shared, since women in general did not understand the power of the ballot. The WCTU's mission – and it required perseverance – was to popularize the franchise.

Calgary's clubs did address suffrage through debates and lectures. In the spring of 1912, the First Street Baptist Young People's Union staged a lively debate on women's suffrage, where "it was evident from the keen interest displayed throughout, that Calgarians are by no means disregarding the great political issue which is before woman kind at the present time."[1] The case for the affirmative: firstly, as one of the governed, woman had a natural right to the vote; secondly, she as a citizen had the "inalienable" citizen's privilege of voice in her country's legislation; and thirdly, full suffrage granted elsewhere had triumphed beyond return. Arguments for the negative: "women were already well represented by their husbands and brothers, and the majority of women were content with things as they were"; "even if women had political power they would not have the physical strength to enforce it"; and, a fear-mongering tactic, "the ladies of the militant suffragettes were sure indications of what might be expected when women entered politics."[2] The decor was green, white and purple – the colors of the National Woman's Suffrage Association; the debaters were all men; and the affirmative prevailed. Just three days later, while speaking on patriotic subjects, R.B. Bennett, KC, MP, defended his staunch opinion that women should not be granted the franchise. The 60 members in attendance at the Colonel Macleod Chapter IODE luncheon were told women "would do far more good" exercising their influence in the schools and homes, "quietly and sympathetically" instead of "mixing in the active turmoil of politics."[3] Although there was no local branch of the Canadian Suffrage Association in the city at this time, representatives were, on occasion, invited to speak.

Local newspapers gave generous coverage to these programs, but they were equally generous in their reports on acts of militant suffragettes, especially those in Britain. When these articles appeared, reader curiosity peaked, as did apprehension. The latter feeling is obvious in a mid-December *News-Telegram* reference to an earlier Canadian visit by Miss Barbara Wylie, the militant English suffragette. The writer gloated over the cold reception that Miss Wylie had received in Ontario and Quebec but worried about the "congenial spirits" closer to home among "the Socialists" of Winnipeg. In this rather nasty account, readers were warned that there must be none of the nonsense of the "shrieking sisterhood" here in Canada – Miss Wylie and her ilk should be deported before "any real damage" could be done. The writer huffed:

> Already in Calgary, the free public library has been used for a lecture by Mrs. Yeomans of Winnipeg, on women's suffrage, which many considered an improper use of a building belonging to the ratepayers, and, if Miss Wylie should visit Calgary, it is desirable that the hospitality of this building shall not be further abused by permitting its use for her purpose.[4]

Such adverse publicity may explain why the subject was treated with ambivalence – discretion rather than valor – by Calgary women until a local issue, the reform of civic government, goaded them into exercising their municipal ballot. Their participation in the civic issue enhanced interest in general suffrage and the power it could engender.

Social Conscience Raising

By 1912 Calgary was the fastest growing metropolis on the prairies. Always a boom-and-bust city, it was in the throes of a real estate boom, attracting newcomers at the rate of a 1000 per month. Prosperity beckoned, but it proved a tarnished coin: one side shining with opportunities for employment and a new beginning; the other dulled by exploitation, alienation and neglect. This contrast was vividly addressed in an April *News-Telegram* article entitled "The Other Half." After describing needy cases visited in the company of a dedicated Associated Charities' agent, the author wrote of a Dickensian world of unfortunates:

Away out here in the suburbs or down by the riverside, rents are supposed to be cheap, although when one finds . . . a family of eight living in a roughly built, unfurnished shack which boasted of one room and an impoverished lean-to, one wonders where the cheapness comes in. After a trip through one of these settlements, one is forced to confess that the homes of the "other half" present a pitifully striking contrast to the magnificent abodes of Mount Royal or the palatial dwellings of Calgary's fine residential quarters.[5]

Harsh realities existed here. In this already overcrowded city nearing 65 000 souls, alcoholism, vagrancy, truancy, prostitution and disease frayed the moral and social fibre of the established community. The many who arrived with unsuitable skills and unrealistic wage expectations were soon adrift, down and out. Families faced desperate circumstance when the breadwinner became ill or died. Children of impoverished and overburdened families roamed the streets, the enterprising ones hustling as boot-blacks, vendors of newspapers, messengers. Friendless young girls employed at meagre wages accepted more lucrative opportunities – the support of male companions or prostitution.

Calgary prided itself upon being a city where volunteer organizations were more sophisticated, where their work focused on prevention. Samaritan efforts by civic, church and community groups provided hostels, shelters and homes for those in need but never enough to meet the demand. To avoid duplicating their efforts all charitable organizations belonged to one central co-ordinating agency, the Associated Charities, to which the city contributed trained staff and funds. Under the direction of its superintendent, Reverend D.A. McKillop, the Association assisted men and women in times of economic distress by granting money in exchange for work, paying rents, and supplying food or essential furnishings. It was hoped that such rescue efforts would prevent pauperism and further attendant problems. The Children's Aid Society was desperately in need of new accommodation away from the isolation hospital. Here, under the direction of Reverend A.D. McDonald, neglected or dependent children were sheltered, sent to foster homes or given medical care. Its greatest pride, however, was in its success at moral reform, when delinquent boys and girls were persuaded to abandon petty crime and immoral pursuits.

The well-established and growing WCTU, in concert with the Baptist, Methodist and Presbyterian churches, proselytized against the unrestricted consumption of alcohol, which they identified as the root cause of many social ills. When Reverend McKillop addressed the Naomi Mothers' Society in July of 1912, he attributed the need for the work of the Associated Charities to intemperance: "It is the cause of eighty per cent of the cases of distress and crime with which the Charities have to deal."[6] He justified the closure of saloons by using the analogy of a test employed to determine incurable insanity. The insane asylum inmate was placed in a room with water covering the floor and a tap still running; if the inmate turned the tap off before he wiped the floor, he was deemed curable. Reverend McKillop emphasized, "And that is what we are doing when we are caring for the drink-cursed victims and allowing the saloons to exist. We are mopping the water but leaving the tap turned on." An insanity, in his view. When prohibition forces won out three years later, theoretically, the tap turned off.

At the end of August, 1912, the Reverend A.R. Schrag delivered a similar conscience-stirring address, "Civic Problems and Temperance Work in Calgary," to the West End WCTU. The Minister lamented, "How slow and measured are the wheels of justice in this city and the reason for the slowness is in the legislation. How often the crime of drunkenness is considered bad manners rather than bad morals!"[7]

Civic Indifference and Voter Reaction

The litany of civic complaints as reported in newspapers of the day included lax supervision of places of dubious amusement (pool halls, dance halls, motion picture houses); a dearth of wholesome recreation centres for children and adults; choice property in residential areas being sullied by a proliferation of unsightly billboards, some of which advertised alcohol and cigarettes, thus adding insult to injured sensibilities; the release of prostitutes to return to houses of ill repute upon payment of a token fine; and, the disruption caused by unruly crowds on their way to and from boxing matches held on the city's outskirts. Such criticisms and complaints seem to have fallen on civic ears, not deaf but more attuned to the purveyors of profits. For those citizens intent on changing civic priorities, the beckoning avenue of approach was the upcoming December municipal election.

Specific dissatisfaction with the ethics and competence of city officials heightened during two notorious cases of civic mismanagement. The first was the woefully substandard paving done by hired contractors in 1911, their work being so faulty that the defects in pavements, sidewalks, curbs and gutters were patently obvious by the spring of 1912. The second civic scandal occurred over the unconscionable neglect of patients at the smallpox hospital, an outdated structure lacking water connections and proper furnishings. Under the headline, "Distressing Conditions Said to Exist in the Pest House; Patient Alleges Barbaric Indifference," readers learned that although the food might be good, patients had to do their own cooking, fumigate themselves, sleep under unwashed blankets and use unclean towels.[8]

An in-depth civic probe headed by veteran alderman James Hornby resulted in the release of the comprehensive Civic Investigation Committee Report on July ninth. In a sweeping indictment of City Hall from the Mayor on down, only one commissioner was spared. The Report recommended the removal of J.T. Child, the City Engineer held responsible for "insufficient specifications and very incapable inspections" of the street work contracted in 1911. It called, as well, for the immediate dismissal of Dr. Estey, the Medical Health Officer, and R.W. Fox, the Sanitary Inspector, held jointly accountable for the conditions at the smallpox hospital. Mayor Mitchell was severely censured with regard to the hospital scandal because he knew of the situation and chose to remain silent. In another instance related to sanitation, His Worship had instructed Dr. Estey to withhold the enforcement of the sanitary bylaw respecting house connections – technically an illegal act. In general, as the city's chief executive officer, the Mayor was censured for unwarranted interference in depart mental matters in violation of the bylaws of the city. The Commissioners were censured for their practice of "saw-off," in which they endorsed each other's projects, even if they disapproved of them, in exchange for support of their own proposals.[9]

Ten days later, and in a lighter vein, the *Morning Albertan* published a front page satire on the paving scandal in the form of a clever parody of Poe's poem, "The Raven." The rhymer, Harry Burmester, attributed his inspiration to this curious news item: "The City of Calgary has an expert who is going about rapping, tapping the sidewalk, to ascertain by acute ear-judgment, whether or not the recently laid sidewalks are of the requisite thickness." The closing lines proved to be prophetic:

Will the people now bemoaning flaws in asphalt and in stoning
Try to plan for an atoning ere the present regime's o'er,
Will they harpoon all the guilty or elect them as before?
Echo answered. - NEVERMORE[10]

The "expert" and aldermanic hopeful was one Thomas Albert Presswood Frost. His initials coupled with his tapping test earned him the irresistible sobriquet "Tappy." The name stuck much longer than the paving materials, and Tappy was later sued for what one might call "Frost damage."

Voter reaction was not slow in coming. On July 30th, under the auspices of the Direct Legislation League, 200 of the affronted citizenry met to form a Citizen's Progressive League. Chairman George Ross explained that the League's purpose would be to generate such interest in public matters that responsible citizens would come out to vote and worthy citizens would seek public office. Civic reform proponents also wanted a co-ordinating body able to translate the women's votes into social and political action. Within the city of Calgary there were now 1600 women voters who, if organized, could certainly impact on civic affairs.

At the local level, Calgary's women had been granted the municipal franchise on the same basis as men for almost 20 years, with one fine distinction. If a wife owned property, her husband could vote as tenant, but the corollary did not apply. Those women 21 years of age and over, married, widowed or single, who "enjoyed the franchise" were property owners to the assessed value of $200, or tenants living in a property assessed at $400. As was the case for men, women could vote for three aldermen in each of the wards in which they were assessed for property. The problem was that many Calgary women did not know they, in fact, "enjoyed the franchise." If these talisman votes were to be garnered, a canvass was required to identify voters and explain their own obligation to make certain that their name was on the voter's list.[11] In some cases, this entailed additional personal effort, including a certificate of proof from the assessor's office.

Timing the Women's Civic League/Local Council Option

Just two days after the launching of the men's Citizens' Progressive League, the women's page of the *Morning Albertan* suggested that Calgary women should now form their own equivalent. The author, who signed herself "An Interested One," pointed out that if women exercised the 1600 votes they already had, they could assure election of any reform-minded candidate chosen by the men's Civic League. She urged:

> There is a great need, right here, of woman's hand in both the moral and social uplift, as well as in the actual civic affairs. We have had unrest and disturbance, in our city government, and while our men have formed a civic league, to aid in the re-construction of said government, what is to hinder our women bestirring themselves, and turning their energies in the same direction?[12]

As their first major move, the civic league enthusiasts scheduled a September 12th women's meeting in Paget Hall. The chairwoman, Mrs. G.W. Kerby, was a strong proponent whose husband, the Reverend Dr. George Kerby, Principal of Mount Royal College, now served as one of the ministerial representatives on the men's Civic League board.

Over 100 women keenly interested in the civic league question heard advocates give inspiring accounts of work being done in American cities. The Secretary of the American Women's Club, Mrs. Heilge, who had gained a detailed knowledge of civic league work while in the United States, likened Calgary to Kansas City, which had faced similar challenges in trying to cope with a rootless population, especially the friendless young girls likely to be befriended for immoral purposes. The League there established a hotel for these girls and had women volunteers appointed deputy policemen authorized to accost any suspect male companion. Mrs. Newhall, who had been a League member in Toledo, Ohio, then listed the achievements in her former city, where 50 women's clubs instituted public playgrounds to keep hundreds of children off the streets. Due to their efforts, sanitation standards were monitored, reported and improved. Again, Calgary was identified as fertile soil for similar seedings. She reiterated Mrs. Heilge's view that the organization should be a federation of all women's societies with no exclusions. Her closing words, "we must have no caste, no dress, only – womanhood," may have been an oblique reference to the status-conscious Council of Women advocates. The last speaker, Mr. Tregillus, president of the men's Civic League, wanted very much to have a ladies' counterpart. Appealing to the women's collective civic conscience, he pointed out that it was their duty to help solve present city problems. His assurance: their vote, well-organized, would have power and influence.[13]

The audience was very receptive until Mrs. Harold Riley, well aware of the potential for competition if another federated organization formed, seized the moment. She urged that a decision on the civic league be held in abeyance out of deference to the impending visit of Mrs. Edwards, who had already been asked to form a local council in Calgary. Mrs. Riley, who had been a committee member of the Edmonton Local Council before moving back to Calgary and knew whereof she spoke, assured her listeners that a Council of Women could accomplish the same work as a women's civic league. The Council was a superior organization: national in scope and thus a strong force for legislation. A Canadian organization, she felt, would probably receive better support from the women in Alberta's other cities. This remark reveals that Mrs. Riley had a more ambitious agenda in mind.

Mrs. Riley's references to Mrs. Edwards, with whom she had worked in Edmonton, and to the Council of Women as a Canadian organization were both well-timed. The fact that Mrs. Edwards was coming reminded listeners of a commitment already made to a respected authority on councils of women. It also reminded the WCTU forces that Mrs. Edwards was one of their leaders. Moreover, due to fortuitous coincidence, the city was in a patriotic mood. Just a few days earlier, the Women's Canadian Club and the IODE had co-hosted an impressive reception in honor of their Royal Highnesses the Duchess of Connaught and Princess Patricia during the viceregal visit of the Governor-General. It was an important occasion for clubwomen because the Duchess was honorary president of both the National Chapter of the IODE and the National Council of Women. The excessively deferential addresses of welcome commended their Highnesses for their ennobling influence on the women in the young Dominion. Patriotic fervor had not yet abated.

This stalling stratagem of awaiting Mrs. Edward's visit worked. Maude Riley's own motion that, "the organization of the league be deferred until after Mrs. Edwards, of Macleod, who proposes to speak about the National Council of Women, comes to Calgary," carried.[14] Thus did Maude Riley sidetrack independent League momentum.

A motion was also passed appointing Mrs. Newhall, Mrs. Jamieson and Deaconess Lampard as a three-member Committee of Investigation into the civic league question. Its mandate was to gather information on civic leagues and to determine the relationship which would exist between a women's civic league and the Local Council of Women. Of the women charged with this responsibility, Mrs. Newhall chaired a committee of the American Woman's Club; Mrs. Jamieson, a founding member of the YWCA and the Women's Musical Club, was also the widow of Calgary's "best ever Mayor" and was familiar with civic affairs. Deaconess Lampard represented the Anglican diocese. It was anticipated that Mrs. Newhall would, upon her return, present the findings of the Committee of Investigation and that the Report would be given at a public meeting where the civic league question would be decided by the women in attendance. Not all happened as expected.

In the interim, examination of the civic league option continued. An early October *Albertan* update informed readers that, "a diversity of opinion" existed, "among the members of the committee, and among other club women in Calgary, as to the relative efficiency of a local council and a civic league to carry out the aims of those women interested in civic affairs." Those women acquainted with the nature and work of the Council of Women preferred that civic work be carried on within its standing committee structure. It was quite feasible. By this time the Investigating Committee had consulted Mrs. O.C. Edwards and the NCWC secretary in Toronto, and the responses were reassuring. Civic campaigns undertaken by local councils had been very successful. The national body could provide authoritative publications on civic bylaws relating to sanitation, pure food, curfew, municipal franchise, education, etc., as well as expert advice.

Others, however, preferred an independent league with members able to focus solely on civic concerns, able to act quickly. *The Albertan* examined this option in the context of the league becoming an affiliate member of a local council.

The independent league could outline a more comprehensive policy than the
local council; yet the united strength of the local council would be behind any
policy which met with the approval of the various other clubs. The local council
is a comparatively slow moving body which is representative rather than
radical, a body of supporters rather than agitators.[15]

The most interesting aspect of this debate is its conciliatory tone. If a
women's civic league formed it would federate with a local council.[16]

Time was of the essence. Capitalizing upon the momentum, civic
league advocates pressed their case effectively while Council of Women
aspirants awaited Mrs. Edwards. Because of her National Council and
WCTU eminence, Henrietta Muir Edwards was much in demand as a
public speaker on temperance, women's rights and enfranchisement. Her
powers of persuasion were well-known in the West. When reporting on
her October 24th addresses to the Women's Canadian Club on the subjects of "War and Peace" and "The Woman's Maintenance Act," *The*
News-Telegram described her as "a forceful, logical speaker, . . . quite
worthy of the reputation which has been attached to her – that of being
one of the cleverest, most progressive women in Alberta."[17] A *Calgary*
Daily Herald writer who described her as, "one of the best women platform speakers in western Canada," predicted that her influence would
be the deciding factor.[18] The Local Council standing committee advocates
sincerely hoped she would, indeed, prove the deciding factor. But they
had to wait until October 26th before Mrs. Edwards was available to meet
with representatives of women's associations to advise on the formation
of a Local Council.

Local Council Launched

In the autumn of 1912, when Henrietta Muir Edwards came to organize
Calgary's Council of Women on October 26th, she was almost 63 years
old and had lived in Alberta for nearly a decade. Her history of commitment to social service went back much further and had its roots in her
devout Baptist family in Montreal. In 1874, as a young woman of 25, she
and her sister, with their father's help, had established a boarding house
for poor working girls in east Montreal, providing them with a reading
room and instruction classes. From this beginning, The Working Girl's
Association evolved. A precursor of the YWCA, the Association also
sought employment for the underprivileged. Henrietta Muir used her
talent as a gifted miniature and portrait artist to help fund these projects.

In 1876 she married Dr. Oliver Cromwell Edwards and moved from
Montreal to medical outposts in what is now Saskatchewan. In the
absence of a Baptist church, she changed her religious affiliation to
Anglican. At the turn of the century, the Edwards family returned briefly
to Ottawa, where Mrs. Edwards served as president of the YWCA and
on the Board of the Home for the Friendless. After a short stay in

Montreal, they moved west again when Dr. Edwards became Medical Officer to the Blood Indian Reserve near Macleod, Alberta.

Despite advance publicity, attendance at the meeting was disappointing, only half that for the earlier civic meeting. Just a few days prior to this, on October 21 and 22, the *Albertan* published two special detailed excerpts of the national and local constitutions on its women's page, "giving definite, accurate information of the organization and work of local and national councils." Ironically, this publicity may have had just the opposite effect. Although impressive, the details of the National's executive committee may have been a bit overwhelming. The committee consisted of a president, an advisory president (the Countess of Aberdeen), honorary vice-presidents (wives of the lieutenant governors), elected vice-presidents, provincial vice-presidents, recording secretary, treasurer, presidents of local councils (ex officio), the presidents of nationally organized societies in federation, and the conveners of 15 standing committees. Those women's groups which functioned simply with table officers, a committee or two, and a few, if any, bylaws must have found the explanation of Council of Women's parliamentary constitution and federated structure dauntingly complex and cumbersome.

The procedure to be followed when preparing the agenda for an annual local council meeting might also have discouraged some potential affiliates whose agendas were already full:

> *A preliminary agenda for the annual meetings is prepared in a similar manner to that described yesterday for the National Council [i.e. sent out to each federated association two months before the meeting]. This agenda is considered and adopted or amended by each affiliated society, and a final agenda incorporating amendments, etc., is then prepared and distributed to each society for consideration at the monthly meeting previous to the annual meeting of the Local Council.*

Despite such prescriptive procedures, the constitution guaranteed the independence of a local council when it affiliated with the national body with one exception. There was a standing order that all matters brought before the provincial Legislature by a local council must first receive the endorsement of the executive committee of NCWC. This restriction meant that municipal government was the only level to which a Local Council could present resolutions or petitions without the NCWC endorsement. In the not too distant future this would frustrate Calgary's efforts to petition the provincial government. Although complex, the constitution of the Women's Parliament did have a prestigious Canadian heritage. It had been drafted at Lady Aberdeen's request by Dr. John Bourinot, then clerk of the House of Commons.

Fortunately for Mrs. Edwards and her organizers, the majority of important city groups were represented by the 50 women who attended the October 26th meeting. The knowledgeable Mrs. Edwards described the kind of work being done in other locals while stressing the importance of avoiding religious and political party controversy, cautionary advice also given by Lady Aberdeen when she came to organize the 1895 Local Council. Mrs. Edwards' recommendation that the officers be representative of as many religious denominations as possible suggests that she may have had some concern that the council be broadly based.

Until the first annual meeting could be held at the end of January, Mrs. R.R. Jamieson was elected interim president, along with seven table officers. Her executive comprised: first vice-president, Mrs. G.W. Kerby; second vice-president, Mrs. E.A. Cruikshank; third vice-president, Mrs. W. Pearce; fourth vice-president, Mrs. P.J. Nolan; treasurer, Mrs. P.S. Woodhall; recording secretary, Miss Burns; corresponding secretary, Mrs. F.S. Jacobs. Calgary now had a Local Council of Women.

The aggregate memberships of these women covered a range of women's groups. As well as having gained experience in board positions with the YWCA, the Children's Aid Society and the Women's Hospital Aid Society, Alice Jamieson was active in the Presbyterian Church. Emily Kerby, as wife of the former pastor of Calgary's influential Central Methodist Church had become the mainstay of both its Ladies' Aid Society and its Women's Missionary Society. She was a charter member of the Woman's Canadian Club and one of those credited with founding the YWCA where she held the office of honorary president. Mrs. Cruikshank, wife of Lieutenant Colonel Cruikshank, became second vice-regent of the IODE (Colonel Macleod Chapter) when it was formed under the auspices of Senator and Lady Lougheed in 1909. She was also recording secretary of the recently formed West End WCTU, on the Management Committee of the VON and honorary president of the Calgary Woman's Literary Society. Mrs. Pearce, who served on the same VON Committee, was also a member of the Hospital Aid Society and the Children's Aid Society. Mrs. Nolan, wife of a leading Calgary lawyer, was regent of the IODE (Colonel Macleod Chapter), and an executive member of the Alberta Woman's Association and the Extension Society of the Roman Catholic Church. A veteran leader in Calgary's central WCTU, Mrs. Woodhall had also served two terms as vice president in the Alberta Saskatchewan WCTU; Miss Burns, a member of the Hospital Aid Society. Mrs. Jacobs, president of the Calgary Woman's Press Club, was also a member of the Business Woman's Club. The interim executive did not include an officer of the American Woman's Club.

The founding meeting addressed the pressing civic league option. On a motion by first vice-president, Mrs. Kerby, the meeting recommended the appointment of Mrs. Newhall, Mrs. Jamieson and Deaconess Lampard as Local Council's standing committee on civic work. Because these women had been appointed earlier as the three-member Committee of Investigation, this motion could have been a pre-emptive move designed to have a standing committee of local council already struck before the Committee of Investigation gave its report. One wonders, however, if Mrs. Newhall, Mrs. Jamieson and Deaconess Lampard felt compromised? They must have.

When LCW's interim officers discussed the standing committee's recommendation four days later at their first executive meeting, there were second thoughts. At this juncture Mrs. Jamieson expressed reservations. As it had been before, the concern was expressed that committee work could be seriously handicapped by the unavoidable absence of its intended chairman, Mrs. Newhall. The LCW executive were then persuaded by their president, vice-president and corresponding secretary to defer action until after the Committee of Investigation presented its report to the public meeting on the civic league question.

Press propaganda favoring a separate organization continued. The writer of an October 30th *Morning Albertan* article entitled "Will Calgary Women Organize A Separate Civic League?" opined that there were many women who preferred an independent civic league with affiliate status over a standing committee appointed by Local Council. Work could be accomplished more expeditiously without time-consuming consensus negotiations with other Local Council members. In further defence of this view, the experience of Edmonton's Local Council was cited. In Edmonton the standing committees responsible for civic projects proved transitory, evolving quickly into special organizations in order to accomplish their goals more readily while still retaining their connection with the Local Council through affiliation. Three days later an item "The Formation Of The Civic League" in the *News-Telegram* attributed some of the civic league opposition to a few patriots who opposed the formation of a civic league because it was an American idea – a rather ironic coincidence given that the Council of Women was also an American idea.

Events took an interesting turn on November sixth, when a very large public meeting was held in the public library to discuss the long-awaited Committee of Investigation Report and to take action. The outcome of those discussions could be attributed to the absence of the convener, Mrs. Newhall, but more likely it was due to a well-organized opposition lobby led by Maude Riley. Mrs. Jamieson read the Committee of Investigation report, which "favoured the organization of an independent league in affiliation with the Local Council as being more expedient and at the same time quite as sympathetic with other organizations, as a committee selected by the council."[19]

Mrs. Jamieson's position was not to be envied. She favored the recommendation; she was Local Council of Women's president; she was well aware that her own executive were divided. In defense of the recommendation, Mrs. Jamieson commented that it could include those women who may not want to join Local Council. Mrs. Jamieson also read a letter from Mrs. Cummings of Toronto, NCWC president. The idea of a civic league met with National's approval, but its form was entirely a local matter.

The reply was a clear affirmation of independence at the local level (a constitutional principle), but that may not have been what the interim executive hoped for.

Maude Riley to the Fore

Persuasive, dissenting opinions determined the outcome. The first to speak in opposition, Mrs. Harold Riley, argued that a separate league would overlap with Local Council while at the same time drawing on a much smaller membership support base. Mrs. Jamieson's second vice-president, Mrs. Cruikshank, also opposed the recommendation, contending that "she could see no other reason for, nor object or aim of a local council, other than for civic reform work."[20] Mrs. Spence, Mrs. MacDonald and Mrs. C.A. Stuart all held that Local Council should be allowed to prove its worth in this undertaking. On the other hand, Mrs. J.A. Clarke supported the report contending that special committees were cumbersome and unwieldy, a case in point being the sanatorium committee of the Canadian Club, which took eight months to accomplish anything.

The impasse was broken by a compromise proposal from Mrs. Heilge of the American Women's Club, which was supported by Mrs. Kerby. Their suggestion that the Local Council give this civic committee all the executive powers of an independent league met with general approbation. A confirming motion granting conditional approval received almost unanimous support. It read, "we, the women here assembled, do not deem it expedient to form a civic league until the Local Council of Women be given a chance to deal efficiently "[21] The standing civic league committee's mandate: it could determine its own membership and carry out work without prior consultation unless the added support of Council's affiliates was desired. The constitution required that the convenor and officers be appointed by Local Council. Compromises notwithstanding, it was Maude Riley who carried the day.[22]

Newspapers tracked the progress of the newly formed LCW Civic Committee because of the impending municipal election and the potential 1600 women voters. With its officers and some policies predetermined by the Local Council, the Civic Committee launched a public organization meeting. Two categories of membership were solicited: a representative from every organization in Calgary; individual women interested in civic work. Women were assured that the committee was empowered to appoint subcommittees and to initiate campaigns without reference to the Local Council of Women.

Many were called but few came. Very few. Only 16 interested ladies, one one-hundredth of eligible women voters, met to plan strategy when the Civic Committee held its first public meeting at the library on November 25, 1912. Not an auspicious beginning – more like a boycott – but what transpired proved very interesting indeed.

Voter Canvass Leavened By Frost

The press – understood to have been invited – were frozen out, and a select guest, Mr. "Tappy" Frost, warmly welcomed in. A motion to exclude reporters now and henceforth was supported unanimously. As chairman pro tem, Mrs. J.A. Clark, urged "Many things which will be discussed at our meetings would be harmful to the public." *The Albertan* reporter meekly retired. Whereupon Mr. Frost, aldermanic candidate in Ward I and secretary-treasurer and envoy of the men's Civic League, was admitted to the "enclosure," whereupon he advised the ladies on how to canvass and card index the names of women voters. For exemplary illustrative purposes, the former Baptist minister used voter cards from Ward IV. The following day the *Albertan* sniped, "It is understood that these sixteen women will attempt to canvass the women voters of Calgary, . . . for a purpose not allowed to be printed in the local papers." The chairman of the Ministerial Association then added his group's corporate blessing and assurance of co-operating with the "secret plans of the assemblage." A final tidbit presented as leaked information was that a letter was being sent to Calgary's women voters who could not be personally canvassed, "asking them to be sure to go out and vote 'with as much intelligence as possible' on election day."[23] In those days, intelligence meant information.

Mrs. Clark's explanation that the press was being excluded because matters under discussion "would be harmful to the public" was certainly tactless if not downright offensive, in light of the fact that this committee was hoping to attract a large number of city women to its ranks. What she probably meant was that the meeting would discuss election strategies. One strategy was soon evident. The Civic Committee sent a letter to Calgary's women voters notifying them of a public forum on December six, 1912, where the 40 candidates for the offices of mayor, alderman, and commissioner would be invited to speak to women voters. For their part, the women voters were to assess who would be "the most moral and progressive" candidate worthy of their support. Voters' lists were available for the benefit of women who wished to ask questions and confirm their eligibility. This time many voters came.

The Women's Forum – A Tactical Triumph

Local Council of Women and its Civic Committee set a precedent at its first public forum. The editorial writer for the *Morning Albertan* lauded it as "better attended than any other municipal campaign meeting . . . , better conducted, . . . more interesting, . . . the most businesslike meeting that has been held."[24] This newspaper, ardently behind the clean-up-the-city-with-clean-candidates campaign, headlined its detailed December seventh front page coverage "Candidates Raked by Merciless Fire of Cross Questioning by Women."

Mrs. Kerby, who chaired the meeting, rallied the women by repeating the comment of a man she had overheard on Eighth Avenue: "We could run these elections all right if only these darned women could be kept out." The candidates themselves were called to account by being required to address a prepared list of questions read out by Miss Annie Foote, secretary of Local Council's Civic Committee:

1. Will you support building bylaws that will provide such accommodation as will conserve the convenience, comfort and health of the occupants, especially of the girls employed in offices and stores?

2. Will you endeavour to have the law regarding noxious weeds strictly enforced within the city limits, not only in the parks, but on the streets and vacant lots?

3. Will you use your influence to enforce the present bylaw which forbids so-called boxing bouts within the city limits?

4. What are your ideas concerning the disposal of sewage?

5. Will you use your influence with those who have the authority to control Sunday trading?

6. Since the police authorities of this city are in a degree at least the servants of the city council, will you as a member of that council use your power to see that equal justice and punishment is meted out to the men and women found in houses of ill fame?[25]

From the outset those women in attendance at that Friday's mass meeting scorned rhetorical tactics. The *Morning Albertan* reported, "Aldermanic candidates who attempted to pass over polite platitudes and fulsome flattery were promptly reined up by the chairwoman, and by women in the audience who rose at most unexpected moments with most unexpected questions." When aldermanic candidate Alexander Ross made the observation that he was glad to know that the women were there to be addressed as men, the chairwoman corrected, "No, not as men, sir! As women." When Mr. Ross tried the recoup "As women, having the same rights as men," Mrs. Kerby corrected him, "As women with our own rights." At this juncture, the candidate got on with his speech.

On behalf of the women voters of Calgary, Mrs. M.S. Russell of the Women's Hostel presented tough questions to mayoralty candidate R.A. Brocklebank on the delicate subject of his "real" real estate interests in the thriving houses of ill fame in South Coulee. In a cleansing attempt, Alderman Brocklebank did admit to building the first houses but washed his hands of any knowledge of the dirty linen now laundered therein. When questioned concerning his presence in a notorious cafeteria during a police raid and the subsequent fortuitous absence of his name from the police charge sheet, he disclaimed any knowledge of that sin of omission.

The candidates, being quite well-attuned to audience bias, all assured listeners they stood for a clean city. Frost, who had tutored the women at the "closed" committee meeting, spoke for moral, humane and sanitary reform in general and for a curfew law, in particular to protect vulnerable young girls. His avowed support for the latter received tumultuous applause. The audience clasped candidate Frost to their collective bosoms, figuratively speaking.

Thomas Alfred Presswood Frost does seem to have been candidate credible to reformists of both sexes, and a colorful civic personality besides.[26] An Englishman by birth, a Baptist minister by early avocation, Frost arrived in Calgary in 1896 in response to a call from the First Baptist Church, where he preached for two years before moving on to other Canadian congregations. In 1904 he left the ministry and returned to Calgary to follow more earthly pursuits, acquiring extensive real estate, exploring for natural gas and promoting The Alberta Interurban Railway Company, of which he was vice-president. Mammonish pursuits notwithstanding, Frost, a man of social conscience, served as a justice of the peace and commissioner of the juvenile court.

Voter turnout for the December ninth civic election was the largest ever. Over 5400 cast ballots in the high profile mayoralty contest. Every man the Progressive (Civic League) sponsored was elected to the 1913 Calgary City Council, among them Mr. Frost, W.J. Tregillus and George Ross. Only two incumbents were returned. The *Calgary News-Telegram* predicted:

> *A year of reform is ahead of Calgary. Nearly every member of the new council has a program to submit to his confreres and to the citizens, and, in addition to these plans, the new mayor and the new commissioners, while not revolutionary, will advance proposals looking to the improvement of municipal conditions.*[27]

Was the year of reform ahead due to the impact of women voters? Mrs. Ida E. Baker, who aired her views on temperance, suffrage and morality in a *Morning Albertan* opinion column, believed this to be the case. "It is reasonable to assume that the vote of many hundreds of women at the recent election helped to force the happy issue of the hour."[28] The *Albertan* published the day after the election retrospective attributed the upgrading of council's calibre to the women's campaign, vote and "elevating influence." A later estimate of the number of women who actually voted was 1200, or 75 percent of those eligible. Given that these numbers forced "the happy issue of the hour," then the standing Civic Committee of the neophyte Local Council had dealt "efficiently" with its first challenge. More importantly, the public presence of women was made clear.

Local Council of Women also became a public presence, as was always the intention of the influential women of the day. Its threatened pre-emption by a women's civic league seems, in the context of the powerful lobby led by Mrs. Harold Riley, a discordant event.

Chapter Four

Positioning For Power

∽ ∽ ∽ ∽

The Club Scene

Positioning for power in Calgary's women's organizations was an important strategy at a time when reform-minded women could vote in municipal elections only if they met certain property qualifications and could not vote at all at the provincial or federal level.

By 1912 the number of women's societies in Calgary had grown to over 40, as westward-moving Canadians and immigrants from Britain and the United States contributed their mosaic of innovative ideas and personal experience to the club movement. In addition to the church and hospital societies, there were groups formed from common patriotic, professional and cultural interests. The patriotic societies were the most exclusive of these. The influential Imperial Order Daughters of the Empire (IODE), the prestigious Woman's Canadian Club and the elitist Alberta Woman's Club promoted British and Canadian loyalties at a time when immigrants from other nationalities were perceived as unenlightened threats to established values. An excerpt from a 1913 speech given to the IODE in Calgary by Miss Constance Boulton, President of the Women's Canadian Club of Toronto, affirmed the role of imperialist organizations.

We Canadians must, in order to preserve our national and imperial unity, demand of the foreigner in our country due respect for our institutions and national customs, our flag and national anthem, and by so doing we gain the respect of the whole world. In Women's Canadian clubs and other patriotic societies, British subjects only, either born or naturalized, should be allowed to be members and have voting privileges.[1]

Even if American women, those from "the other side of the line," were considered somewhat of an exception, they could not join those Canadian clubs which required the oath of allegiance to the King. Recognizing this environment, the American Woman's Club, which formed in Calgary on March 29, 1912, with almost 100 women in attendance, tactfully avoided overt American patriotism. "It is not the object of the club to advance any cause not strictly Canadian nor to encourage patriotism to the United States."[2] Although eligibility was based upon being an American or the wife of an American, the AWC's special aim was to attract women

excluded from existing patriotic organizations. One complimentary observation on the calibre of the women in this immediately popular society
was that it represented "the brightest and the most educated women
across the border," many of whom "have had wide club experience and
have been actively associated with the leaders of many modern movements for women on the other side."[3]

A contemporary analysis of Calgary's women's clubs appeared in the
Minneapolis Sunday Tribune in early 1913. It was reprinted in the *Morning
Albertan* because the woman interviewed in that American city was Mrs.
Bert Cummings, formerly Miss Irene "Uno" McLachlan, a clever journal-
ist and popular young clubwoman in Calgary who wrote for the women's
page of the *Calgary News-Telegram*. While on a winter visit to Minneapolis,
Mrs. Cummings had been asked about the status of the women's suffrage
movement in Canada. Uno, an American by birth, had worked for
newspapers in Port Arthur, South Dakota, Missouri and Lethbridge
before coming to Calgary. Her opinions were also of interest to the
Americans because at this time she was president of the Southern Alberta
(Calgary) Branch of the National Women's Press Club. She made these
astute comparisons:

> The Canadian club woman is energetic, but she gets her initiative from her
> American sister. The Canadian club woman is just beginning to take an active
> interest in civic affairs. She is adopting the broadening standards of the
> progressive women across the border.

> The Canadian clubs are really divided into two well defined groups, social
> and patriotic. The patriotic societies, the "Daughters of the Empire" have an
> intense patriotic fervour which it is hard for the average American to under-
> stand. Every club meeting or public affair of any kind opens and closes with
> the singing of God Save the King. The King's picture is the first one flashed on
> the screen at every moving picture show and the work of the women's clubs
> simply reflects the national life of the country. The social clubs, of course,
> explain themselves.

> Tea is the "open sesame" to the inner circle of these clubs. A round of teas
> composes the afternoon diversion of the average woman of position in Alberta.
> To the uninitiated, the most striking feature of this side of Canadian life is the
> endless repetition of the same thing, day after day, without seeming to tire the
> women in the slightest degree. A week of such perpetual teas would bore an
> American woman to distraction.[4]

Mrs. Cummings did identify Canadian women's emerging interests as
civic affairs, the larger sphere of the home and community. It was this
emergent energy that the new Local Council of Women hoped to co-ordinate.

Local Council Mounts Broad Membership Campaign

When the interim executive of the Calgary Local Council of Women drafted a proposed constitution on October 30, 1912, it also agreed on a membership campaign – every woman's group in the city would be invited to join. Local papers reported that letters would be sent to the presidents of church organizations including the ladies' aid, missionary society, girl's club and altar society; to the WCTU and the YWCA, the Mother's Societies, the Canadian Woman's Club, the American Woman's Club, the Alberta Woman's Association, the Art Association and the Anti-Tuberculosis Association. The presidents of prospective federates were assured that their society would retain its independence and would not be committed to the aims of any other affiliate. Local Council's purpose was to unite all women's societies in the city into a central council to pursue common concerns, but, as in Lady Aberdeen's day, sectarian and party politics were to be excluded.

These letters also included a list of 18 NCWC standing committees. The names of some identify important concerns of those times: suppression of objectionable printed matter; equal moral standards and prevention of traffic in women; care of the feeble-minded; care of the aged and infirm poor; the problems of childhood; vacation schools and supervised playgrounds; home-making; agriculture for women; citizenship; immigration; peace and arbitration; employment for women; public health. Keeping special local interests in mind, the interim executive suggested that committees could be established to improve women's wards in jails, to prevent use of women for immoral purposes, to strengthen women's property rights legislation, to support and enlarge local hospitals, and to improve schools and playgrounds.

With the exception of equal delegate representation, the proposed comprehensive, complex constitution adopted by the interim executive mirrored the model suggested by the National Council. Calgary's executive would consist of a president, one or more elected vice-presidents, ex-officio vice-presidents (affiliate presidents), a corresponding secretary, a recording secretary and a treasurer. Including the affiliate presidents meant that the executive size would fluctuate in proportion to the number of federated societies. Local Council officers would be elected from among those women nominated by each member society and by the executive committee of Local Council. Although above reproach in theory, in actual practice subsequent dissatisfaction with the annual nomination slates suggests that the executive choices predominated. Individual officers and individual members could not nominate. The restriction was completely consistent because a local council's *raison d'être* was as a federation of member societies. Standing and sub-committees would be appointed by the executive, the president and corresponding secretary being ex-officio. This power of appointment and de facto membership meant that committees served at the pleasure of the executive.

The one deviation from the constitution suggested by NCWC was delegate allocation. Instead of equal representation, as was anticipated from earlier publicity, the founding meeting opted for proportional representation and the interim executive determined the formula. Affiliates would be allocated one delegate for every 25 members up to 100, and one delegate for each additional 50. If a society composed of both men and women joined – the Anti-Tuberculosis Association was a case in point – only the number of women members counted. Because the constitution specified that the president of each member society must be designated first delegate, the small groups could only send their president. Each delegate carried an instructed vote determined by her own society, not by personal choice. Although all other members of affiliates could attend Local Council meetings and participate in the discussion and debate, only the delegates could vote.

Why was this proportional representation chosen in preference to equal representation? The larger organizations represented at the founding meeting may not have wanted their vote diluted at meetings, so they interpreted the directive that "Each society belonging to the council shall have three or more votes (exclusive of that cast by the president) as may be decided upon by the council," both literally and in their favor. However, proportional representation offered the means to another important end. The Council of Women was a lobby organization, and a weighted formula would attract, at the outset, the large organizations with the membership numbers needed to give credibility to Local Council's lobby base. The choice of proportional representation was therefore a strategy chosen to launch a high profile alternate to a separate Civic League.

Fees were set at one dollar a year for each society sending one delegate and a dollar more for each additional delegate, a scale which promised considerable revenue. Three regular meetings were to be held annually (the last Saturdays of January, May and November), with the new Local Council's permanent executive to be elected at the January 1913 meeting. Although special meetings on an important matter of the moment could be held at the request of any affiliate with two days advance published notice, the three general meetings a year meant that the large executive would actually conduct most Local Council business. Possibly the decision to include affiliate presidents as ex-officio vice-presidents anticipated this; however, demands on the time of the ex-officio vice-presidents could be excessive, because these women were also the presidents of their own active organizations.

This draft constitution was still subject to adoption by the permanent executive and to endorsement from member societies. In the meantime, it was sent on to the National Council for approval along with Calgary's application for branch membership.

WCTU Claims Honor of Being First to Join

By the third week of November, 1912, the Calgary Local Council of Women consisted of the interim officers appointed at the October 26th organizational meeting and the delegates appointed by the four affiliated societies. The Central WCTU claimed the honor of being the first to federate when its affiliation resolution passed unanimously on November sixth. With a membership of 77, the Central WCTU named three delegates: Mrs. Langford, its president, as well as Mrs. Humphries and Mrs. Bruce.

In an historical context, the distinction of being first was not inappropriate, because the WCTU had belonged to the original Local Council of Women. It had waxed and waned in Calgary since a small branch formed in Calgary in December of 1886, when Mrs. Betts, wife of the "esteemed" Pastor of the Methodist Church, where the meetings were held, served as president and Mrs. A.C. Priest as secretary. On the agenda in those days was a request to join with the *Women's Journal* in petitioning Parliament for the abolition of liquor permits in the North West Territories. At that time it was noted that the supportive editor of the *Calgary Herald* had "kindly offered space in his Journal for the insertion of any matter connected with the Union or the temperance cause generally."[5] Such press support notwithstanding, infrequent newspaper references to early WCTU activities in Calgary suggest that its progress was intermittent but that it probably revitalized at the turn of the century. By 1900 it was strong enough to circulate a successful petition for a curfew bylaw which R.B. Bennett, MLA, presented to the city fathers on February ninth of that year. In the fall of 1909, when proposed provincial legislation threatened to disenfranchise Calgary women, the WCTU, led by Mrs. P.S. Woodhall, planned a mass meeting of protest. The meeting was cancelled only after reassurance from the Minister of Public Works, Calgary's Honorable Mr. W.H. Cushing, promised the municipal franchise would now be extended to all Alberta women who met the property qualifications, not just those in Calgary and Edmonton. Three years later, on October 26, 1912, when the Local Council of Women formed, Mrs. Woodhall became its treasurer.

The American Woman's Club, which joined just one day after the WCTU affirmed its enthusiastic support for the new Local Council, had intended to be the first, "to show its appreciation of the federation of local clubs and to show its willingness to co-operate in the endeavour by women for the betterment of Calgary."[6] On November ninth, the ten-month-old Calgary Women's Press Club joined, its prompt federation probably due to the fact that the president, Mrs. F.S. Jacobs, held the office of corresponding secretary on the new Local Council. This rather exclusive professional group of talented writers and journalists, a few of whom were members of the Canadian Women's Press Club, began with only seven members and grew slowly. What they lacked in numbers they made up in endeavor, including a study of Canadian women writers, the commemoration of Dickens' Centennial Anniversary, and special invitations to contemporary women writers and to women eminent in other fields. Their professional encouragement was so sustained that by June of 1913 the members claimed to have, "entertained a larger number of distinguished guests than any other woman's club in the city."[7] The Woman's Canadian Club, the fourth affiliate, was the status acquisition. Formed in Calgary in 1911, its purpose was clearly patriotic: to foster patriotism, to encourage the study of the institutions, history, arts, literature and resources of Canada, and to unite Canadians in such work for the welfare and progress of the Dominion as may be desirable and expedient. Like other organizations, it enlightened and motivated members by inviting guest speakers distinguished in the fields of religion, politics, education, the arts and contemporary concerns; however, it was not just a "listening" society. Soon after the WCC formed, its members began the lobby for a tuberculosis hospital in Calgary. Now with a membership of 300, the Woman's Canadian Club chose eight representatives to the Local Council. In addition to the president, Mrs. C.A. Stuart, they included Mrs. Anderson, Mrs. Harold Riley, Mrs. George Lane, Mrs. Lawson, Mrs. E.H. Riley, Mrs. Carson and Mrs. A. Price. These four organizations probably sent 20 delegates in all to the Local Council, of which three-quarters came from the Canadian and American Clubs.

The YWCA Holds the Balance of Power

The realities of proportional representation imploded when the five-year-old YWCA, the city's fastest growing and largest women's group, joined at the end of November. With a membership now of 825, it was allocated 18 delegates, more than twice that of any other federate. In a split decision or contentious issue, the YWCA would control the balance of power.

The local history of the "YW" was a success story. Mrs. George Kerby and Mrs. Thomas Underwood mentored the first YWCA, which formed in July of 1907. Under their aegis, a rented and furnished boarding house, a home away from home for 14 homeless young girls, was readied by early November of that year. The need for such an amenity was so great that in 1909 the YWCA Board purchased six lots as the site for a large new building. They were paid for by public subscription, a tag day, a women's edition of the *Calgary Herald* and a booth at the exhibition. The new $60 000 YWCA building, complete with splendidly furnished meeting rooms, a library, swimming pool and gymnasium, opened on February 16, 1911. This facility was immediately filled to capacity, and once again women had to be turned away. In September an annex was opened in the Underwood Block. The YWCA also served meals, provided instruction classes, an employment bureau for women domestics and a traveller's aid service, the costs of which were shared with the WCTU. Every train was met so that young women upon arrival were directed to the "Y" or other suitable interim accommodation as a measure of preventive care until they found employment. The operations of the YWCA became so extensive that, by 1912, it was managed by a board of 50 women who, according to the president, Mrs. Underwood, "had not once quarrelled but had settled all matters amicably, saying what they had to say to and not of each other."[8]

Despite the publicity which attended affiliations and delegate appointments, only 14 societies had joined by the time of the Council's First Annual Meeting. At the very most, one-third of the women's societies belonged, which was disappointing considering that every woman's group in the city was invited (and expected) to join. However, Local Council's aggregate membership did look impressive as a lobby since the larger women's societies had federated: the YWCA, the Woman's Canadian Club, the American Woman's Club, the WCTU and some churches.

Moreover, proportional representation did not deter some smaller groups. The Crescent Heights branch of the WCTU elected officers, voted to join the Local Council of Women, and named its president, Mrs. Lebeau, as delegate, all at its founding meeting. The Women's Hostel became a member on December 16th, with its president Mrs. A.M. Scott designated first and only delegate. A board managed the hostel, which was a large home used as a temporary boarding house for Old Country women newly arrived in the city. It seemed adequate when it was first established, able to accommodate up to two dozen British immigrants, but now so many were turned away that there was a pressing need for a new building. The well-known interdenominational Naomi Mothers' Society also federated and delegated its president, Mrs. Rumrill. As the Society's name suggests, its main purpose was to offer mothers guidance in exemplary parenting. Its regular meeting program for the year 1913 indicates the stress placed on the spiritual and moral upbringing of children. The topics for discussion included "God Hearing And Answering Prayers," "Giving The Girls Occupation – The Best Safeguard Against Temptation," "The Poison That Lurks In The Moving Picture Houses," and "When The Boy Is Grown – The Hour When He Claims The Right to Settle Matters For Himself."[9]

One organization affiliated when its own viability was in doubt. The 35-member Business Girls' Club (also referred to as the Business Women's Club) joined on January sixth while it was still very much in an embryonic state. Founded by businesswomen in October of 1912, the club hoped to attract self-supporting working girls from the estimated more than 7000 in the city. But initial interest in the organization was so minimal that several meetings were required to establish it, an uncommon problem at a time when clubs mushroomed. The three special mothering aims of the club were health and sanitation, rest and recreation, and moral protection of self-supporting working women and girls.

Pro tem officers only were appointed at the December meeting and affiliation with the YWCA, which entitled club members to enjoy the privileges of both organizations for one fee, was postponed until February when the founders hoped that "the club would be in better running order."[10] The founding group's decision to join Local Council early on suggests that their agenda required lobby support. Miss Mabel Childs, president pro tem, became delegate. When the LCW held its Annual Meeting on March 29th, "the president, Miss Childs, presented a motion asking the local council to petition the various merchants in the city to provide chairs for saleswomen employed."[11] This mothering concern was valid. In those days, with the exception of one store, girls in Calgary's shops and department stores were not provided with seats. They stood nine and ten hours per day and for 12 hours on Saturdays. After three months of combined effort by the Council of Women and the Business Women's Club, all 42 Local Council's federates had signed the petition by the time of a June 20th meeting. Several aldermen had promised support as well. At this juncture, rather than present the petition to City Council in the usual manner, the Business Women's Club proposed a more expedient route. The city's Medical Officer of Health, Dr. Mahood, was asked to incorporate the recommendation in a Board of Health Bylaw, and he agreed, asking that all pertinent documents be forwarded to the Board of Health. "I shall expect a strong deputation in support of this," he cautioned.[12]

Henrietta Muir Edwards' suggestion that the interim Council officers represent as many religious denominations as possible does not seem to have been a factor in early affiliations. At the time when Local Council launched its membership drive at the beginning of November of 1912, there were at least 29 Protestant mainstream churches, along with about eight other variant denominations in the city.[13] Even if at the First Annual Meeting the remaining five affiliates of the 14 were all church societies, and they may not have been, it is important to note that non-sectarian societies were in the majority. Comparatively few church groups joined during the first three months, although the Central Methodist Ladies' Aid Society had affiliated by December fifth.

Although proportional representation seemed acceptable to some clubs at the local level – as might be inferred from the fact that a few smaller societies had joined – it was challenged by the National Council. When the Calgary Local Council executive met with Mrs. Edwards in January, 1913, just a few days prior to their annual meeting, she advised them that their delegate formula was not in conformity with National policy. Under the intriguing headline "Local Council Are Not Constitutional," the News-Telegram of January 22nd reported that Mrs. Edwards had pointed out that, in her opinion, either method was constitutional but if Calgary Local Council of Women adhered to proportional representation, it would be the only one in Canada which did not distribute representatives equally. After much discussion, an amending motion by Mrs. C.A. Stuart brought the Council in harmony with National. Each society would be admitted equally on the basis of four delegates, including the president.

To the frustration of the doers, the wrangling and confusion caused by delegate apportionment stalled other important agenda items. A writer for the *Calgary Standard* quoted one of Local Council's exasperated members as saying, "If we don't do more, we won't have six women coming to the next meeting."[14]

First Annual Meeting Reconvened

Tortuous retraction procedures lay ahead. The equal delegate amendment to Calgary's proposed constitution now required due consideration by the annual meeting. If approved there it would have to be circulated to all affiliated societies for their study and approval, a procedure which could prove time-consuming. Although it was now impossible to adopt the constitution by January 25th, it was carefully explained at that time. Mrs. A.M. Scott "in a very lucid speech" (meaning in plain words) stated, "The Council was meant to combine societies of all sorts and to broaden sympathy and understanding between them. Each society, while independent in itself, was yet part of a great whole, which served to push the feminine movements." She quoted Mrs. A.M. Cummings, of the National Council executive; unlike Henrietta Muir Edwards, she was unequivocal on the matter of delegate allocation. "Proportional representation at present in practice [in Calgary] was against the rules of the constitution, each society of necessity, to enjoy an equal number of votes, and to pay equal entrance fees." There had been no deviation from the founding principle espoused in Lady Aberdeen's day.[15] This ruling instituted equal representation, effective immediately.[16] Formal adoption of the proposed constitution somewhat nullified the annual meeting. It had to be reconvened at the end of March.

The election of the executive was also postponed at the January 25th meeting, even though a list of officers had previously been circulated to some affiliates and had been accepted. The nominations procedure was complex, and there had been a timing problem with it from the outset. At the January eighth Local Council general meeting, Mrs. Spence charged that the election of a nominating committee at that time was unconstitutional – the committee should have been in place two months ago. The constitution specified that the report of the Nominating Committee and the preliminary agenda had to be sent to federates two months before the annual meeting to allow input from the affiliates. In this case, two months earlier meant November 25, 1912. Not possible, protested the ladies, because at that time the full executive (interim officers and first delegates) was not yet in office. Mrs. Spence raised another pertinent technicality, namely that the additions suggested by the various clubs after they had studied the preliminary agenda then had to be included in the final LCW annual agenda and the final agenda must be sent out two weeks prior to the meeting. (In this case, on January 11.) Mrs. Spence was credited with occasioning much delay; however, the majority prevailed. It was resolved, under the circumstances, to proceed with election of the Nominating Committee at once and to send out the proposed slate without first stage input from the affiliates. Each federate would now have to call a special meeting to consider these nominees. Small wonder, then, that on such short notice elections were not held at the January annual meeting. By then, according to the *News Telegram*, "some of the nominated officers had withdrawn and . . . new nominations must come before the societies."[17] Both the *Calgary Daily Herald* and *Morning Albertan* explained the postponement differently – the recording secretary neglected to bring the Nominating Committee's report. Under the circumstances, an understandably strategic oversight!

Despite nomination and election conundrums, when the Council of Women reconvened its annual meeting on the last Saturday of March, Mrs. Jamieson, Mrs. Kerby, Mrs. Pearce, Mrs. Jacobs, Miss Burns and Mrs. Woodhall were all re-elected, proof that the interim table officers survived the early months with their credibility intact – a remarkable vindication. An even better indication of support for the pro tem executive was the surge in membership. By the first week of March, 42 societies belonged.

Procedural Wrangles Not Uncommon

Calgary Local Council of Women was not alone in facing procedural problems. Constitutional amendments, elections and rules of order were important matters to Calgary's capable and ambitious clubwomen. A gleaning of reports of annual and other meetings provides examples. Mrs. Heilge, an expert on "red tape," regularly conducted brief parliamentary drill sessions for the members of the American Women's Club. The women's pages reported arguments over whether a Nominating Committee member should let her name stand for office. In some groups there was an assumption that incumbent officers would be returned or at least that the Nominating Committee's executive slate would be elected by acclamation. Ratification sometimes proved elusive.

On the last day of January, 1913, two newspapers recounted a severe and angry confrontation during the election of officers for the Woman's Canadian Club. The *Morning Albertan* especially piqued curiosity with the query "Was Mrs. Harold Riley Double-Crossed By Canadian Club," and a subtitle, "Feminine Oratorical Fireworks Add Piquancy To Annual Meeting." A telling opening paragraph reads:

> The election of a recording secretary for the Woman's Canadian Club at the annual meeting yesterday afternoon provoked one of the bitterest and most hotly-argued contests in the history of women's clubs in Calgary. Charges of

underhandedness and scheming were made against the retiring president, Mrs.
C.A. Stuart, and other members of the club by Mrs. Harold Riley.[18]

It transpired that Maude Riley had agreed to accept re-nomination as recording secretary with the assurance that the Nominating Committee's support was unanimous. Aware beforehand that Mrs. Fred Currey was also interested, Maude Riley had taken the precaution of soliciting her private promise of no opposition. To Mrs. Riley's dismay, her confidante accepted a nomination from the floor. Mrs. Riley lost her temper. "Warming to her subject," she exposed the *modus operandi*, "she accused Mrs. C.A. Stuart, the retiring president of conspiring against her candidacy by telephoning to Mrs. Currey and canvassing in the latter's favour over the phone." Mrs. Stuart "denied the allegation." Both candidates withdrew their names then resubmitted them after laudatory testimonials from loyal sponsors. The ballot was taken. Mrs. Riley lost by two votes, left her chair of office and targeted her verbal missile, "I think this is contemptible." Mrs. Stuart did not comment.[19]

Forty-Seven Societies Provide a Broad Base

By the time Local Council submitted its first annual report to NCWC in April of 1913, 48 affiliates were listed. They covered the spectrum of women's organizations and church societies were now in the majority. The following profiles highlight the new diversity. A unexpected omission is also noted.

Of those mentioned earlier, the influential Calgary branch of the Alberta Woman's Association's membership was restricted to university graduates, and to the wives of members of university senates and boards of governors. The Calgary branch was the first to lend support to the City Planning Commission's proposal to regulate the billboard nuisance. This endorsement was viewed as a kind of coup because the Association's women were considered the "socially elect." At least four of the executive, Mrs. C.A. Stuart, Mrs. Harold Riley, Mrs. P.J. Nolan and Mrs. A.M. Scott, were also prominent on Local Council. The purpose of the Woman's Association was to promote higher education in the province, but like other women's groups, its members were also interested in community affairs.

The Colonel Macleod Chapter of the IODE had an auspicious beginning in Calgary in October of 1909 when Senator and Lady Lougheed hosted the founding meeting in their stately home, Beaulieu. Thirty-one ladies were inducted into the Order by Toronto's IODE leaders who were travelling west by private rail car to organize chapters. Calgary's chapter was given the name Colonel Macleod to honor its distinguished local soldier and to symbolize its interest in "the welfare of the soldiers of the empire." Officers elected were regent, Mrs. Pinkham (wife of the Anglican Bishop); vice-regent, Mrs. Lougheed; secretary, Mrs. Spence; treasurer, Miss Foote; and standard bearer, Mrs. Nolan. The next day, Miss

Jackson, one of the Toronto officials, visited all the city schools to explain the order to children and to ask teachers to accept applications "from the children who will be made members at a future date."[20] The IODE would continue its special interests in patriotic education, sponsoring an essay competition with topics chosen to "lead boys and girls to study the history or stirring events or illustrious persons of their own or the motherland, and to fill them with respect and love for the Empire."[21]

The Society for the Prevention of Tuberculosis, a branch of the Dominion Association, owed its origin in 1911 to the Woman's Canadian Club's campaign for a TB sanatorium in Calgary. In those days TB, "the white plague," was ubiquitous, claiming victims irrespective of age. Desperate sufferers with infected lungs who moved to Calgary's high dry climate to seek relief found medical care here minimal. Many had to make do for themselves, living in tents where air was fresher and where such isolation protected others. At the November 16th public meeting organized by a special mayor's committee, more than 80 men and women founded the Anti-Tuberculosis Society. Its aim: to work for public education on the prevention and cure of tuberculosis and to press for provincial funding to purchase local land and erect a sanatorium. Noteworthy founding officers and executive included honorary president, R.B. Bennett; president, Mr. A. Price (the CPR Superintendent); vice-presidents, Mayor Mitchell and Dr. Anderson; Mrs. C.A. Stuart, Corresponding Secretary; and Mrs. Harold Riley and Mrs. Wm. Carson. The last named was certainly not the least. Marion Carson would remain and then head the Women's Auxiliary which formed in May of 1914. The new Auxiliary wanted members not too busy in other clubs to furnish the hospital with amenities, to visit long-term patients and to improve staff working conditions.

The Young Women's Benevolent Society was a charity which existed to aid other charitable causes. Under the presidency of Mrs. J.H. Woods, this small group functioned informally without a constitution and by-laws, its one requirement being that every member had to be a conscientious working member willing to attend meetings regularly and punctually. Joiners, per se, weren't welcome.

Two leading professional groups joined – the Calgary Women Teachers' Association and the Graduate Nurses' Association – as did the Calgary Women's Musical Club and the Calgary Women's Literary Society, both important cultural groups in the city. The Calgary Women's Musical Club, re-established on a permanent basis in the fall of 1912, fostered and encouraged an appreciation of music in the higher forms and promoted young musicians. The older Calgary Women's Literary Society, formed in 1906, was unusual in that its membership was limited to 35 with a waiting list. Its purpose was to encourage the study of literature and appreciation of the best. Members' dues were designated for a charitable cause.[22]

There was one unexpected absence. The Victorian Order of Nurses, which owed its origin to the National Council of Women, did not federate, even though Mrs. A.M. Scott, a member of Local Council's executive committee, was the Order's president, and Mrs. Spence, Mrs. Cruikshank and Mrs. R.R. Jamieson all served on the 1913 executive. The object of the non-sectarian VON, established in Calgary in 1909, was to supply a trained nurse to the sick and afflicted at minimum cost if the recipient could afford to pay; if funds were unavailable, the service was paid for by the Order out of its subscriptions. From the outset the VON experienced difficulty in raising subscriptions as well as opposition from the Registered Nurses's Association which feared competition from the VON because the latter charged a mere 50 cents a visit, and only if the patient could afford it. But its fortunes gradually improved so that by the autumn of 1913 its membership had grown to at least 75. Even then it did not join.

Church organizations enjoyed a slight majority, as was the case with the original Local Council. In 1896, three Methodist, two Anglican and one Catholic society comprised six of the 11 affiliates; by 1913, 26 of the 48 federates, again a slight majority, were church or missionary affiliations, and all except two were Protestant. This time 13 ladies' groups from two newer Protestant denominations, the Baptist and Presbyterians, swelled the ranks and Methodist groups had more than doubled, to seven. The most singular member was the Woman's Alliance of the Unitarian Church. There were only ten such societies in all of Canada, among which the three-year-old Calgary Alliance ranked third in membership. It was the entrepreneurial ladies of this society who launched the first "Made in Calgary" show to raise money for their new church building.[23] The number of Anglican affiliates increased by one and the Roman Catholic remained at two. This analysis suggests that the second Local Council of Women attracted the more activist, reform-minded denominations.

The shift from a minority of sectarian affiliates to a majority occurred after the January 25th meeting. Why? Although the change to equal representation would attract smaller church groups it is more likely that local publicity concerning projects and petitions undertaken by Local Council was the deciding factor. By early January of 1913, both the new city council and the neophyte Local Council of Women, in a symbiotic relationship, undertook to mentor the moral wellbeing of young girls and women. The prevention and control of immorality and prostitution, delicately referred to as "the social problem" or "the social evil," called for the unified effort of church and other reform groups. Implementation of restrictive legislation also required the co-operation of municipal authorities. The time seemed propitious, because Calgary's 1913 City Council contained a reform-minded majority elected by reform-minded voters, and there were promises to keep. On the new council was Alderman Frost, who had earlier promised a curfew bell to protect vulnerable young girls.

Local Council's Handmaiden Role

Both papers relished reporting Alderman Frost's adherence to this campaign proposal. While ranking the issue as less important than municipal construction and services, the *News-Telegram* did admit a curfew should be reinstated (the March 1900 curfew had lapsed) to keep hundreds of young girls off the streets at night lest they fall victim to immoral enticements. Frost followed through on his election promise by giving the new City Council notice that at the next Council meeting he would introduce curfew legislation prohibiting girls under 18 unaccompanied by a parent or guardian from being on the streets after 9:00 on winter nights beginning in October and after 10:00 p.m. from April on. All concerned ladies – and this would include members of the Civic committee, the WCTU and the Naomi Mothers' Society – were urged to attend. The meeting provided surprising intelligence. Alderman Frost launched forth with startling revelations: 200 girls under 18 were on the verge of motherhood, their downfall accommodated in rooms above popular grills and their transportation provided by licensed chauffeurs.

It was civic policy to seek advice from the City Solicitor before passing municipal legislation, a useful delaying tactic for a Council somewhat less enthused than its petitioners. Legal requirements ground down Alderman Frost's moral improvement wedge. The City Charter specified that a petition must be supported by one half the population (a daunting 35 000 names) and a curfew must be rung precisely on the hour. A timely problem because there was no bell to ring. The explanation given: "The last bell did the flip-flap act about five years ago, and carried 'Billy' Nutt ceilingward with some violence. The rope broke and Mr. Nutt landed on the floor with a thud, while the bell turned a double summersault that put its gear out of commission for all time."[24] A tale indeed well tolled.

In the aftermath of his vital statistic about the number of girls on the verge of illegitimate motherhood, Tappy Frost had some explaining to do. His dramatic revelation had tarnished Calgary's shining city image, and some of the loyal citizenry protested. Aptly described as a spellbinding speaker, Mr. Frost allowed that he had resorted to hyperbole under the stress of a two-minute time constraint which did not allow him to clarify that this figure also included single women. The erring flock was not all lambs; some were on the shady side of eighteen. The distinction was not lost on sectarian reformers working toward a more permanent solution. This time the appeal would be carried to a higher authority, the provincial government. In the process, the Local Council of Women would be invited to marshall its lobbying force.

Calgary Local Council of Women joined the Ministerial Association's campaign for a detention home for immoral women when Mrs. Ida Baker proselytized the January fourth executive meeting on the pressing need for a provincial reformatory for prostitutes where they would be detained on court order and taught a rehabilitative trade. A form of compulsory moral reclamation, it was deemed necessary because at that time arrested prostitutes simply paid a fine then returned to ply their trade. Mrs. Baker was a very determined woman, and it seemed to her that neither the city nor the province was making an effort to curb immorality. Fines merely added to city coffers. Although there were already two rescue homes for fallen women in the city (one operated by the Presbyterian women and the other by the Salvation Army), residence there was voluntary. When Police Chief Cuddy was called to account for an ineffectual system, he told the executive that the provincial government made no provision for an institution of detention. In his view, it was time that the provincial morality department accepted responsibility. Spirited discussion followed, whereupon Mrs. Woodhall and Mrs. Riley gave notice of motion to petition the Legislature for the immediate establishment of a home of detention.

The motion came up for discussion four days later at the Council of Women's general meeting. This time a three-member committee from the Ministerial Association – Reverend M.A. McLean of the Olivet Baptist Church, Reverend A. Esler of Grace Presbyterian Church and Reverend A.S. Tuttle of Wesley Methodist Church – joined Mrs. Baker in discussing "the social evil." Proposals varied. The Local Council subsequently appointed a five-member committee that included Deaconess Gordon of the Presbyterian Home for Girls, Mrs. Russell, who was on the Board of the Women's Hostel, Mrs. Glass and Mrs. Underwood from the YWCA, and Mrs. Riley, to study the problem and the best ways of dealing with it and to present their report at the next meeting in January. After further committee deliberations, Deaconess Gordon advised segregation. Children from age 11 to 17 should be housed in a reformatory away from the influence of mature prostitutes.

Two petitions were subsequently prepared for presentation to the Legislature. The first, from the affiliated Baptist Olivet Mission Circle, asked the Local Council of Women to,

> petition the government of Alberta to establish forthwith, to maintain and to control an industrial home for girls of immoral life: such a home to be an institution in which girls shall receive kind, patient and loving care, and shall be instructed in all desirable lines of industry that they may be prepared to live virtuous and useful lives.[25]

The second requested a detention home for immoral women where they would be sent by the court after arrest and payment of a fine. Detention time depended upon inmates showing evidence of mended ways.

Between that time and the March 29th adjourned annual meeting deadline, pressure mounted. Mrs. Riley wanted a petition presented forthwith to the Legislature, regardless of the fact that the legislative agenda was already full for the session scheduled, which ended on March 20th. Time was of the essence, but in order to petition the Legislature, the Calgary Local Council of Women had to follow two preliminary procedures. The constitution of the NCWC required that all matters to come before provincial governments must receive endorsement from its executive committee. This process seems to have worked smoothly, because a letter of approval from National was read at the March seventh executive meeting. The constitution also required the Local Council to circulate the petitions to every member society for a response, a time-consuming undertaking because the meeting schedules of affiliates varied considerably. Some preferred to short-circuit that route, and heated discussion followed at the Friday, March seventh executive meeting. The *Morning Albertan* detailed the "fast and furious discussion:"

Mrs. Cruikshank stated that she had supposed the L.C.W. was in existence to educate the community and was opposed to hurried legislation, to which Miss Coutts replied that it was more complimentary to suppose the community already educated.

Mrs. Spence and Mrs. Pryce were both against anything being done during the present session since two of the large societies included in the local council would not have a meeting before a decision was taken and would therefore not be represented.

Mrs. Jamieson replied that in courtesy to Mrs. Baker she did not feel disposed to wait for another session, and stated that the delay had been caused by Miss Gordon's [Deaconess Gordon's] refusal to give the information which she had been called upon to collect.

She stated further that if a society did not know its mind on the matter it should do so since it was now two months since the matter first came up. Further if no regular meeting met the case, a special meeting should be called.

Mrs. Pryce then said that in the event of a society calling a special meeting for every emergency there would soon be no societies in existence.[26]

After further discussion, this impasse was resolved. Each of the 42 affiliates should indicate its preferred petition procedure before March 15th, whereupon a two-thirds majority would determine the approach.

At this time, the Baptists suspected that the provincial government would shift its responsibility for establishing homes to, "certain churches already enjoying the rescue work." Possibly because the Local Council petitions would now be delayed, delegates from Calgary's Baptist churches convened almost immediately to pass a resolution of support for the Local Council's pending petitions and to protest to the Legislature against public funds being put to sectarian uses. This intervention proved strategic, because the Local Council of Women did not present its petitions to the Legislature by March twentieth. At Mrs. Riley's suggestion, they waited until April fourth, when Premier Sifton was in Calgary, thus saving the costs of a trip to Edmonton. After listening to Mrs. Riley, Mrs. R.R. Jamieson, Mrs. M. Cruikshank and Mrs. F.S. Jacobs, the premier promised to give his attention to the matter.[27] In the ensuing years, the premier's benediction "to give the matter his careful consideration" would terminate many an earnest invocation made by supplicants to a higher power.

Frank Opinions Were the Mode of the Times

Press coverage of the Calgary Local Council of Women's meetings might lead to the conclusion that this organization was a fractious one. Not necessarily. Frankly expressed opinions were the mode of the times. During 1913 the Woman's Canadian Club, the Alberta Woman's Association and the IODE argued hotly as well, prejudice exposed, the contentious issue of widening membership. Sometimes those women who exchanged verbal thrusts in Local Council meetings were carrying grudges from these clubs. Constance Errol of the *Albertan* criticized the mutual tensions in the Woman's Canadian Club and the American Woman's Club over various proposals to admit each other's members. "If the matter ended there little harm would result, but a spirit of animosity is apparent between members of these two clubs when they meet on common ground, as in the Local Council of Women."[28] Errol strongly advised the Canadian to set the example by admitting their "close relations" and "near neighbours" – the Americans. The Canadian Club did lead by relaxing its policy, but not without well-publicized verbal duelling.

In late June of 1913, Mrs. G.W. Kerby presented a motion that the women of other lands residing in Canada be received into the Woman's Canadian Club as associate members.[29] Her motion was backed by a well-researched address in which she pointed out that foreign-born men were admitted to the Men's Canadian Club with the proviso that they could neither vote nor hold office. In the debate which followed, Mrs. McDonald and Mrs. Wolley-Dodd supported including foreign-born women if the same powers were withheld from them. Then, after explaining the relevant clauses of the Canadian Club's present constitution, the first vice-president of the club and wife of Calgary's superintendent of public schools, Mrs. A.M. Scott, spoke her mind. In contrast to Mrs. Kerby's tolerance, her barbs revealed a patriotic bias which must have discomfited some, Mrs. Kerby concluded:

> as a Canadian who had never lived under the American flag, and who would willingly live at Timbuctoo or at the North Pole rather than have the Stars and Stripes waving over her head, she wished to point out that the constitution said nothing of being a Canadian subject or of owning allegiance to Canada but that Britain was the word used all through. This, she argued, changed much of the

argument that had gone on, and most of Mrs. Kerby's speech. She wished,
however, to say that she would vote on the motion as amended, as she wished
to be broad, and the club to be the same.[30]

Under the Union Jack *noblesse* obliged! Mrs. Kerby's motion was passed almost unanimously, mixed benedictions notwithstanding, and there seems to have been no lingering resentment. No closet patriot she, Mrs. Scott became president of the Woman's Canadian Club in 1914.[31]

How *La Crème* Rose to the Top

Local Council was structured so that clubwomen became influential leaders by popular designation or by personal stratagem. In theory, it was to operate as a parliamentary democracy where leaders like Mrs. Jamieson were chosen by the wish of the majority.

Alice Jane Jamieson (née Jukes) was born on July 14, 1860, in New York City. Of Puritan stock, she was a descendant of Miles Standish on her maternal grandfather's side. In the spring of 1882, she married Reuben Jamieson in Springfield, Ohio, whereupon the couple immediately took up residence in Toronto. In those days, as a wife of a British subject resident in Canada, Alice Jamieson also became a British subject. Their marriage produced five children, one of whom died in infancy. Reuben Jamieson was a railway official, so the family moved from place to place in Canada, eventually arriving in Calgary in 1903, when Mr. Jamieson became general superintendent of the western division of the CPR. In this young and growing city, Alice Jamieson soon became an active club member. A cultured woman, in 1904 she helped found the Woman's Musical Club, serving as its first secretary. Almost a decade later, in May of 1913, she headed the committee invited to organize a Ladies' Auxiliary for the newly formed Calgary Symphony. A founding member of the YWCA, she also belonged to Grace Presbyterian Ladies' Aid, the Hospital Aid Society, and in 1913 served on the executive committee of the VON. When her husband was elected Mayor of Calgary in the 1908 and 1909 elections, her interest in civic affairs grew.

Why Mrs. Jamieson was named in September of 1912 to the original three-member Committee of Investigation into civic league formation is not noted in available sources. Nor is there an explanation of why she was elected interim president of the Council of Women in October. She was certainly the woman who had a dual experience in women's societies and civic functions. We do know that when the LCW nominating committee prepared the list of nominees at its January eighth meeting, hers was the only name proposed for president because she had, "so ably filled the position for the past three months." As a further confirmation of peer regard, she was appointed convenor of the Civic Committee in April after Mrs. C.A. Stuart resigned due to ill health. By this time civic work was of such importance that the committee now included the entire executive. Above all, she must have had special personal qualities. It seems from accounts of her participation in discussions that she was diplomatic, an intelligent kind of arbiter who could be trusted to carry out her obligations mindful of democratic procedures.

Calgary journalist, Elizabeth Bailey Price, writing in the April, 1917, edition of the *Women's Century*, explained just how crucial her Council leadership was.

> [D]uring her four years of office she had guided the Local Council of Women
> with infinite judgment and tact, through its embryo stages in a new city and
> on through the troublous times of war. And just as every educational move-
> ment brings to light its leaders, every war its great generals and the records of
> these leaders are the records of that movement . . . so when the wave known as
> the "Emancipation of women" swept over Western Canada, it created its
> women leaders and to follow the lives of these women is to follow the progress
> of the movement, and this is true in the life of Mrs. Jamieson.[32]

Local Council was also structured so that an ambitious clubwoman could rise in the organization by personal stratagem. The constitution specified that the president of a federate became vice-president ex officio on Local Council's executive and first delegate with attendant voting power. If an aspiring clubwoman was not president of her own club, she could still be appointed one of its delegates to Local Council. The odds improved for a woman who belonged to smaller organizations or to several federates. Assuming that such a person was a persuasive officer in her own clubs, she could influence the vote at this initial level, then carry an instructed vote to support her particular project or resolution within the Council of Women executive. For her, one of the most import-ant positions in Local Council would be the convenorship of the commit-tee related to her special interest.

It was probably Maude Riley who epitomized this kind of acquisition of power. With the possible exception of the office of president or first vice-president, Mrs. Riley could have held any office she wished on the interim Local Council of Women which formed on October 25, 1912.

Alpha Maude Keen was born in St. Mary's, Ontario, and received her first class teaching certificate at the School of Pedagogy in London. When she came to Calgary to teach at Nose Creek school on the city's outskirts, she proved to be the survivor after four teachers had left their unruly pupils in a period of as many months. In 1907 she married Harold Riley and moved to Edmonton when her husband was appointed provincial secretary for the newly formed province. In 1908, when the University of Alberta came into being, he also became its registrar. While in Edmonton Maude Riley founded the Edmonton Women's University Club and became a member of the Edmonton Local Council of Women committee which met with the premier to request improvements in women's rights legislation. However, her rise to power in Local Council work occurred in Calgary.

By the fall of 1912 she was also a prominent clubwoman in Calgary. She had helped found the Calgary branch of the Alberta Woman's Association in late October of 1911 and served as corresponding secretary until the May 1913 annual meeting. At this juncture, it was decided officers should "go round" and Mrs. Riley was elevated to president. Both Mrs. C.A. Stuart and Mrs. Fred Currey, both of whom featured in the earlier Canadian Club election confrontation, no longer served. As president, Mrs. Riley would now be ex-officio and first delegate on the Local Council executive, some compensation for the loss of delegate status in the Woman's Canadian Club. In better times, mid-December of 1911, she, Mrs. Stuart and Mrs. Cruikshank were the three Canadian Club delegates selected to present a petition to Premier Sifton asking for provincial aid in the establishment of a provincial sanitorium for the treatment of tuberculosis in Calgary. On this occasion Maude Riley enjoyed a dual mandate, because she was also identified as the secretary of the Anti-Tuberculosis League. When the League affiliated with Local Council she, the secretary, acted as first delegate, possibly because the president was a man. She served on the 1912 executive of the Woman's Literary Club, was a member of the IODE, the YWCA, and the Women's Press Club. When the latter organization undertook to host the Canadian Women's Press Club on June 13, 1913, en route from their triennial convention held in Edmonton, she was appointed convenor of the joint Women's Press Club and Local Council of Women Entertainment Committee. June 13th was a highly publicized occasion, and Maude Riley's name preceded most.

In the civic league formation debate she turned the tide in Local Council's favor, her authority enhanced by her lobbying experience in the Edmonton Council and attendant work with Henrietta Muir Edwards and friendship with Mrs. Arthur (Emily) Murphy of Edmonton.[33] Although she was not named a member of the interim Local Council at the October 26th organizational meeting, within two weeks she was among the eight delegates appointed from the Woman's Canadian Club. On January fourth she was one of those who initiated the motion that Local Council petition the Legislature to establish a detention home for immoral women, and by March she had been given authority to judge the appropriate time to petition Premier Sifton. When the executive of the provisional Calgary Local Council of Women formed its first Legislative Committee, Maude Riley was appointed convenor, and she in turn appointed her own ten committee members – Mesdames Cruikshank, Langford, Sycamore, Budd, Glass, Hume, Scott, and Miss Foote, Deaconess Harriet Lampard and Deaconess Gordon. This was the position she had wanted all along. She held that convenorship for the next 20 years and therefore headed the committees presenting petitions and resolutions not only to city authorities but also beyond the local level to provincial government – the level at which she first sensed power. She went on to become Convenor of Laws on the Provincial Council of Women and succeeded Henrietta Muir Edwards as President.

Twenty-one years later when the Local Council celebrated its coming-of-age on January 21, 1934 at a gala banquet held in the Elizabethan room of the Hudson's Bay Company, both Alice Jamieson and Maude Riley were among six women honored for having "made a place for themselves in the life of the community and province." Both were presented with life memberships in the National Council of Women. On that occasion, Maude Riley stated that she had made the Calgary Council's founding motion.

Chapter Five

Out with Moral Stave and Shovel

തെ തെ തെ

There is just one piece of advice we would give – or rather offer – the ladies who participate actively in public affairs. It is this, – "Do not become extremists on any one topic, especially if it be of a sociological nature. On such questions as temperance and the social evil, an extreme course will get you nowhere. Be good enough to paste this inside your spring bonnets. "
Bob Edwards, **Calgary Eye Opener**, March 14, 1914

The Agenda Furore

The favored instrument for co-ordinated action was the petition or resolution which either originated within the Local Council's executive itself or was submitted by the societies belonging to the Council. These proposals were then passed on to each affiliate, whose members discussed the format, approved or disapproved, then instructed their own LCW delegates to vote accordingly. Member societies were thus committed to endorsed causes, and the Local Council was committed to its leadership role.

No doubt the most sensitive "Social Problem" resolution that Local Council received in its early years came from the WCTU in February of 1914. It caused such a furore that Calgary's Council of Women decided thereafter to require a two-thirds executive vote in favor before resolutions could be circulated to member societies.

During the third week of February, the *Morning Albertan* reported a three-part resolution, brought in by Mrs. P.S. Woodhall from the WCTU, which asked the Local Council to endorse its request "that certain specific punishments be given men for certain offenses." Specifically, that there be "more drastic punishments for offenders in cases of small children." Although euphemisms were used, one of the recommended punishments was the lash, the other castration. In accordance with accepted procedure, the Council executive included this WCTU resolution on the April agenda sent to member societies, along with other resolutions asking for the provincial franchise for women, for prohibition of white help in restaurants run by black or yellow people, and for tax exemption on non-revenue producing church property.

In those days, in polite circles at least, the franchise and church taxation weren't hush-hush subjects, but castration certainly was. Some ladies of delicate sensibilities within the Canadian Club, Mrs. Wolley-Dodd among them, branded the subject as too indecent to warrant discussion in the presence of "young or unmarried women." She tried a pre-emptive censuring motion against the Local Council, but this was duly ruled out of order because the WCTU motion was already under debate. When the three-part vote was taken, the Canadian Club endorsed the section requesting "severer punishment for offenders in cases of assault," but defeated the second part – the method of that punishment. The third section was tabled, or, as the *Herald* reporter worded it, "flogging was left over until the next meeting."[1]

Three days after the Canadian Club upset, the *News-Telegram* ardently defended the Local Council's executive while taking the other two organizations to task. It began with the Canadian Club: "surely a club which has for its aim the welfare and progress of the Dominion, and which is composed of the thinking women of the city, is able to discuss a question such as this without having its beautifully, serene outlook disfigured." Such misguided modesty, the argument went, actually impeded moral reform. "When women cease to be artistically shocked and learn to sanely face such issues as this, then, and not till then, has the work of stamping out some of the terrible conditions which exist, gained a foothold."[2] Censure should not fall on Local Council's executive, which had adhered to its constitution, but upon the WCTU, which initiated "this very indecent suggestion," if it would "in any way soothe the injured modesty of the Woman's Canadian club." Instead of being censured, the writer felt Local Council's executive was to be commended for its broad-minded, unprejudiced outlook.[3]

Bob Edwards, who usually called a spade a spade, handled the subject delicately, using sly euphemism:

> The Calgary Women's Council, we are given to understand, are on the eve of issuing a manifesto of some sort – a kind of proclamation, protocol or encyclical – under the terms of which, in the event of certain contingencies duly tabulated in the Agenda, a few surprising and novel alterations in the human landscape are contemplated. Wherefore it might be as well for some of our handy men around town, when they espy an angular female approaching with a pair of barb wire pliers, to make for the high places and wig wag the S.O.S. signal to the nearest station. The idea, which in theory is not altogether a bad one, is said to have originated in Brazil where the nuts come from.[4]

The furore did abate in time for "The agenda" and its several resolutions to receive overwhelming support at the Council's mid-May meeting, the special victory being the high profile WCTU-initiated resolution, which passed by a majority of 108 votes (124 in favor and 16 opposed).

With the dissension caused by the WCTU resolution in mind, the same meeting also strongly endorsed Local Council's change of policy regarding resolutions. "[In] the case of any resolution being deemed questionable, the executive by a two-thirds majority may send the resolution back to its source for amendment. Or any resolution not considered suitable for inclusion in the general agenda may be sent to the societies separately."[5] Not a radical change, but one that was quite acceptable to the National body, which followed the same policy.

Whether or not the contentious agenda contained a proposal to tax consumers of alcoholic beverages is a matter of doubt, but Bob Edwards inferred it was. A noted imbiber himself, he could not resist a waggish comment: "All drinkers paying the tax will be required to wear a tin tag. The plan has been objected to by one of the ladies' husbands on the ground that there is not enough tin mined to supply the demand for tags."[6]

Recycling – The Curfew Bell

By 1912 the sounds and effects of the 1900 curfew bell on Calgary's unsupervised children were pretty much hearsay. That bell had ceased to toll after a few years, and the matter rested until the spring of 1912, when mothering women concerned with the numbers of children out after nine o'clock turned again to the curfew solution in the hope that the old bylaw still on the city's books could be reinstated. Apparently not, for when the Local Council of Women re-emerged in the fall of that year, the curfew surfaced as a minor civic election issue, and a by-law petition became one of the new Council of Women's first projects. As noted earlier the 35 000 signatures required on a petition stonewalled the process. But the ladies of the Women's Council were gifted with long memories.

The cause lingered long in the memory of one particularly persevering and capable member, Mrs. C.R. Edwards, Local Council's Health Committee convenor, who faithfully and conscientiously brought needed improvements in community health to the attention of civic authorities. She also truly believed in the efficacy of the curfew bell as a crime prevention measure. By 1920 Mrs. Edwards was well aware that local petition requirements had eased considerably. Twenty-five percent of the votes cast in the year's previous mayoralty contest was now all that was required to elevate a petition to plebiscite status on the civic ballot. Sensing that the number would not be daunting – Calgary's voters were not noted for turning out *en masse* to anoint mayors – she proposed to the Council of Women's mid-September executive meeting that City Council be requested to register votes for or against a curfew in the upcoming December civic election. With the help of her supporters, she obtained the required 1700 signatures and a few to spare by the deadline, and the matter was put to plebiscite.

Editorial pundits that year focussed on city gas rate increases and aldermanic pay, not on the curfew. By 1920 press and popular enthusiasm had waned, and the few curfew opinions offered were negative in tone. One disparaging comment appeared on the editorial page of the *Herald*. "A curfew bylaw . . . will be a joke as well as an annoyance. There are other and better ways of accomplishing the end sought."[7] An election day item in the *Albertan* advised instant defeat, labelling the bylaw "foolish, senseless, buttinski legislation" which interfered with parental responsibilities and childhood. Readers were reminded that children should be allowed to "grow up without being early introduced to the police and punished for no other crime than being alive."[8] Nevertheless, there must have been an organized lobby in favor of the bylaw. The plebiscite "Are you in favour of the City of Calgary passing a Curfew Bylaw requiring that all children, 15 years of age or under, be off the Public Streets of this City before 10 o'clock each evening, except when under proper control or guardianship or for some unavoidable cause." passed by a majority of 1598 votes.

Implementation was some time in coming, and it came in rather mysterious ways. During the June 1921 LCW Annual Meeting, the *Herald* updated readers on the status of several civic reforms requested by the Local Council. Curfew legislation, an "amendment which the Women's Council has been asking for the last two or three years," had been passed by the Legislature. But other hurdles materialized. In the summer of 1921, Mrs. Edwards, who considered herself a leading "agitator," felt personally insulted by a particularly sarcastic *Albertan* item which read, "when the curfew signal is given, the policemen will go forth and club the smaller children off the street and every person will be happy everafter." Mrs. Edwards responded in dead earnest via a letter to the *Herald* editor clarifying that she had checked with Chief Ritchie, who gave his word that under no circumstances were Calgary's police allowed to club a child. After stressing that the role of the curfew was preventive not punitive, offering election statistics on the strength of curfew support, and citing a few instances in which she would like to do a little clubbing herself, Mrs. Edwards closed with a personal warning, "should it ever come to my knowledge that a policeman clubbed my child I should wage just as strong a campaign for his removal from the force as was waged for a curfew bylaw."[9] Outraged, Mrs. Edwards held to her moral high ground.

Calgary children were not destined to hear the gentle toll of a curfew bell, for city fathers had in mind a more assertive device. In mid-July, the *Albertan* archly reported that the cannon's roar "will intimate to the children the hour at which they must be off the streets." This intelligence should have caused responsible parents to view with alarm the alerting effect on their own slumbering offspring. However, the effect upon errant ears must have been efficacious, because Chief Ritchie pronounced in December: "We have had no trouble whatever in the enforcement of the curfew bylaw, and we have so far received no complaints." The reason for not leaving well enough alone is not given, but about that time a siren "devised" by the street railway superintendent was under serious consideration. The prospect of its shrill wail replacing the cannon's rude roar received the approval of the original curfew lobby.

Of all social control measures, the curfew was probably one of the most recycled. As recently as 1993, the police commission followed through on a citizen curfew proposal to control teenage night crime in Calgary. A six-month in-depth study laid that idea to rest. Costs aside, the two most relevant findings were that Calgary's teenage crime occurs mainly during non-curfew hours and that under Canada's Charter of Rights and Freedoms, the curfew could be judged an unjustifiable restriction on personal liberty.[10]

The Virtue of Thrift – Copper Coinage

Undertaken as part of a 1913 campaign to bring down the city's unconscionably high cost of living, the introduction of copper coinage proved a viable exercise, despite some early resistance from those with dollars at stake. The copper coinage proposal originated at a time when the nickel was the smallest coin used in Calgary. The introduction of coppers, as initially proposed to the January 26th Annual Meeting by Mrs. F.S. Jacobs, promised to be a very practical application of the old adage "A penny saved is a penny earned." Using as a statistical base the 3000 members of Local Council, Mrs. Jacobs calculated that butchers stood to make $60 (6000 pennies) a day at their customers' expense by "rounding up" the price to the nearest nickel when the actual cost of the meat was two cents lower. Three days later, with women shoppers trying to cope with Calgary's high cost of living clearly in mind, the executive decided to petition the local Board of Trade.

Both Lethbridge and Edmonton stores accepted copper coinage, so its introduction in Calgary appeared a timely Local Council undertaking. Calgarians had previously shown indifference to small currency, considering cent pieces cluttered their purses, and the city's merchants fell right in line. In boom times particularly, the fashion here was extravagance not economy. Now that the city was in a recession, the practice of economies seemed a moral responsibility. Wastefulness was not only foolish, it was sinful.

Five businessmen were invited to the January 30th executive meeting to present their views. They were influential people: the manager of the Hudson's Bay Store, the president and the secretary of the Board of Trade, Mr. Price-Jones (probably the city's most prominent local merchant), and the president of the Industrial Bureau. The Manager of the Hudson's Bay store, Mr. James Baker, clearly on the defensive, declared himself, "absolutely and utterly opposed to the whole idea . . . it would entail tremendous work for little additional good."[11] Mr. C.G. Devenish, President of the Industrial Bureau, opposed the idea on the basis that copper coinage was a nuisance, more trouble than it was worth. The others either were of two minds or altruistically supported the introduction as benefitting the poor, the thrifty housewives and those children who rarely received nickels. Local Council's executive harkened back to its mothering instincts and prepared the following resolution for circulation to its affiliates:

> Whereas economy in the smaller details of life means the greater good of the whole community and whereas in the buying of necessities it is not always possible to have exactness of measure, weight and change, therefore be it resolved that we ask the Calgary board of trade to use its influence in inducing tradesmen to adopt the use of the copper cent.[12]

By the March 25th general meeting of Local Council, 33 member societies had endorsed the copper coinage resolution. Even the City Council "thought the time was now ripe for its general use" and came onside, but when the Board of Trade asked the city's retail merchants for their support, that body refused. By the first of August, the retail stores, with one exception – Price-Jones Limited – still refused to accept copper coins. According to one calculation, their intransigence denied Calgary's homemakers a savings of nine percent.

Limited success in merchants' stores notwithstanding, there was more than one route to saving a penny. The Council made inroads by encouraging women to obtain pennies at the banks and spend them at the flourishing public market that was established that spring by the Consumers' League, which evolved from Local Council's Home Economics Committee. Under the direction of Georgina Newhall, now League president, members lobbied market merchants by explaining that the coppers saved paid streetcar fare and encouraged thrift by "careful buying." As a further strategy, League shoppers were advised to patronize only "the merchant who tried the experiment." Mrs. Newhall noted, "this gentle boycott leavened the whole in a few weeks."[13] By autumn, copper coins were here to stay.

The Ruthenian Problem

In those early years, when Canada was absorbing waves of immigrants from countries other than Britain, not all newcomers cast aside their traditional ways upon arrival and embraced the prevailing British-Canadian values. During the summer of 1913, Calgary's reform-minded Local Council women, led by Emily Kerby, targeted Ruthenians (Austrian and Ukrainian immigrants from the provinces of Bukovina, Galicia and TransCarpathia), most of whom settled in rural areas, as a prime example of a foreign population whose ways threatened Canadian values. Whether or not the Council's Canadianization agenda was unduly discriminatory against Ruthenians – or Ukrainians as they preferred to be called – seems a moot point now, but women of patriotic sensibility felt they epitomized anti-social foreign ways sorely in need of mending. A situation wherein men who neither wrote nor spoke English could vote; wherein the practice of child marriage flouted existing Canadian law and girls were effectively denied a proper education – clearly it begged remedying. By late summer, the Calgary Local Council of Women had prepared three petitions designed to correct the Ruthenian problem. All came to naught.

Local Council's restricted franchise proposal emerged from a suggestion made by Mrs. Price during her July 24th farewell speech to the Women's Canadian Club. While expressing a few views on the women's suffrage movement, she recommended that before women campaigned for their own suffrage they should first curtail universal male enfranchisement to eliminate the enormous "ignorant vote" factor already being exploited by unscrupulous politicians and political agitators. If not culled beforehand, she warned, existing abuses would only be compounded when ignorant women gained the vote on the same terms as men.

Emily Kerby crafted a follow-up petition for consideration at the July 30th Local Council executive meeting. It requested that the provincial government "limit the franchise for men so that no man who cannot read and write the English language be allowed to exercise the franchise." In making her case from a feminist perspective, Mrs. Kerby urged that men who treated women as slaves, enforced child marriage of girls, and refused to learn English had no right to the vote. The executive agreed that restricting the franchise was a "logical first step toward a successful woman's suffrage."[14] An appropriate literacy test, it was thought, would be the reading and writing of the British constitution.

Two other "Ruthenian problem" petitions followed. One asked the provincial government to take steps to prevent child marriage of girls. Existing legislation required parental consent for the marriage of those under 18 in Alberta. The other petition asked for residential schools where girls would be taught school subjects in English and would be "trained in all branches of housework, gardening and dairying," the intent being to keep the girls in school long enough to learn Canadian ideals and ways before they married.

By the time the executive met in mid-September, complications had arisen. One of these was securing the National Council's permission in time for the fall meeting of the Legislature. With NCW's 1913 Annual Meeting now over, and with no prospect of that executive meeting until November, Calgary's own executive decided to ask NCW's Emergency Committee for permission by using the argument that the concern was a regional not a national matter. National did not respond quickly. At least two months elapsed before the Local Council received qualified permission: it must first have the backing of Alberta's other Councils of Women before approaching the provincial government, which would make it impossible to meet the fall Legislature deadline.

Closer scrutiny of the literacy test by some affiliated societies then revealed that the British Constitution was not a "definite code or set of laws" but a nebulous concept which encompassed "all the common and parliamentary laws and also laws of precedent in Britain." Confronted with this very daunting revelation, the words "Canadian Constitution" were substituted – in those days, that meant the British North America (BNA) Act.

Meanwhile, there were early indications of a problem with the restrictive marriage petition. Having examined the issue closely, the Women's Press Club members felt that stricter enforcement of the marriage law would be ineffectual in a culture where parents arranged the marriages. Because the Ruthenians wanted young girls to become young mothers, preventing the marriage of girls under 18 would only increase the social problem of illegitimacy. Changed legislation would have more impact. The Women's Missionary Society of Knox Presbyterian Church concurred: "The society decided that as Canadian Law allowed these marriages with the parent's consent, that such a petition would be useless, and that new legislation would have to be made to get at the root of the matter."[15]

The objections presaged defeat. The marriage restriction petition lost by nine to eight at the October Local Council meeting; however, a one vote loss was not hope abandoned. A determined Emily Kerby and other disappointed advocates considered the narrow rejection a grave, albeit temporary, setback which might be reversed after further enlightenment. In hindsight, the persuasive argument that preventing these early marriages would allow the girls more years of "Canadian" schooling must not have been clearly made.

As the Local Council's first vice-president, Emily Kerby undertook the role of harsh enlightener. In December of 1913, both papers reported a great deal of background information on Ruthenians taken from Emily Kerby's "masterful" address to the Naomi Mothers' Society. Cassandra-like in tone, it contained a curious mix of fact, fiction and dire prophecy. Mrs. Kerby explained that in rural Alberta, where most of the 70 000 Ruthenian immigrants lived, compulsory education regulations were simply ignored. The immigrants cocooned their children in traditional custom – the boys might attend school during the winter months, but the girls were kept at home, "taught to cook, keep house, pray, and hoe in the garden." She warned, "lack of education, in English and in civics," and the work of their own agitators among a population posed a potential threat to "Canadian laws and people" which would have dire consequences. "You women may turn this question down and put it away from you now," Mrs. Kerby added, "but the day is surely coming when you will give your sons to settle the disturbances arising from this."[16]

Ruthenian girls, she emphasized, were doubly handicapped. Besides being denied a formal education, girls had no say in their own marriage

and no protection under Alberta laws. Ruthenian fathers reigned supreme, and they wanted "under age" marriages because in their culture,
where families grew to 12 or 15, it was considered a disgrace if by the age
of 15 a girl was "not married and the mother of one or two children."
Emily Kerby's compassionate observation that child marriages caused
young women to age very prematurely could not be disputed, but two
further observations pertaining to congenital conditions – "the preva-
lence of one dead eye" and "unknown skin diseases" – would be challenged as irrational today.

As preferable as it might seem to restrict child marriage, it was almost
impossible to garner general support for restriction of consent. That
parental option also served to remove the soul-searing stigma of illegitimacy within the Canadian establishment itself. Special schools for Ruthenian girls, the longer process, offered a better hope. When the Calgary
Local Council of Women presented its petition asking the provincial
government to establish the school, Premier Sifton listened sympathetically and promised to address the proposal after his government had
established a school for the boys.[17] He was in no hurry. The premier saw
Ruthenians in a different light, and he felt their advantages outweighed
the disadvantages. Having proved their survival skills in Alberta's harsh
climate and soil regions, they had shown themselves to be tough enough
to break the land and stay, as well as desperate enough to prevail against
privation. The province needed them.[18]

The Canadianization of Ruthenian girls was addressed by another
organization. In the spring of 1917, the provincial WCTU proposed a trial
project for the Ruthenian area northeast of Edmonton. If the government
would set up two-room schools where one room could be used as a
demonstration and social centre, the WCTU would supply a domestic
science teacher to train girls in the Canadian way of keeping house and
cooking. Later that year, in the December issue of *Woman's Century*, Nellie
McClung, who described Ruthenian women more charitably as "hard
working and gentle," provided more information. Neighborhood women
would be encouraged to gather at the demonstration centre to learn
"modern sewing ... home-nursing, and the care and feeding of children,
and many other things." In fact, Canadian values probably became the
priority because the WCTU decided upon a social worker, "a consecrated
Christian woman," who would live with the teachers and use her own
judgment to help Ruthenian women realize "it is not their duty to let their
daughters marry at such an early age."[19] Just over a year later, Louise
McKinney, provincial president of the WCTU and MLA for Claresholm,
confirmed that the WCTU had sent the social worker.

Equal Franchise – Theirs for the Asking

*In view of the fact that there is little or no protection for women and girls
in the province of Alberta in cases of assault, and in view of the fact that their*

word is not accepted against a man's word, it is moved that we petition the government to grant the franchise to the women of Alberta, realizing that we must have some say in laws that make for protection of our girls.

Albertan, November 29, 1913.

So read the Local Council's equal franchise petition, which originated within the Social Services Committee headed by Emily Kerby. Its mothering genesis was the notorious Chinaman-Polish girl assault case, which also brought calls for women policemen and for the appointment of women to serve as juvenile court judges.

Early discussions about how women should press for the franchise differed, but there was general agreement that, in Alberta, where women already enjoyed the municipal vote, the provincial vote would be forthcoming without violent confrontation. Moreover, Emily Murphy and other feminists were convinced that the provincial franchise was there just for the asking. This view proved naïve. More effort lay ahead than was ever anticipated. Three long years, three large delegations and thousands of signatures later, Alberta's "theirs-for-the-asking" equal franchise legislation was finally assented to in due course on April 19, 1916, by the "powers-that-be."

The preliminary spade work for equal votes with men, or full franchise, was undertaken by the WCTU before the 1912 Calgary's Local Council even formed. Part of the problem faced by the WCTU then was that its energies were committed to the province-wide prohibition movement, which at that time depended upon the existing male vote. If women's votes were to swell the ranks, there had to be another province-wide campaign to enfranchise women before the prohibition referendum. This was no easy undertaking. Alberta's already municipally enfranchised women, unless fired by some special issue, had proven themselves unresponsive to that ballot, so there was much consciousness-raising to be done if they were to embrace the equal franchise movement in time.

Local Council strategists in Calgary may have intentionally deferred an overt equal franchise campaign until 1914, deciding instead that the best time to ask for the provincial franchise was after women had clearly demonstrated their "enjoyment" of their municipal ballot. From its outset, in a series of well-publicized moves, the Local Council's Civic Committee oriented women on voting procedures and local issues, the highlight being the seminal December 1912 women's pre-election forum. Then, early in 1913, the Women's Council took another step: it petitioned to have the City Charter amended to make women eligible for public school trustee. In anticipation of the 1913 municipal election, new women voters were registered, and at the appropriate time, the Local Council selected an above-reproach woman school trustee candidate. That year, conduct of the pre-election forum showed new sophistication. "The women changed their tactics this year, and instead of a printed list of questions read by a gentle-voiced lady to each candidate, the women allowed each man five minutes for his spiel, heckled him with unexpected vigour, and finally dismissed the male element and settled down to talk it over."[20] Women were again urged to vote for reform-minded candidates (15 out of 23 hopefuls) and to do one thing new – vote for School Board candidate, Annie Foote. They responded.

Furthermore, by late 1913, the Local Council's restricted franchise proposal vis-à-vis the Ruthenians had been winnowed out, to be supplanted by a concerted campaign for equal franchise. Speaking to the January 1914 Annual Meeting on the Social Services' Committee's equal franchise petition, Emily Kerby seemed somewhat uncomfortable about this obvious shift to a new priority.[21] After putting forth her case, she clarified: "Last year we were talking restricted franchise and now you may think what does equal franchise mean now? What will they be talking about next?" She justified the new goal by explaining that an "eminent legal man" in the know had assured her the restricted franchise would be legislated "in the near future" so that, "no foreigner will be allowed to vote unless he can both read and write the English language."[22] That matter seemed to rest in capable male hands. (And rest it did, as time progressed.)

A thoroughly convinced Emily Kerby put her case for "the prosecution" of equal franchise to that January Annual Meeting in vintage Kerby style:

> You ask why is the necessity for equal suffrage. We do not recommend asking it on the usual grounds – equality with men. We do not want equality with some men but there are hundreds and thousands of good men who are willing to give women and girls good laws, but they are handicapped by the men below the average. . . . Don't tell me the old story about woman being placed on a pedestal. Things are usually placed there on account of their value or for protection. Men are afraid the possession of the franchise will drag women down, but men do not hesitate to drag down the pedestal. . . . We did not lose any of our womanliness in the recent civic election, why should we in provincial or Dominion?[23]

The province-wide campaign strategies began to surface by January of 1914. At its Lethbridge conference the United Farmers of Alberta agreed to put the question of support for women's suffrage on the final day's agenda and voted unanimously for it; the Calgary Suffrage Society announced that because the Local Council had taken up the franchise question, it was no longer needed.

Without doubt, the Calgary Local Council of Women had taken on a complex obligation. Over and above its other ongoing commitments, it had to process the petition through its own time-consuming vetting procedures, secure the endorsement of the other local councils, speak to the unconverted and collect signatures. More streamlined organizations soon seemed to have passed it by. By the time the Local Council's executive endorsed the Social Services Committee's equal franchise petition a month later, in February, it still had to be sent to the affiliated societies.[24] At this juncture, the Protestant church based Association of Temperance and Moral Reform Workers had already passed its own franchise resolution; the United Farmers were circulating their petitions in the country districts; Louise McKinney's WCTU was covering the small towns, and the Edmonton Political Equality League was on the campaign trail. It was April before the Local Council sent out its petition to its own affiliates along with that month's agenda and mid-May before the Local Council finally got its petition campaign underway. Vast in scale and concept, the provincial petition campaign survived the disruption of the outbreak of World War I, and everything came together by the October first deadline insisted upon by Professor Alexander of Edmonton's Equal Franchise League.

On October tenth, a 15-member delegation of women and men met with Premier Sifton to present to him a total of 44 000 signatures, 7000 of them from the country.[25] Simply put, the petition presented from Calgary by Mrs. Jamieson asked that the word "male" be stricken from the appropriate paragraph in the electoral act where it appeared in front of the word "persons."

What transpired was mainly preliminary, because both sides showed due deference to the pre-emptive outbreak of War. Premier Sifton advised against contentious issues coming before the Legislature right now and against entailing expenditures on new voter lists when those monies could be diverted to the war effort. After expressing his broad-based concern as to whether equal franchise was strongly supported in rural Alberta, a suave premier leavened disappointment with fulsome flattery. The premier was reported to have spoken "in the highest terms of the systematic and dignified manner in which the women had pursued their campaign."[26] "Many of the men," he said, "could take a leaf from the books of their unenfranchised sisters in this matter."[27] One of those unenfranchised sisters, Annie Langford, astutely anticipated a stalling tactic. The moment the premier queried whether there was country support, she pointed out that the petition's 7000 rural signatures had been garnered by the Farmers' Unions and the WCTU. But a greater concern overshadowed all else, and Professor W.H. Alexander of year-old Edmonton's Equal Franchise League deferred to wartime priorities. He explained that the real purpose of the meeting was to demonstrate the calibre of work done by organizations across the province. It was another trial run, but according to the *News-Telegram* and the *Albertan*, the delegation departed "with every hope that the object of their petition will be granted." The delay did have special portent. A vote on prohibition was in the offing.

Spring, hope and promises returned. Calgary's "always willing" Mrs. Jamieson came to join an even larger and more representative delegation, headed now by Edmonton's Nellie McClung. This time the Premier switched tactics. He did not evoke wartime priorities but called upon male precedent, as it were. The prohibition vote must be taken by those enfranchised at the time the prohibition petition was taken up. Elizabeth Bailey Price wrote of the three-time exercise in frustration:

> WE ALBERTA WOMEN *have always boasted that we have only to ask for equal suffrage and it would be granted. We've asked twice and we've been "turned down." We've asked politely, too; we've got names, we've followed every tactful by-way, but although our delegates have been politely received, yet the fact that they didn't get what they asked for is staring us in the face. It is glaringly befronting us.*[28]

The Premier's closing message urged more spade work. "Go back again, . . . use your influence on individual members, and secure the sympathy of the government as a whole, then, perhaps, . . . at the next session there may be changes in the franchise laws."

It was a crucial setback. The movement had been driven by a sure and certain feeling that only the women's vote could make Alberta dry. Each municipality voted on its own, and now the women could not cast ballots in the July local option prohibition vote. But, as the adage goes, "When a door closes, a window opens."

One month before the July 21st vote, the WCTU launched a city-wide women's petition signing campaign at a special meeting chaired by Local Council's president, Alice Jamieson. On that occasion, the provincial president, Louise McKinney, gave the keynote address. She urged that women workers collect the signatures of all women over 21 by door-to-door canvass. Drawing upon her recent canvassing experiences in southern Alberta, this battle-scarred WCTU veteran of the cause warned just how divisive the prohibition issue was. It could alienate personal friendships. Her own friends in one town would not even entertain her when she there came to speak in public. Prohibition could even be challenged as unpatriotic. One woman's organization would not endorse it because of the comfort rum rations brought in winter to the soldiers in the trenches. She warned that women were just as divided as men on prohibition, although their reasons might differ:

> Some women will not listen because they do not believe in women speaking on such a subject in public; some because they think prohibition is depriving people of their rights; some because they won't do without it in their cooking, on their tables and some more because they don't care if their husbands drink as long as they give them all the money they want.[29]

She had found that women's moral vision didn't necessarily surpass that of men. Some were quite able to consider that abstinence did not apply to them personally.

On June 21, 1915, Alberta voted in favor of prohibition by a majority of 20 000. With the exception of Lethbridge, every city in the province supported it. Calgary's 3000 majority had been greater than anticipated, with considerable credit due to Bob Edwards. This rather notorious non-teetotaller knew whereof he spoke when he came onside (albeit with some reservations) through the pages of his widely-read *Eye Opener*. Moreover, the women's signature petition fared well, with 5000 names affixed in Calgary alone. The Local Council of Women was not credited with the achievement – that was a WCTU triumph – but all of the women interviewed by the *News-Telegram* for post-victory rhapsodic comment, among them Mrs. Fred Langford, Mrs. A.M. Scott, Mrs. F.M. Black, Mrs. William Carson and Mrs. Sydney Houlton, were also Local Council influentials.

On victory night, after the polls closed, jubilant prohibitionists joined in an Eighth Avenue "parade de triomphe," the strangeness of which could only be seen today in a Hallowe'en procession. The next day's *News-Telegram* provided this mesmerizing account:

> As thousands of happy Calgarians passed, cheers were given for R.C. Edwards, W.M. Davidson, G.M. Thompson, [three of Calgary's four influential publishers] . . . and for a time Bedlam was let loose. Then came the "piece de resistance" of the whole affair – the laying away of John Barleycorn himself. . . . On a float near the head of the procession had been planted a tattered and forlorn-looking figure, topped with a death's head and on placards surrounding the effigy were the words, "Farewell to John Barleycorn," and "Here Lies John: There Will be No Resurrection."

A skeleton was attached to a gun carriage, and upon another float lay a gigantic bottle of rye, "with its business end to the west." Every parade needs a band, and the Salvation Army provided theirs, but only the music of the "patriotic airs" could be heard above the noise.[30] The "wets" drowned their sorrows at Calgary's bars and drank until those wells ran dry or until, at the unkind stroke of ten, the bars shut down.

With the prohibition vote settled upon Premier Sifton's ground rules, the final obstacle to the equal franchise appeal seemed removed. But the issue of limiting the franchise to those who could read and write English resurfaced again in October of 1915. It threatened to pose a further, last-minute obstacle, created this time, ironically, by one of Local Council's own affiliates. The Women Teachers' Association of Calgary insisted upon the principle of limited franchise, whereupon women would have to pass a qualifying literacy test. Opponents of this "schoolmarmish" idea felt that such a proposal would offer the government another excuse for refusal. It would be far better to accept the franchise on the present terms – equality with men – and then work to refine ballot restrictions to include both sexes. Although the Calgary Local Council did offer to include the request, it held out little hope. Emily Kerby explained that a previous delegation had already raised the idea only to be told by the Premier that if women wanted enfranchisement, they would have to accept it on the same terms as men. The Women Teacher's Association was advised to send its own delegate to re-enforce its case.

Premier Sifton's held out hope for the fall session proved prophetic. An anecdotal retrospective of that 1915 victory provided in 1921 by Byrtha Louise Stavert, a long-time member of Calgary's Local Council and the Women's Press Club, provides a lively account of the final appeal: "The war was a year old and woman's ability to serve the state had been amply proven when another delegation went up to Edmonton. This time . . . Mrs. Jamieson was the only Calgary woman to present the claims of Alberta women for enfranchisement but she was met in Edmonton by Mrs. McClung . . . and Mrs. Emily Murphy." The delegation was invited to speak before the Legislature, and Alice Jamieson was the seventh in line. Local Council's president, who had headed the first delegation, now had her final say. Alberta's women were not just asking the Legislature to grant them their privilege, they were asking for their rights. It was her hope "that the premier of Alberta would be 'the first in Canada to grant women full citizenship rights.'"[31]

Louise Stavert then described how Nellie McClung, "striking a characteristic pose," wrapped up debate. "Well gentlemen, you have listened to this flow of eloquence from the mouths of these ladies and all I can say is that there is nothing left for you to do but come across."[32] They did, and the franchise resolution passed with one dissenting vote from a man "who said he voted the other way because he didn't want the women to get the vote too easy." They didn't.

Although Alberta's was the first Legislature to vote for equal franchise, by the time the enabling legislation was assented to, on April 19, 1916, Manitoba and Saskatchewan had already passed theirs. Flattered as Sifton may have been by the prospect of Alberta becoming the first province to grant women the franchise on terms equal with men, and notwithstanding the fact that he personally introduced the first reading of the equal franchise legislation, in Alberta the mills of his Legislature ground slowly.

The March first debate on the second reading of the Bill proved a highlight, and the *Calgary News-Telegram* sketched the "Glory-be-day" scene:

> *When the Alberta legislature opened on Wednesday afternoon on one of the most historic sessions ever held in the province, the galleries of the magnificent edifice were a riot of color and women and girls crowded the speaker's, public and press galleries and even the corridors of the house. Mrs. Nellie McClung, who has done much to secure this boon for her sex, occupied a seat in the press gallery, and with her was Mrs. Arthur Murphy, the talented authoress. . . . Mrs. Jamieson and Mrs. Langford of Calgary were conspicuous onlookers.*

The account concluded:

Throughout the session the women listened attentively to the addresses of the different members, applauding all who spoke in favour of the suffrage movement and hissing their disapproval at the government member who went back on his party and declared his intention of voting against the bill.[33]

This distinction was earned by the government member, Mr. L. Boudreau, St. Albert, when he offered his opinion that "interference of women in public matters would cause them to lose affection for their children."[34] His comment was captioned "Here's a troglodyte" (caveman).

There were two outcomes of particular relevance to the Council of Women movement. When passage of the equal franchise bill became a certainty, Nellie McClung called an emergency meeting on March second at her Edmonton home for the purpose of forming a Provincial Laws Committee as the first step toward "directing women's use of the franchise in the best possible way." By mid-March its mandate was clear: legislation "dealing with a woman's interest in her husband's estate, equal parental rights, red light abatement, and proportional representation."[35] Mrs. O.C. Edwards was chosen to organize new local councils in as many communities as possible so that other women's associations away from the cities could be brought in. Indeed, by the end of March it did emerge as a Council of Women Provincial Laws Committee, and by the fall it had grown to include an impressive membership: the presidents and convenors of Calgary, Edmonton, Red Deer, Olds, Medicine Hat, Lethbridge and Macleod, as well as the provincial WCTU and the United Farm Women. Meanwhile, when the Laws Committee became a reality that previous spring, it was decided to ask that all legislative proposals within the province's jurisdiction be exempted from preliminary vetting through the National Council. Mrs. Harold Riley proposed a further step, suggesting the formation of a Provincial Council of Women. The expectation was that Manitoba and Saskatchewan would follow suit.

With the women of the three prairie provinces now entrusted with the ballot and those in British Columbia likely to be next, hopes rose that the women's franchise movement would quickly gather momentum in 1916. This did not happen. In Quebec the anti-suffrage movement was strong, and in Ontario, a proposed women's franchise bill did not even pass its second reading in the Legislature. It was turned down for the same reason that Premier Sifton had given in the fall of 1914 – it was too divisive an issue in wartime.

Another 1916 expectation was that provincially enfranchised women could vote federally. Parliament debated an enabling resolution on February 28th to no avail, although only one of the six supporters hedged. M.P. Edmond Proulx endorsed single women's suffrage but warned of the risk in marriage, "a house divided against itself on political lines" could fall. Richmond's M.P. G.W. Kyte, a rigid adherent to the "sturdy oak-clinging vine" tradition, railed against the whole idea, "Woman's suffrage was an evil only fit to rank with divorce," said he. The debate ended with Premier Borden's pronouncement that, "the whole question of the federal franchise would be considered in the near future, and with it the matter of woman's suffrage, which would be taken up, not on the basis of single provinces, but as regards the whole Dominion."[36] A year later, with the women of five provinces now enfranchised, Canada's constitutional lawyers advised that the Dominion Act did not affirm this voting privilege.[37]

That spring, Nellie McClung launched a federal franchise petition campaign on behalf of the Equal Franchise Board. Calgary's Local Council, under the presidency of Emily Kerby, supported the campaign. A highlight of the April 13th special meeeting was the encouraging letter received from R.B. Bennett. Calgary's M.P. now promised his "hearty" but qualified support. He advised the franchise should be given "reservedly" to cull those of foreign birth, especially those of alien enemy birth.[38, 39]

Bennett's caution anticipated restrictive federal legislation. On September 20th, 1917, the Borden government passed its controversial Wartime Elections Act which, among other things, limited women's franchise to the immediate relatives of soldiers and to women in the armed forces. The federal franchise had come, as it did provincially, in due time and after due consideration of the terms viewed appropriate in wartime by the Dominion's political strategists.

The Woman's Platform

The Woman's Platform was not the credo of a new feminist political party, nor was it the platform of any other kind of political party. It was a statement of guiding principles which Councils of Women prepared to encourage women to cast their ballots independently, for the most worthy candidates, irrespective of political affiliation. In those days, feminists and social reformers believed that the power of the woman's ballot, thus selectively focused on ideals, could bring about political and moral reform. Enfranchised women could one day force party politics above circumscribed personal survival strategies into the realm of the common weal.

On May 24, 1918, Canadian women aged 21 and over were granted the federal franchise. In July they received the right to stand as Members of Parliament. Shortly thereafter, the NCW undertook the preparation of a Woman's Platform in anticipation of a 1920 general election.[40] After receiving unanimous endorsement at the executive meeting in March of 1919, the project was launched by a circular letter which solicited opinions on important issues from women's organizations and individuals across the country. Respondents were told that time was of the essence because the document was to be ready for adoption at the annual meeting that June in Regina. It was not. There was disagreement over the content, and convention time constraints did not permit debate on whether past progress or new challenges should be incorporated. The postponement disappointed many, but NCW's *Interim Report*, published in January of 1920, indicated the response level was high. There was "no poverty of expressed opinion as to wrongs that should be righted, or legislation needed to improve the condition of women and children." Mrs. Adam Shortt of Ottawa and her 18-member Platform Committee, which included Alberta's Emily Murphy, Irene Parlby and Alice Jamieson, selected and summarized the most urgent and fundamental reforms. The concerns were not new but, rather, a timely reiteration of "those social problems for which tens of thousands of Canadian women had been giving their energy, time, and money during the last half century."

An apolitical document, it contained a mix of the practical and the ideal, of mothering, feminist and socialist aspirations. The format listed truth, justice, righteousness and loyalty as the four guiding principles and grouped specific reforms into three categories – political, social and industrial. Where duplication occurred, it was a deliberate co-ordinating strategy employed to bring about universality in those particular areas. Particular political goals, such as equal moral standards in public and private life, a speaking knowledge of English or French as a ballot prerequisite, and thrift in the administration of public and private affairs have yet to be achieved.

The welfare of children was such a paramount concern that child welfare sections were to be an integral part of Public Health Departments at all levels of government. With Quebec and British Columbia having opted out of prohibition by 1920, and the federal government having lifted wartime prohibition, lost ground had to be regained. Otherwise, the Social Standards lists differed. Uniform marriage and divorce laws (with no financial barrier) and the raising of the age of consent to 18 years were federal goals, whereas the provincial agenda was dominated by additional concerns for the health, educational, financial and legal vulnerability of the family, such as segregation of the feeble-minded, school medical inspections, free and compulsory education, physical training, no sex discrimination in technical training, mother's pensions, equal guardianship of children, dower rights and income. With the exception of prohibition and compulsory registration and cure of venereal disease, most became part of Canada's social fabric.

Except for the addition of a provincial minimum wage and eight-hour day work week, Provincial Industrial Standards mirrored federal. Both levels of government were asked to implement equal pay for work of equal value in quality and quantity, no sex discrimination policies in employment, collective bargaining, industrial co-operation and profit-sharing policies.

Formally adopted at the 1920 Annual Meeting, the Woman's Platform was intended as a lobby instrument. NCW's Federated Associations were asked to give the Platform their "widest publicity" and women were asked to personally "urge upon the members of the commons and senators, as well as upon candidates for election, their views as expressed in the Platform."[41] Readers were reminded that the distribution of the woman's platform did not mean that the National Council endorsed the idea of a woman's political party. This organization had no intention of moving beyond established party lines, but it did intend to educate women voters in time for their first federal election. That long anticipated event occurred just six months after National Council's delegates convened in Calgary for their Twenty-eighth Annual Meeting.

Chapter Six

Weaving Golden Threads of Thought

ↀ ↀ ↀ ↀ

The onlooker at such a congress as the twenty-eighth annual gathering . . .
is conscious of a deep desire for a master brain which could separate unerringly
all the golden threads of thought spinning about in the confusing, whirling
piles of straw and dross, could weave them into a coherent pattern, could then
envisage a complete, strong, beautiful fabric representing the sum total of all
worth while thought and effort circulating in the convention mill.
"What they did and did not," Woman's Century, June-July 1921.

In June of 1921, the Calgary Local Council of Women hosted the first
NCWC conference held in Alberta. Although bringing the Twenty-eighth
Congress to the foot of the Rockies did suggest to some a new horizon
envisaged from a greater height, the organization's own horizon would
change very, very slowly indeed. Decades later it would seem to some
that only the foothills had been scaled while others were climbing the
mountains.

The Twenty-eighth Annual Meeting was the first held after the 15 000
member Women's Christian Temperance Union had finally joined the
NCW, bringing its activist record of battles won for prohibition and
women's franchise. Feminism was in vogue, and new doers would make
their presence felt in a changed political landscape where federally enfranchised women anticipated their first election. Those visionary Council women who wanted to carry the organization into new frontiers
foresaw that if the National Council was to attract younger members, the
dominance of the old guard and the organization's tenacious adherence
to traditional procedures must diminish.

Two years earlier this tenacity had cost the organization its Winnipeg
Council. The critical point had been reached at the 1919 Annual Meeting
in Regina, when proxies blocked well-prepared constitution revisions
and watered down major proposed action on important issues to "approval in principle" status. The Winnipeg LCW subsequently withdrew
its NCW affiliation in protest, and the shock waves jarred the 400 000
member body to consider reducing its use. When rampant rumor predicted a western breakaway, Calgary's loyal Emily Kerby, writing as

"Constance Lynd" in *Woman's Century*, issued a rallying call to rejuvenate the mother organization instead:

> *The old National is all right in her ideas. True, she has a little too much Red Tape, and several yards of wire entanglements, before you can reach her, but her heart is right. Don't forsake our mother in her old age, let us stay and support her. Let us buy her some new clothes; replace the tape with elastic, and the wire entanglements with strands of silver. Let us rejuvenate and adapt her to the new role her children occupy, viz., citizenship.*[1]

There was no further disaffection, and hope renewed with the affiliation of the WCTU and with the adoption of the Woman's Platform in 1920.

In June of 1921, eight nationally federated societies, eight provincial councils, and 28 local councils sent their delegates to National's Annual Meeting to debate proposed and pending legislative reforms, Canada's current economic, educational, health and citizenship problems as well as one pending political aspiration – the Women Senators resolution.

Those women who gathered in Calgary now represented a broader cross-section of society with more divergent views. Their body politic included "women magistrates, members of Parliament, journalists, doctors, successful business women, nurses, many notable figures in the social or philanthropic circles of the various provinces and the usual impressive number of veteran home-makers, thoughtful mothers of families and useful citizens."[2] There was not necessarily strength in such diversity. Sometimes indecision prevailed, and golden threads of thought came unravelled.

The Herald's pre-conference editorial promised the Congress would be a superb event. Readers were assured that the National Council's leadership comprised many "brilliant and devoted Canadian women" who were "keen students of affairs," exemplary in their unsurpassed ability to conduct meetings strictly in accordance with the rules of debate and parliamentary procedure while carrying out their grand mission – the well-being of the Canadian home and the women and children therein – through evils remedied, reforms secured and legislation passed.

The host Council was a very credible federation of women's societies in its own right. Forty-seven Calgary community and sectarian organizations belonged. Church societies accounted for over one-third of the membership, while the other groups included five Mothers' Clubs and four WCTU branches. Separate influential associations, such as the YWCA, the Woman's Canadian Club, the American Woman's Club, the Women's Press Club, the Business Woman's Club, the Calgary Graduate Nurses' Society, the Housekeepers' Association, the Women's Auxiliary of the Tuberculosis Society and the Women's Musical Club, provided a balanced reflection of women's traditional and contemporary interests.[3] Although no overt suffrage society belonged, the Calgary Local Council had achieved an enviable municipal office record and the *Herald* anticipated that visitors would want to know:

> *Calgary is very proud of the fact that every woman occupying a public office in the city has been a member of the council with such outstanding examples as Mrs. R.R. Jamieson, first president of the council, and now police magistrate; Mrs. P.S. Woodhall, president and member of the School Board; Mrs. Fred Langford, magistrate and chairman of the School Board; and Alderman (Mrs.) Annie Gale, member of the City Council.*
>
> *Other women who have figured prominently in the community are Mrs. William Carson, member of the School Board, and president of the Society for the Prevention of Tuberculosis; Mrs. E.P. Newhall, who as convenor of domestic science, both in the local and the National councils, has waged a vigorous campaign on behalf of the consumer against the high cost of living, and Mrs. Harold Riley whose splendid work for the welfare of children is receiving Dominion-wide recognition.*[4]

Rising to the Occasion

For the nine-year-old Local Council, this Congress provided an opportunity to showcase the National movement and to foster local relevancy. Interested members of the public were invited to attend. Host committees planned for six months in advance to assure that Calgary would offer the very best in western hospitality. Mrs. Kerby reported the social program, now confirmed, to the May 20th Local Council meeting:

> *Thursday night . . . the delegates will be taken by scenic car to the Keith Sanatorium provided the bridge now under construction is completed. Friday there will be the big civic reception in the grounds surrounding the Lougheed home. . . . Saturday the delegates will spend in Banff, where tea will be provided at the "Y" club house. Monday night, a motor drive will be taken about the city. . . . Wednesday afternoon the delegates only will be entertained at the Burns' ranch, Midnapore.*[5]

There was to be a closing grand banquet at the Palliser Hotel. At this time, and whenever else deemed appropriate, the Congress would be graced with the distinguished presence of elected dignitaries, among them the Premier, the Deputy Minister for Health and Calgary's Mayor. Each rose to the occasion. At the convention's Monday morning opening Mayor Adams declared, "No convention has assembled in the city to which I could extend a more hearty welcome than to yours, which is working for the good of the city, the province and Canada as a whole."[6] Honorable Charles Mitchell, Alberta's Deputy Minister of Health, addressed the afternoon session. He credited women's organizations as being the major influence behind the creation of his two-year-old department, which provided nursing services to rural areas lacking doctors as well as health inspection of rural school children. The expansion of Alberta's rural hospital system, he declared, now set the standard for the Dominion. When Premier Stewart addressed the delegates on Wednesday evening, he acknowledged the Provincial Council's remarkable success with petitions:

We have direct evidence in the government of the influence of your annual meetings. . . . This body of women is so active, so enthusiastic and earnest in its work that it is useless to refuse them when they approach the government with their petitions or suggested amendments to provincial laws. In this province we have only refused the council once, and that was when it wanted us to interfere with Dominion legislature.[7,8]

Local press coverage of information-saturated sessions and layered luncheon speakers was generous and free of serious criticism with one exception – an *Albertan* editorial decrying the senate resolution. Opinions of leading delegates – Dr. Stowe Gullen, Emily Murphy, Charlotte Whitton, Maude Riley – seasoned accounts, while by popular demand, Nellie McClung, the celebrated western feminist, prohibitionist and novelist, became a pre-emptive speaker who made a few objective observations on how the National Council could best serve Canada. When one of NCW's leading feminists, Dr. Stowe Gullen, accepted a last-minute invitation to speak to a joint Canadian Club luncheon, she cleverly dispelled a prevailing illusion concerning women's unique brain size. Operational foibles, heated arguments and logistic flaws were highlighted later in the summer edition of the *Woman's Century*.

The press and the public came to Central Methodist Church and on the evening of June ninth, the particularly distinguished "thronged" Lougheed's beautiful Beaulieu and strolled among grounds transformed into a veritable fairyland by colored lights strung among the trees and shrubs. Civic reception guests were greeted by Calgary's president, Mrs. Woodhall, the National president, Mrs. Sanford, the hostess, Lady Lougheed, Alderman Mrs. Annie Gale, Mrs. R.R. Jamieson, Mrs. G.W. Kerby, Mrs. Harold Riley, and Mrs. T.B. Mofatt, president of the Woman's Canadian Club.[9]

On the same Friday as the civic reception, the noon program was changed to include Nellie McClung, whom the delegates longed to hear. In an inspirational "by their deeds ye shall know them" admonition, the West's celebrity urged the National Council to take the forward path; to act as the social conscience for the nation; to form the social cement binding the country's diverse factions together; to work for peace; to support public men; to encourage women to stand for office then loyally support the chosen ones. In glistening imagery she likened Canada to "a pile of sand, each grain in itself beautiful, but needing a social cement to bind all together to make a beautiful temple." Before closing, she delighted delegates with a glimpse into *Purple Springs*, her latest Pearl Watson novel. Tremendous applause followed words of thanks tendered by Lady Gibson and seconded by Mrs. Willoughby Cummings. After adding her personal expression of appreciation, NCW President Mrs. Sanford coyly posed a compromising request, "I have only one fault to find; you said 'You have a wonderful organization'; I want you to say 'We have a wonderful organization!'"[10] In her cheerful reply, Nellie McClung ignored the remark.[11]

Dr. Augusta Stowe Gullen replaced the Honorable Mary Ellen Smith, who was unable to address the Men's and Women's Canadian Club luncheon on June 14th. Like her famous mother, Emily Stowe, Dr. Gullen was a medical doctor, and as feminist president of the Canadian Suffrage Association, she was well-qualified to update her audience in both realms. "The cause of women is the cause nearest to my heart," she declared. Women were held back not by physical limitations but by lack of training and opportunity. "It is not long since the world laboured under two opinions, first that woman was a supernatural being, and second, that her brain was too small to admit of training."[12] The small brain syndrome was not confined to the female of the species, she teased, since some of the strongest male adherents to the theory were themselves found to have undersized brains.[13] In her speech this feminist argued that husbands should not take economic advantage of the marriage partnership by pauperizing their wives, for where else would a partner work without remuneration?

Actual Progress and Aspirations

The conference proper opened on Monday, June 13th with official greetings and reports of the table officers. Then the main work began – a combination of standing committee and special reports, final approval or rejection of previously circulated resolutions, with the emergency resolution option available to address valid immediate concerns. All of it was interspersed with pre-scheduled and pre-emptive procedural and constitutional matters which, on occasion, aborted any sense of continuity.

The Provincial Councils' diverse reports charted actual progress and aspirations elsewhere in Canada. Mrs. S.E. Clement, Manitoba's vice-president, stated there had been many requests for information on her province's very progressive social legislation in the area of mother's allowance, workman's compensation and child welfare laws. But their ongoing request for the establishment of a public health portfolio "had been laid on the table for future consideration."[14] The successes of New Brunswick's Council seemed smaller in comparison – sanitary protection of foods in stores and slaughter houses as well as the appointment of a woman food inspector and two women on the provincial Board of Moving Picture Censors. Miss E.C. Carmichael, vice-president for Nova Scotia, outlined pending matters there. One resolution yet to be presented to the Legislature asked that prisoners be paid at union rates, with maintenance costs to be deducted and the remaining monies sent to their families. Two others asked for improved housing for the mentally deficient and for an amendment to the Education Act to allow women to become school trustees.

Progress made in Ontario, the National Council's power base, was of paramount importance. In an overly lengthy account, Dr. Stowe Gullen remarked that in this, the Council's best year ever, the Ontario Legislature had assented to equal guardianship of children and compulsory mainte- nance of parents by their children. Women juvenile court magistrates would be appointed in large cities in the future. Pending resolutions asked for women jurors, especially in cases concerning women and children, women probation officers and police women. There were also resolutions requesting the remuneration of prisoners or their families, legal status for illegitimate children and a study of conditions in hospitals for the insane. In recognition of the importance of home-making, the government was asked to make domestic science a compulsory subject, and, in deference to Canada's dual culture, to require the teaching of both French and English in public schools. The request for university courses in playground supervision was a further recognition of the Council's early espousal of the playground movement. The Ontario Council's Dominion teaching certificate proposal is still worth considering today. By studying special courses in Canadian education and citizenship, teachers could then teach anywhere in Canada.

An interesting bias surfaced with regard to the banning of foreign publications. Ontario's resolution asking that Hearst Publications be excluded from Canada was retained in Dr. Gullen's vice-presidential account, but the BC Provincial Council resolution requesting that British magazines of a revolutionary nature be barred federally was deleted.[15] Mrs. Scott's defense was that she was only reporting what was a fact in BC, but to no avail. Those were the days of sacrosanct bonds with Empire.

Saskatchewan's graciously deferred report was respectfully terse. Given by the provincial vice-president, Mrs. Peverette, it dealt with the young council's efforts to improve legislation for women and children by asking for an increase in mother's pensions and legal rights for the illegitimate child. Only in Saskatchewan was there a fund in place to aid indigent expectant mothers.

Of all the National standing committee reports that formed the sub- stantive link with local councils, the most important was Laws, and the eminent authority in the field headed it. Mrs. O.C. Edward's 1921 Annual Report was ranked by the *Herald* as, "The most constructive and by all odds important report that has so far been presented to the meeting. . . ." The *Albertan* concurred. In the moral march of progress along the Woman's Platform, Mrs. Edwards was able to announce that the Committee's request for the age of consent to be raised to 18 years had been granted. This was a final federal victory after two decades of advocacy. During its April 22nd meeting with the Federal Minister of Justice, NCW's laws delegation had asked for the inclusion of women on juries sitting on cases where women were concerned; for extension of the indeterminate system of sentence for those men and women convicted of sexual offenses under the criminal code; for the abolition of fines as punishment for crimes of an immoral nature; for a uniform divorce law; for adultery to be made a crime; for wife desertion to be made an extraditable offense. Many were unresolved concerns, as was the request for women to enjoy the same rights to homestead as men.

Calgary's Mrs. J.J. Hall gave NCW's Mental Hygiene report in the absence of the National convenor, Mrs. Stead. Its content would not be considered politically correct today, but in those days there was a pre-occupation with the "mental illness menace" and its cause. After reassuring delegates that there had been great advances in the public's knowledge of mental hygiene, the convenor listed five principles which were "universally acknowledged to be true:" (1) Insanity is a disease which may be cured by proper remedial measures; (2) Feeble-mindedness is an inherited condition and is incurable; (3) Manual labor has been proved an invaluable remedial measure in the treatment of insanity; (4) Segregation is essential in preventing the increase of feeble-mindedness; (5) The insane and the feeble-minded should not be housed together and treated in the same manner. Statistics were used to prove that criminality and vice had a direct relation to insanity. On the basis of Montreal and Toronto statistics, the report targeted immigrants as one source of the feeble-minded and advised stricter mental examinations of the foreign-born before they were admitted to the country, making it possible to cull the subnormal before they became a Canadian problem. This advice was not so discriminatory as it seems, because a later recommendation from the Citizenship Committee proposed mental examination and subsequent registration of all subnormal cases within Canada in addition to mentally deficient women of child-bearing age being "supervised" – meaning, not allowed to reproduce.[16]

The idea still prevailed that the foreign-born, left to themselves, posed a threat to existing Canadian values and unity. In this context, Dr. Gullen, National's Citizenship chairman, proposed two approaches. Immigrants' knowledge of Canada should be a qualification for admittance, and once here, they should be Canadianized, not "left to themselves to form units apart and alone." NCW's Civics Committee proposed that adult "foreigners," both new and natural-born, could be Canadianized through contact with civic clubs which explained to them "the science of government and all problems of reconstruction." A follow-up comment suggested that local councils assume that role. Immigrants' children should take their citizenship courses in schools, in English of course.

The recommendation for uniform curricula in all Canadian schools, as proposed by NCW's Education Committee convenor, Mrs. Horace Parsons, provoked a prompt rejection. One reporter noted that it "was sent down to instantaneous defeat on the sensible ground that what we wanted in educational standards was not stultifying uniformity but intelligent variation to suit localities and inspiring initiative in educators."[17] The Committee itself did propose an interesting educational innovation: credits for home work – sweeping, dusting, wood-chopping – in order to recognize the talents of those children who did not excel at academics.

In 1921 Canada was still in the post-World War I reconstruction era. Canadians felt morally obligated to meet the medical and pension costs of its returned soldiers and to pay off the war debt, but the national economy had languished for almost four years. The Dominion was in an economic slump because Canadians were engaged in a kind of buyers' strike in the hopes that if purchases were withheld, prices would fall. The trade-off, however, was rising unemployment. The weapon of buyer thrift had proven to be a two-edged sword.

Mrs. McIvor, the energetic convenor of NCW's Home Economics Committee, began her Buy-in-Canada campaign months before the Annual Meeting. In a special January mail-out, she asked Local Councils to urge their affiliate members (and hence thousands of women) to purchase Canadian or Empire-made goods, not American. Based upon the premise that women held 90 percent of the buying power, Mrs. McIvor felt they could make a difference. Her faith knew no bounds. Canadian money kept in Canada would prove the panacea which paid off the war debt quickly, provided funds for the development of Canada's untouched mineral wealth, narrowed the unfavorable US trade balance and raised Canadian currency to a par exchange rate with the United States.

Mrs. Murray's in-depth report on federal taxation also addressed the need to generate debt reduction revenue. After criticizing the recently imposed sales tax as one which fell very heavily on the ultimate consumer and praising succession and income taxes because they fell on those best able to pay, NCW's Taxation convener then laid down four fundamentals for equitable taxation: "One, that taxes should fall lightly on industry; two, that they should be easily collectible; three, that they must be as certain as death, and four, that they should fall equally on all."[18] The Halifax feminist and editor was quite rightly judged to have a "clear and courageous grasp of a big subject."

Tensions – The Old Guard Versus the New

The "distinct cleavage between conservative and advanced opinion" noted by the *Woman's Century* reporter surfaced on several quite different occasions. One was during discussion on a proposed matrimonial law amendment. Existing marriage laws allowed a widower to marry his deceased wife's sister, but a widow could not marry her deceased husband's brother. The amendment to remove this discrimination "roused delegates to fever height." Traditionalists who supported the present law invoked, "the Church and clergy as their final court of appeal," while equal rights advocates "backed themselves up by science and the medical profession." There was also sex discrimination in the legal marriage age, less protection being offered to young girls. Dominion-wide the limit for boys was 14, but the limit for girls varied from 12 years in Quebec to 16 years in British Columbia. The Atlantic provinces and Saskatchewan required only parental consent when the contracting partners were minors. Alberta's law, which legalized marriage of girls of 14 in order to offset an illegitimate birth, provoked a considerable amount of vigorous protest. But there were others who defended it because of their religious and moral abhorrence of illegitimacy.

Another split occurred when the National Council of Women renewed its affiliation with the Social Services Council of Canada despite strong opposition from the Old Guard – identified in the *Woman's Century* report as Miss Carmichael, Mrs. O.C. Edwards, Mrs. Murray and Lady Gibson – who feared that NCW might be seen as recognizing a younger counterpart organization as being bigger and better. This situation suggests that newer movements were proving more attractive. Once passed, however, NCW's strong participation suggested a "If you can't beat them, join them" strategy. The conference named 18 NCW members to the Social Services Council's nine standing committees, a majority of which formed counterparts to National's own committees.

The health of NCW's body politic received its usual review in the form of proposed constitution and bylaw amendments. The carrying of the proxy (silent) vote again came under discussion at the meeting. Participation by proxy was an accepted Council procedure necessitated by NCW's desire to keep all its councils participating in annual conferences when distances and costs precluded their attendance. This procedural accommodation lent credence to NCW's claim to Parliament of Women status, but the proxy had two inherent flaws – it depleted actual attendance, and it sometimes predetermined important decisions, leaving only minor matters up for on-the-floor debate. This was at odds with the basic premise behind the Council of Women movement, which was that it would provide a forum for delegates from diverse backgrounds and persuasions to debate important concerns in order to persuade others to join in concerted action.

The smouldering proxy issue flared at the meeting during a time-consuming debate on a restrictive amendment which would allow only provincial vice-presidents to carry the proxy votes from federated associations. After a lengthy discussion the amendment passed, only to be followed by another contentious item: a compromise motion which would allow federated associations the option of sending a written-in vote on agenda matters to the corresponding secretary prior to the meeting. Viewed by supporters as being a move in the interests of "democracy and justice" it was opposed by those who considered it an extension of the *in absentia* proxy and felt it could further deplete attendance. The Queen's Alumnae and Social Service Council of Canada delegate, Charlotte Whitton, vividly warned this change would, "kill the women's parliament because the dead hand would strangle the living presence."[19] She urged that no action be taken.

The write-in backlash also worked against one innovative idea which would have expanded NCW's membership beyond its urban middle class base. Some delegates, Mrs. Harold Riley among them, felt that the Council of Women movement could and should encompass women living in remote areas and those in poorer circumstances by accepting their written-in opinions and votes on council matters. After identifying this membership extension proposal as a kind of *in absentia* variation of the proxy, that recommendation was deferred to the next annual meeting.

One conservative "mothering" resolution directed at acquiring future members seemed timely but carried only after vigorous debate. The proposal that girls' auxiliaries be instituted was certainly not radical. Precedents did exist in other organizations, the Women's Institutes being one. A more innovative move would have been actual membership. That idea had been explored in the January 1920 issue of *Woman's Century*, when an editorial writer urged that now was the psychological moment for Council of Women to lead the way by including young girls in its membership. Not by putting "old heads on young shoulders" or laying "the burdens of the day on the girls" but by formulating plans whereby "girls' work might be more closely knitted up" in the movement. She based her proposal upon the altruistic theory that girls would join in appreciation of the changes already wrought by Councils of Women – improved living conditions, fairer laws, better pay and greater educational opportunities.

No doubt sensing the difference between theory and practice, the conservative NCW opted for a notice of motion that girls' auxiliaries be attached to local councils with the proviso that the local councils involved should bring a recommendation to the next annual meeting, where the matter would be voted upon. Its presenter, Mrs. Willoughby Cummings, a charter NCW officer who believed that a feeder organization was vitally important to National Council's future, re-enforced her advocacy by examples. Auxiliaries could form themselves into study and social groups, contact new girls coming into the city and check on their circumstances, undertake special community work, identify special girl problems and bring them to the attention of the Local Council. Mrs. E.M. Murray lent her qualified support provided that young matrons would join.

But others felt quite threatened by the presence of young girls, and 25-year-old Charlotte Whitton, who could easily have been the granddaughter of NCW's president, Mrs. Stanford, or its convenor of laws, Mrs. O.C. Edwards, and the rest of the over-70 group, capitalized on the obvious generation gap. Putting apprehensive thought to words, she quickly cross-stitched a few shining threads of caution.

Miss Whitton pointed out that no group is as likely as a group of young girls between the ages of 16 and 25 to get the idea that everything else is 20 years behind the times. (A touch of hyperbole here, since one would hardly consider women in their 20s to be young girls.) Her rationale was that because young girls defer more to knowledge than experience, they might show disrespect. The delegate for Queens Alumnae and Kingston suggested a different solution. Without comment, the June 16th *Albertan* reported: "She would like to see the girls brought in and put in the gallery or on the footstools of local council."[20] After such a tactless remark, it is highly unlikely that young girls on the threshold of the roaring '20s would willingly submit to that humbling experience. (How Charlotte Whitton ever managed to be elected chief magistrate of Canada's capital city, and Canada's first mayor at that, should intrigue political historians.)

Miss Lucy Doyle, Dominion President of the Canadian Women's Press Club, felt that there was already over-organization in Canada and that the Councils of Women and the mother members therein should set such a fine example that young girls would want to join. Calgary's President, Mrs. Woodhall, seems to have wrapped up debate. She was of the opinion that there were already too many societies to take girls out of the home; she would prefer a council movement to bring them back home!

Want Women in the Senate Forthwith

The pending Women in the Senate resolution, which read "Resolved that the National Council of Women request the governor-general-in-council that women be forthwith appointed to the senate in Canada," was certainly more endorsed than debated by influential speakers. Emily Kerby, who seconded the proposal, explained that the presence of women in the Senate offered the best hope for the passage of moral reform legislation. Emily Murphy and Dr. Augusta Stowe Gullen concurred. No one seems to have mentioned what many already knew: that the Federated Women's Institutes headed by Emily Murphy since its 1919 founding had already passed such a resolution at its outset. Charlotte Whitton, who cast Kingston's lone opposing vote, clarified that she personally favored the idea, as did the Queen's Alumnae.

NCW's level of support does seems surprising. Because senatorships were patronage appointments to a bastion of male privilege, entry there should have been anathema to some. The overriding factor must have been frustration over defeats of earnestly hoped for parliamentary legislation which would have improved the lot of women and children. Prohibitionist forces within the National Council were outraged when the Senate vetoed a delaying bill which would have awaited the soldiers' return from overseas and a subsequent national referendum before discontinuing wartime prohibition. The Senate had also rejected an amendment to the criminal code which would have protected children under 16 from sexual and alcohol abuse in the home – a mothering concern if there ever was one.

By 1921 Emily Murphy was able to inform delegates that a backlog of 150 divorce applications now awaited the all-male Senate.[21] No women were there to hear the woman's side. It was eminently clear to many, Emily Murphy and Emily Kerby among them, that the work of conversion lay within the Senate, and women must have a presence there if Canada's reconstruction era was to be a period of moral renewal.

Emily Kerby's reason for endorsement accepted, her unqualified support seems surprising. A year and a half earlier Calgary's "Constance Lynd" had held the Senate up to ridicule and proposed abolition in a *Woman's Century* article. "[W]hat is the use of paying some ninety men the sum of $2500 each, annually? Men who too often have their position through 'political pull,' or as a gift, for services rendered to a party, or as a sort of 'pap' to the man, who in a constituency has done the 'underground work' of the party, yet who has never been successful in winning an election." If the Senate could not be abolished by legislation, then there was another way that august body would self-destruct. If men faced the prospect of a senate comprising at least half women, they would promptly abandon the institution anyway![22]

When Calgary's Local Council debated the resolution in the spring of 1921, it had already been opposed by the Women's Labour League, which considered the Senate "a decadent institution" and one of "the narrow ruts of special privilege inherited from the past."[23] But the Council swung totally in favor of the resolution after it was pointed out that the British House of Lords (equivalent of Canada's Senate) "had turned back the appeal of [British] women for a law to protect their sisters from the menace of white slavery 99 times."[24]

The reason given for Kingston's opposition vote at the 1921 convention was not reported. However, an *Albertan* editorial writer provided a strong case for the negative, and in doing so took the NCW to task for not asking for the Senate to be abolished. This "undemocratic institution" was not worth the time of enfranchised women. It was "an expensive luxury," "the foundation stone of patronage and election dishonesty," "a reflection on the Canadian ability to govern itself." The conference was reminded that it had other more important matters to attend to. "If the National Council of Women would use as much effort in trying to abolish the Senate as it is using to open its doors to the women of Canada, it would accomplish as much as all else that it has undertaken since it started its session in this city" was the writer's view.[25]

Delegates may have endorsed persons over principle. A later analytical *Woman's Century* editorial pointed out that the apolitical National Council had voted without due consideration of whether this resolution could be construed as political meddling. "The NCW cannot afford and must run no risk, if it means to remain in existence longer than the next federal election – now very close – of being even suspected of exploitation by this or that interest, party or individual."[26] The wishes of Emily Murphy and Augusta Stowe Gullen had automatically been followed out of respect and appreciation for their feminist efforts. Although the editorial did not identify Mrs. Murphy as a candidate, she was, and NCW's vote endorsed her.

Emily Murphy had been proposed by the Montreal Women's Club two years earlier when a vacancy occurred with the death of Alberta's Senator Talbot. Her appointment seemed possible even then because she came from a staunch Conservative background and the Conservatives were in power. A rather discreet sounding of influential politicians at that time also indicated support. However, when Prime Minister Borden was approached, he offered the opinion that the appointment of a woman senator would be unconstitutional under the British North America Act, which used the term "persons" as a qualification and women weren't persons within the meaning of the act. The BNA Act could only be amended by the British Parliament at the request of the Canadian House of Commons. The Prime Minister left the matter there.

When Borden resigned in July of 1920 to be succeeded by Arthur Meighen, hope renewed. Even though there was still only one Alberta vacancy, the *Morning Albertan* sustained reader interest with a November update on the revitalized, "very vigorous canvass of Conservative members of the House of Commons and of prominent Conservatives in Montreal and Toronto," as well as Magistrate Murphy's "qualifications for senatorial honours," which included the vice-presidency of the NCW, national presidency of the Canadian Women's Press Club, and presidency of the Edmonton Women's Canadian Club. Her advocacy was well-known within these organizations. "Mrs. Murphy has repeatedly drawn the attention of women's associations in Alberta to the need of women on the Senate in order to get through certain amendments to the criminal code advocated by the National Council of Women, and hitherto vetoed by the senate." Support was not confined to women's groups. Party strategists interested in garnering women's votes for the next federal election felt such an appointment might prove quite popular "among newly enfranchised women of the country."[27] The Conservatives did nothing further because government law officers still advised that senatorial eligibility as defined within existing legislation in the BNA Act excluded women.

Lobbying continued, however, and if politics be the art of timing, the timing was even better by June of 1921, when Emily Murphy informed delegates that four or five Alberta vacancies would probably need to be filled after the pending redistribution of seats. Although she allowed that the meaning of the word "persons" was still a vexing problem, Emily Murphy felt that there was no legal barrier to women entering the senate.

She was mistaken. The legal meaning of the word "persons" became crucial. Eight years would pass before that vexed word encompassed women – and when it did, the political landscape had changed. The Liberals held power, and there was no Senate vacancy in Alberta.

Banquet Closes in Stately Style

The *Herald*'s account of NCW's 1921 closing banquet began, "The big dining-room of the Palliser Hotel, which has been the scene of so many important functions, afforded the setting of what might be termed an epoch-making event." That evening shimmered with golden threads of thought, all most eruditely woven. Mrs. Harold Riley led with the loyal toast to the National Council, which she credited with having done more for the women and children of Canada than any other organized body. "Wars would cease when the nations ceased to take motherhood as a matter of course, and placed the mother on the highest human plane, giving her, and that priceless gift of God, her babe, a fighting chance."[28] The *Herald*'s account lauded Mrs. Kerby's toast to the press as a "brilliant satire, set in the gold of a very sane version of what the press might in future become." The Mayor's representative, Alderman J.W. Hugill juxtaposed two toasts to "Sovereign Woman." His tribute began with an elegant quote from Richard Sheridan, "Women govern us; let us render them perfect. The more they are enlightened, so much the more shall we be. On the cultivation of the mind of woman depends the wisdom of men." It closed in artless western style, "And now, in the stately language of the rancher and the cowboy, I looks toward you all and I also bows. I hopes I catches your eye."[29]

Before the Conference ended, National's President, Mrs. Sanford, in thanking the host Council pronounced the Calgary meeting to be "one of the most outstanding sessions that body had ever held."

Epilogue

The continuing lobby by women's organizations proved ineffectual until the leading advocate, Emily Murphy, took the legal route. Along with four other petitioners, she exercised a provision in a section of the Supreme Court Act which allowed a group of five interested citizens to seek interpretation of a doubtful constitutional point within the BNA Act. The credentials of Alberta's "Famous Five" read well: Emily Murphy of Edmonton was the first woman police court magistrate in the British Empire; Mrs. Louise McKinney of Claresholm was the first woman elected to a Legislature in Canada; Mrs. Irene Parlby of Alix was Alberta's first woman cabinet minister and, after BC's Mrs. Mary Ellen Smith, only the second in the Dominion; Mrs. Nellie McClung, now of Calgary, had been MLA for Edmonton in the Alberta Legislature; and Mrs. Henrietta Muir Edwards of Macleod was the National Council of Women's eminent, respected veteran Convenor of Laws. Their group petition was sent to Canada's Minister of Justice, who judged the meaning of the word "persons" to be worthy of clarification.

In 1928 two counsels argued the case pro and con for four hours before Canada's Supreme Court. The Crown argued that only "expressed legislation" could extend the suffrage to women, and Quebec's objection was that if women were admitted to the Senate, it would affect appointments to its legislative council because the qualifications in that province were the same.[30] When Canada's Supreme Court ruled unanimously that the term persons within the meaning of BNA Act as it applied to the Senate meant males only, the five women petitioned for an appeal to Canada's highest court, the Privy Council in London. Prospects improved there. The Hon. N.W. Rowell, acting for the appellants, sensed the bench's receptive attitude and noted that the Government counsel, Eugene Lafleur, presented facts without strong argument. On October 18, 1929, the issue was resolved by the British Privy Council, which ruled that "persons" included women, and therefore women, as "qualified persons," were eligible to be called to the Senate.[31]

Great was the rejoicing, especially in Alberta and among its five petitioners, most of whom were quoted, with Emily Murphy leading:

> *That the members of the judicial committee of the Privy Council have given a wider and more favorable interpretation to the word "persons" than that of the honorable members of the Supreme Court of Canada, is a matter of much gratification to myself and my co-appellants in Alberta. The same is applicable to all the women of Canada whom we have had the high pleasure to represent in a long and somewhat arduous struggle for full political rights.*[32]

Emily Murphy was not destined for the distinction of being the first woman senator in Canada and the British Empire. Four months later that honor was bestowed upon Mrs. Cairine Reay Wilson, a member of Ottawa's upper class Liberal establishment with impeccable party credentials. She was the daughter of the late esteemed Liberal senator Robert MacKay and the wife of a former Liberal MP, Norman Wilson. Eight years previously she had founded the Ottawa Women's Liberal Association; then she worked to found the National Federation of Liberal Women of Canada, in which she held office. By faith a Presbyterian and by good works a YWCA supporter, this former president of Ottawa's Woman's Canadian Club and fluently bilingual mother of eight was of pleasing mien as well, "The new woman senator looks amazingly young to be the mother of a family starting to grow up – old enough for senatorial honours but still on the sunny side of forty."[33]

Mrs. Wilson's appointment did not signify the beginning of the end of male imbalance in Canada's upper house – far from it. Between then and June of 1994, only 30 women entered the red chamber, less than one-tenth of the number of men. As of that June there were 86 men and 15 women in the 104-seat Senate with three vacancies to be filled.[34]

Chapter Seven

Silver Threads Among The Gold

ᏧᏩ ᏧᏩ ᏧᏩ ᏧᏩ

Calgary last hosted the National Council of Women Conference in May of 1978 at the Banff Springs Hotel. In keeping with the mountain setting, the Eighty-fifth Annual Meeting chose for its theme "New Heights," an examination of the NCW's past, present and future. Eight and a half decades since its founding, the venerable federation seemed caught in a time warp. Too much reliance on its long history of commendable achievements and complex constitutional procedures had impeded and outmoded it. Senator Joan Neiman, chairperson of the Senate Caucus and National Council's honorary laws convenor, was asked to address the problem. The invitation may have come too late, because a more contemporary women's lobby already enjoyed a higher profile.

In a hard-hitting, knowledgeable keynote address to the Banff Conference, Neiman advocated nothing less than a thorough housecleaning. Her advice was to "Scrap the resolution system, tedious parliamentary procedure, and the bland compromise statements which finally result."[1] She asked delegates a few soul-searching questions intended to determine if the time and effort spent was truly worthwhile, if their affiliate membership was well and carefully vetted, if funded projects were truly beneficial. Her inference was that most queries would be answered in the negative.

She contrasted the obvious paradox of how much had changed in social and economic conditions since the federation founded in 1893, and how little the Council itself had changed. Now, in order to make the most of the special talents and interests of working women with precious little time left over for their own families, let alone volunteer work, the Councils must become more accommodating and less stringent about outmoded, time-consuming procedures, especially its resolution process. Neiman cautioned that today's issues require a very sophisticated understanding of social and technological implications. Continuing to process a large number of resolutions calls into question whether each can be thoroughly investigated before being vetted by affiliates and councils themselves; whether subsequent amendments erode their original integrity; whether they are redundant even before presentation. She cautioned that credibility and relevancy matter a great deal when making important presentations to different levels of government, especially at the federal cabinet level. Faced with a proliferation of lobby groups, Ottawa now wanted to reduce cabinet meetings to once every two years, a point that was not lost on the NCW. Its request for a brief cabinet hearing in the autumn of 1977 had been refused and was finally granted in June of 1978 as a result of persistent lobbying by the president, Ruth Hinkley. Quite aware of this situation, Neiman advised that, from now on, NCW's new measure should be quality rather than quantity. Lapsing into near-western lingo she advised, "you will make governments move a little more smartly with a few good blasts rather than a bunch of buckshot!" Better to focus each year on a few major issues of greatest relevance to women, she suggested, even if it involved utilizing the outside expertise of a highly credible special interest organization. NCW could serve as its vetting agency, distributing a proposal nationally to determine grass roots support before the initiating organization took further action. This new type of vetting role offered relevancy.

Senator Neiman had delivered a change-or-die alert, but Maureen McTeer, NCW's honorary vice-president, did not agree. McTeer, whose husband Joe Clark was then Leader of the Opposition, possessed considerable political savvy. It was her feeling that the Council's traditional broad-based approach on women's issues had stood it in good stead and would continue to do so, if improved upon. She also believed that, although NCW's consultative process did not promote quick action, "government respects the opinion, comments and research done by Council because of its long history of commitment and involvement."[2] In her defense of tradition she gladdened the hearts of the traditionalists in the audience – for there were "more than a few grey hairs" among those gathered there. Indeed, older delegates predominated, particularly in National Council's leadership, where the officers' *vitae* included executive service within their chosen organization, usually up to the presidency, and Council positions at the local and provincial level. *Herald* reporter Elaine Smith felt that the seniority factor did not bode well for the future and that the age mix of Calgary's Council would better serve the organization. "In Calgary, the Local Council of Women has overcome the problems of structure and procedure by giving younger women 'a piece of the action'," she explained. "They are encouraged to speak out at meetings, take leadership roles and assume responsibility right away."[3]

Although this reporter did not elaborate further, younger women were attracted to the Council during the leadership of a sequence of contemporary-minded presidents – Joni Chorny, Gwen Thorssen and the current president, Betty Shifflett – who incorporated the local Status of Women movement as it emerged in the 70s. By 1978 the Local Council's affiliate membership numbered at least 35, and the base was broad indeed. There were the abiding church societies representing Protestant, Catholic, Orthodox and Jewish faiths; business and professional women's groups; the social University Women's Club and Faculty Women's Club; as well as the political groups, Conservative, Liberal and Social Credit women's associations. Community, national and international charitable and service organizations also belonged – the YWCA, IODE, LOBA (Ladies Orange Benevolent Association), Soroptomists, CNIB, CANSAVE, the Salvation Army Children's Village and UNICEF. Among the newer social action groups were the Senior Citizens' Council, the Family Life Education Council, the Calgary Birth Control Association, the Elizabeth Fry Society, the Calgary Women's Emergency Shelter, the Rape Crisis Centre and the Status of Women Action Committee. For the most part, these embodied contemporary feminist concerns.[4] At the 1978 Banff Conference, Senator Neiman did not mention that there was a rival national women's federation, but there was: the young and contemporary National Action Committee on the Status of Women (NAC). Centennial NCW historian, Dr. Naomi Griffiths, noted that by 1978 it was already perceived by others as the leading women's issues lobby.[5] NAC had been formed a mere six years previously, in 1972, as an outgrowth of the Royal Commission on the Status of Women and with some nurturing from the Council of Women.[6]

In their reports of the Conference, the press featured Senator Neiman's criticisms and included Ruth Hinkley's comment that a committee had already been established to review National's procedures.[7]

A Standing Ovation and a Surprise Osculation

But two memorable moments during the grand banquet went unreported in the press. Conference organizers had expected the first of these – the banquet address delivered by Frances Wright. Frances had been proudly chosen to showcase to the national level one of Calgary's most charismatic, promising young women. At that time she represented the Status of Women Action Committee on Local Council, and her convictions and ability had carried her into the federal political arena as Liberal candidate for Calgary Centre. Her speech brought a standing ovation.

The unexpected political statement which followed her speech brought no standing ovation, but it did bring a moment's silence. The convention host committee had every expectation that Alberta's minister without portfolio, the Honorable Stewart McCrae, would be forthcoming as the provincial government's emissary; however, confirmation proved elusive. Then, at the 11th hour, came the surprise revelation that Mr. John Kushner, MLA, would bring greetings.[8] Kushner arrived at the last minute, as bemused as his hosts. Without doubt he knew he was at the Banff Springs Hotel, but whether he knew with whom was questionable. Seated at the head table along with Ruth Hinkley, Senator Neiman, Prime Minister Trudeau's private secretary, Mary MacDonald, Betty Shifflett, Dr. Ruth Gorman, NCW's former honorary convenor of laws, and Maureen McTeer, the MLA for Calgary East digested fine food and inspirational address until it came his turn to "Bring greetings from The Province," as it were. Ever and above all else the many-splendored politician, John Kushner envisaged a pending federal election.[9] After a few complimentary remarks about the federal Conservatives, Kushner, in the protocol coup of all time, turned to Maureen McTeer, pronounced her "the Wife of the next Prime Minister of Canada" – and kissed her smack on the lips. The future proved him to be "smack on" in his political prediction when, much to the surprise of many pundits, Joe Clark was elected Prime Minister of Canada the following year.

Epilogue

ɔɜ ɔɜ ɔɜ ɔɜ

There is a tendency which should be guarded against in a woman's organization, and that is to exaggerate the importance of women just as women, and mothers just as mothers.

E.M. Murray, **Woman's Century**, *December 1919*

Like the early Council, the present one is a mothering society, but now the mothering interests are circumscribed, restricted to re-establishing the traditional, conservative, family-centred values as a bulwark against perceived erosion by the contemporary feminist Status of Women movement.

As was the case in Calgary's original 1895 Local Council, sectarian affiliates are once again in the majority, but the mix of these is different than it was. Among the six remaining church societies, four are Roman Catholic, one is Greek Orthodox, and only one is Protestant. The last two Protestant denominations left with the departure of St. David's United Church Women and the Macleod Presbyterian Women's Missionary Society. Only the First Baptist Church Women remain.

The Salvation Army is the only long-standing, community-based association still with the Local Council. The non-sectarian Young Women's Christian Association, the University Women's Club, and the Junior League of Calgary have left. The departure of the pro-choice Calgary Birth Control Association came as no surprise. When they left, it signalled the end of that feminist issue component within the Council.

Today the Local Council's non-sectarian affiliates are the Calgary Federation of Women United For Families, Calgary Pro-Life, Kids First, Serena, and the Crisis Pregnancy Centre. Membership is polarized on the right, having moved to the ranks of the issue-oriented pro-life movement. No longer does it embody the full spectrum of women's organizations: the right, the centre, and the left.

Calgary's present Local Council is also an anomaly because it reflects neither the National Council's federate membership nor its broad-based interests. Tensions are evident. Over the last few years, the Calgary Local Council has rejected specific national resolutions dealing with contemporary feminist issues and has earned the distinction of being the sole strong opponent of a recent NCWC-funded study – sufficiently opposed to protest to the national office, declaring the funded study an illegal undertaking, and to write to the Minister of Consumer and Corporate Affairs to that effect. It was a fascinating adversarial situation, because the Local Council's aims are supposed to be in harmony with its National body, yet neither body had even temporarily withdrawn affiliation.

From its founding years the Council of Women movement was intended to inspire members to exemplify and apply the all-embracing Golden Rule. Its main purpose was to provide a forum where women representing the spectrum of member organizations met on common ground, sublimating their differences to address common concerns. Its challenge was to build tolerance and consensus from diversity. The present situation begs the question: is there another women's umbrella organization in Calgary? There is, but it is much less formally structured. The purpose of the Calgary-based networking society Women Looking Forward (WLF) is to unite women's groups and individuals working towards the equality of women. According to an article entitled "Left-wing groups face REAL challenge," which appeared in the *Calgary Herald* on March third, 1994, Women Looking Forward was by then the umbrella organization for 85 local feminist groups.

Part Two

Highlights

Mrs. R. R. (Alice) Jamieson
Calgary Local Council President
(1912-1916), Canada's First Woman
Juvenile Court Magistrate and
Second Police Court Magistrate
(courtesy of Glenbow Archives)

Mrs. Harold (Maude) Riley
Calgary Local Council Convenor
of Laws (courtesy of
Glenbow Archives)

Mrs. George W. (Emily) Kerby
Calgary Local Council President
(1917). (courtesy of Glenbow
Archives)

Mrs. Fred (Annie) Langford
Calgary Local Council Vice-
President and Calgary's First
Woman Public School Board
Chairman. (courtesy of Glenbow
Archives)

Annie Graham Foote
Calgary's First Woman School
Trustee (1914-1917)
(courtesy of Calgary Board
of Education)

Mrs. William (Annie) Gale
Canada's First Alderwoman
(1918-1923)
(courtesy of Glenbow Archives)

Mrs. E.P. (Georgina) Newhall
President of Calgary Consumers'
League. (courtesy of
Glenbow Archives)

Mrs. P.S. (Lily) Woodhall
Calgary Local Council President
(1920-1921)
(courtesy of Glenbow Archives)

Alfred Cuddy
Calgary's Chief of Police (1912-1919)
(courtesy of City of Calgary Police
Archives)

T.A.P. Frost
Calgary Alderman (1912-1915)
(courtesy of City of Calgary Archives)

Hon. Arthur Sifton
Premier of Alberta (1910-1917)
(courtesy of Glenbow Archives)

Robert Chambers (Bob) Edwards
Editor Calgary Eye Opener
(courtesy of Glenbow Archives)

Chapter Eight

Annie Foote and Gender Balance

∽ ∽ ∽ ∽

In October of 1992, in the wake of the school board elections, a news item appeared in the *Calgary Herald* under the headline "Male Claims Sex A Factor," its point being that in recent years women had dominated both of Calgary's seven-member school boards. The observation was not overstated. In 1989 Catholic School supporters elected four women and three men; three years later, the ratio increased to six to one. In the corresponding Public School Board elections, Calgary's trustees were all women in 1989, and in 1992 only one man was elected. During a post-election interview, one leading Public School candidate expressed the view that his gender had played a part in his 1992 defeat as well as that of certain other male candidates. Voters, he believed, were showing a preference for female trustees.[1]

Before 1913, gender was not a choice; Calgary's school trustees had to be male. Then, in early January of that year, the Local Council of Women prepared a petition requesting a City Charter amendment which would make women eligible for the office of school trustee. The premise was that if women served on school boards, they would identify areas for improvements not noticed by men, and moral standards would rise as a result.

In planning their school trustee strategy, the LCW decided that electing one woman to the Board would be a realistic objective. After all, the one woman trustee precedent had already been set in Edmonton and in Toronto. The women chose Mrs. C.A. Stuart, Mrs. Cruikshank and Mrs. Jamieson to approach City Council, and a petition duly couched in legal terms was ready for executive consideration by the end of January. When LCW's adjourned annual meeting reconvened on March 29, 1913, 33 affiliated societies had endorsed the petition.

The new City Council in office already had in mind major revisions to the City Charter. Pending revisions were prepared and debated beforehand by City Council's Legislative Committee, a recommending body, in mid-May. Amendments passed by City Council then had to be debated and passed by the fall session of the Alberta Legislature if they were to become law before the civic election in December.

The proposed changes would widen eligibility for the offices of mayor and alderman, extend the franchise, and abolish the ward system. Widening eligibility for elected office meant lifting certain exclusions. In those days women weren't the only ones barred. The number of officials excluded was quite comprehensive – "any Judge, Sheriff, Deputy Sheriff, Clerk or Deputy Clerk, any salaried officer of the Dominion, Territories or City." Neither persons in holy orders nor ministers of any religious denomination could serve as mayor or alderman. The same held true for anyone holding a liquor license in Calgary.[2]

With moral reformers now on the City Council, the issue of qualifying ministers as well as women arose. The "fast and furious" legislative committee debate as reported on the front page of the *Morning Albertan* exposed polarized assessments of clergy. Aldermen Tergillis and former Baptist minister Frost, "urged strongly that ministers were among the best citizens in the community, were leaders of thought, and most exemplary citizens generally."[3] At least three other members disagreed. They argued that ministers' interests were sectarian and factious, in juxtaposition to the broad municipal interest. The negative prevailed and the legislative committee voted unanimously, albeit temporarily, to leave this exclusion in place. Whether this consensus was due to anti-clerical bias or to a matter of principle is debatable. The *News-Telegram* concluded that Alderman Crichton's condemnation of ministers as "sectarian, narrowminded and bigoted," unable to view public matters clearly "owing to the warping of their mental vision," determined the decision. The same report commented "This argument, delivered without prejudice, was unfortunately felt to adequately represent the feeling of the committee," then he made an ironic observation, "publicans and sinners and ministers are still disqualified, and cannot enter the star chamber as the people's representatives."[4]

However, a more worthy, *noblesse oblige* argument did prevail. Mr. L.T. English, secretary of the Alberta Federation of Labour, explained the exclusion was there to prevent church leaders in communities dominated by one religion from being elected to municipal government in order to manipulate matters in the interests of their particular sect. Although a city like Calgary was not at such risk, the committee was advised to uphold vulnerable communities.[5] The committee deferred, its conscience salved.

The most revisionist proposal, however, addressed the exclusion of women from public office. The Legislative Committee had decided to recommend an amendment that would allow women to sit on City Council. The proposed wording change would be gender neutral – replacing "male" with "person" whenever the gender word appeared to the detriment of the gentler sex. During discussion of the proposal, only one alderman was harsh in his opposition. It was the normally "mild and agreeable" Alderman Ramsay who turned churlish:

"Get women back in the kitchen where they belong," he said crossly. *"Women have no business running for office."*

"Oh, tut! tut!" said Ald. Frost soothingly.

When the motion to eliminate the word 'males' came up, Alderman Ramsay had not mellowed,

"Let the women stay home and clean up their kitchens. They have their hands full doing that," said Ald. Ramsay again.

"Whose kitchens are dirty? Why, man, you don't mean to say that women must have dirty kitchens on account of this!" exclaimed Ald. Crichton pacifically.

"Yes I do. I say that the majority of the women who are running around to these meetings lately, have houses that aren't fit to live in. They should be home shovelling the filth out of their kitchens."[6]

The motion carried – and the papers carried the news. A sarcastic editorial riposte in the next day's *News-Telegram* downgraded Alderman Ramsay's social status. "As the other members of the committee are regarded as drawing room company when they make a call, Alderman Ramsay had the kitchen to himself, an event which on other occasions has evidently given him those opportunities for inspection and reflection which are at the foundation of his expert knowledge." Electoral retribution now awaited him. "When he comes to reflect on his official utterances he will have visions of revenge floating before him. The kitchen will be his civic doom if ladies control the next election."[7,8]

When the Local Council of Women wrote Mayor Sinnot in early June with regard to the status of their trustee petition, he sent a brief acknowledgement to Mrs. Jamieson which contained the assurance that he was "personally supportive" of their request.[9] Local Council's letter was passed on to the Legislative Committee, which unanimously endorsed the requested charter amendment.

At this stage the author of a *News-Telegram* editorial lent qualified support to the Local Council of Women's school trustee petition. "A leaven of ladies on the school board would be an advantage," suggested the writer, who favored a minority limit but certainly not a majority. "If the council of women would consent only to an open contest in which no one but ladies might be elected, the result would be unsatisfactory."[10]

On June 23, 1913 the City Council adopted the recommendation of its Legislative Committee. The amendments, which received the assent of the Alberta Legislature on October 25th, qualified both ministers and women.

The idea of promoting women candidates for the two school board vacancies crystallized by mid-November. Readers of the daily papers knew that the women in Winnipeg might nominate a women trustee and that the Lethbridge Women's Civic Club intended to sponsor a woman trustee. Further affirmation came earlier that fall when the Calgary Public

School Board acknowledged the need for women's views on education by establishing a Ladies' Advisory Board of Technical Education to make recommendations on the women's evening classes now offered in four Calgary schools. The Board's mandate was to broaden the scope of technical education to include courses in culinary arts, dressmaking and millinery, drawing, and applied design. Mrs. R.R. Jamieson, Mrs. W.T.D. Lathwell and Mrs. F.M. Black were appointed.

Then, in November, a disturbing but somewhat fortuitous report on school sanitary conditions demonstrated the need for a woman school trustee. City Health Officer Dr. Mahood reported that, with few exceptions, Calgary's 6000 children attended uniformly unsanitary schools where lavatories were unclean, drinking water facilities dubious and windows kept closed – an outright condemnation in the days when serious communicable diseases spread unchecked. Editorial writers in both the *News-Telegram* and the *Morning Albertan* held that had there been a woman on the School Board, she would have seemed more approachable to concerned women teachers and would herself have been more aware of unsanitary conditions.

In the second week of November, the Council of Women appointed Mrs. Jamieson, Mrs. Riley and Mrs. Glass to select a woman candidate for the Public School Board. The ideal choice would be, "a woman who is thoroughly cognizant of the Calgary school system, and one who also understands the needs of children in the school. This woman, in addition to having a keen perception of local conditions, undoubtedly must be a mother who has learned their needs through her own children's experiences, or an experienced teacher."[11] Of the women who met the above criteria, some would be eliminated by the mandatory proprietary requirement: ownership of real estate to the value of $1000, free and clear.

On November 18th the Selection Committee announced its choice, one of Local Council's own members who as secretary of the Civic League Committee had conducted herself with distinction at the precedent-setting 1912 municipal candidates' forum. Miss Annie Graham Foote, the nominee of Mrs. Jamieson, was a highly respected teacher in her late 50s. Originally from Elora, Ontario, she arrived in Calgary in 1893 to teach school, and by the time she retired in 1911, she had taught every grade in the city system. Many of her former pupils were now voters. Almost an equal number of men and women signed her nomination papers; the most prominent groups represented were ministers and the Local Council itself.

The noteworthy signatories of Annie Foote's nomination papers and the Local Council of Women's endorsement were not lost on Bob Edwards. "The names which appear on Miss Foote's nomination papers are quite a sufficient guarantee that this lady is well fitted for the office," wrote the publisher. "The women folk of this city may be implicitly trusted when it comes to a matter of looking after the welfare of the young people. If they say 'Miss Foote,' Miss Foote it is."[12]

Miss Foote was left entirely free to prepare her own election platform. During her first speech to Local Council, she acknowledged their gesture of confidence and her intention to seek their advice and counsel if elected. For their part, the LCW intended to undertake a strenuous campaign to identify, inform and persuade women who met the proprietary qualifications to exercise their ballot. This time the Council set a campaign precedent, sending a letter to all women voters urging them to exercise their franchise and to vote for Miss Foote.

With one woman candidate in the field and two vacancies, the question of another nomination arose and was seriously considered by a group not affiliated with Local Council. Members of the ten-month-old Calgary Woman's Suffrage Society decided a mother would now be a suitable candidate for the other position. Several women who had previously held similar positions elsewhere were proposed, but all declined on the premise that they were not well enough known and could not become so in the time remaining before the election. Their strongest candidate was Mrs. Margaret Lewis, a local leader of the women's suffrage movement who had served on school boards in the old country. Before her arrival in Calgary a year earlier, she had spent 15 years working in the British suffrage movement, and years of frustration with pacifist methods had eventually changed her into a supporter of the militant wing. The reasons for her rather prompt withdrawal from the school trustee candidacy seem contradictory: she was not well known, and she might also jeopardize Miss Foote's chances. Probably the reality was that conservative Calgary voters were still apprehensive of overt suffrage societies, and Margaret Lewis had one under way in Calgary.

When the Local Council of Women held its second annual pre-election mass meeting on December fifth, 23 candidates addressed a large, lively crowd of women voters, and Miss Foote spoke last. In what an enthusiastic *Albertan* described as "one of the most admirable pieces of pre-election oratory offered at the meeting," she stressed her commitment to technical education and evening classes:

> If elected I will support strongly the policy of our present school board and officials in establishing and maintaining courses in manual training, domestic science and other lines of technical work, as well as the teaching of foreigners and others wishing help in our night classes. Such courses and such methods of teaching, added to those that aim at furnishing the student with the knowledge and culture obtained from books only, should give our pupils the all-round development of their powers and equip them as fully as school can for the lifework for which each is best fitted.[13]

When the election results were counted, 4986 had cast ballots, among them 543 women. In a field of four, Miss Foote received 3194 votes compared to 2339 for the other successful candidate, J.C. McNeil. (In the aldermanic race, Alderman Ramsay placed 20th in a field of 23, his fall uncushioned by female ballots. Women had not forgotten.)

For Annie Foote, the triumph was not that she was elected but that she topped the polls. "[H]er victory stands out as one of the most momentous ones in the history of all woman's movements in the Dominion of Canada," enthused the *News-Telegram*.[43] The *Calgary Daily Herald*, a moderate supporter of a woman school trustee during the campaign, sketched this sentimental portrait of Calgary's first woman trustee:

If Miss Foote has a fault surely it is that she is too modest. Asked for her photograph for publication she begged to be excused. She had not, she said, had one taken these 20 years and not having appeared pictorially in print she did not desire to do so now.

In appearance Miss Foote is womanly. As she spoke a kindly smile played round her lips, while the grey tinged hair bears testimony to her life's work, the results of which are now pledged to the service of the people of Calgary.[15]

Although Annie Foote credited "her ardent feminine supporters" with her success, at least half the votes garnered by Miss Foote came from "thoughtful men who never came in contact with her canvassers and who supported her because they believed that a trained and thoughtful woman would add strength to the board," ventured a *Calgary Herald* editorial writer.[16] Because she had topped the polls and garnered the most votes ever for a school trustee, it was suggested that she chair the Public School Board, a distinction she promptly declined. Instead she became head of the School Management Committee, which was considered so important that all five trustees served on it.

The school trustees were facing difficult times. Calgary's boom had ended in 1912, and a full fledged depression loomed. The strings on the public purse would need to be tightened. When the 1914 School Board considered raising the salaries of its secretary-treasurer and assistant superintendent by $300 in recognition of their competency, Miss Foote proved the lone opponent, refusing to change her stand even after half an hour of persuasive argument from the other trustees. Her stalwart commitment to retrenchment received editorial commendation from the *News-Telegram*: "The stand that Miss Foote has taken on the financial obligations of the board is in redemption of one of her pre-election promises, and her steadfastness in resisting the blandishments of her colleagues will be appreciated by her friends."[17] Her integrity, which a pre-election article had referred to as "rock-ribbed," had proved to be just that, but as it turned out, "her moral fibre strong as steel" was questioned less than one month later.[18]

Criticism arose from her support of fellow trustees Messrs. Taylor and Short throughout the Board's dubiously conducted special February third budget estimates meeting. Her voting pattern during that "irregular" meeting suggested untoward participation in a coup and membership in a partisan bloc which disregarded proper procedure. The coup occurred at the outset, when chairman James Short suddenly resigned. He promptly proposed S.Y. Taylor as his replacement, whereupon Messrs. Short and Taylor and Miss Foote quickly voted in favor over the secretary's interjection that the duly elected vice-chairman (J.T. Macdonald) should succeed.

Their voting pattern on school budget items showed consistent opposition to trustee Macdonald. Two of his most significant defeats were the costs of an expanded medical inspection service, of which he was the architect, and a proposal to defer the building of new schools. The *Calgary Daily Herald* described how his medical project was dispatched:

> *The guillotine worked fast and sure, as one head after another was lopped off by Trustees Taylor, Short and Foote. In three minutes, the board, with the exception of J. T. Macdonald, lopped off the heads of the two medical inspectors to the schools, and the City Council was asked to make the medical health officer responsible for the health of the school children of Calgary, in addition to his other duties. The question of the appointment of nurses was cast upon the scrap heap, and in the short space of three minutes one of the most vital questions affecting the health of thousands of the children of this city was settled, in spite of the warning given by Mr. Macdonald, who advised the board to discuss the question thoroughly at a future meeting specially for that purpose.*[19]

Just two months earlier the previous Board had received Mr. Macdonald's proposals with "unanimity and enthusiasm." But the new Board favored economy over paying for upgraded health services. Miss Foote's vote for the cost-cutting measure – her commitment to stringent economies notwithstanding – seems incompatible with the public's expectation that a woman trustee would be more responsive to school health concerns. When she later endorsed the expenditure of $50 000 for new bungalow schools out of current costs instead of supporting Macdonald's reasoned argument that the buildings weren't needed immediately, her commitment became obvious: it was to the voting bloc, not to the economy.

Without naming names, the *News-Telegram* was quick to censure the denial of Macdonald's chairmanship by a partisan faction: "It is not a nice thing to think that either personal or political considerations should play any part in the appointment of the presiding officer, of what should be an entirely independent and non-partisan organization: yet we are forced to say that there is, apparently, an undercurrent."[20] Miss Foote did not escape implied involvement.

Decisions reached in haste at that February third meeting had to be reconsidered with due deference to parliamentary procedure. Cooler heads and legal advice prevailed a week later at the regular monthly meeting. A replay of procedure analogous to musical chairs was advised, and this time the tune was more harmonious. And, as sometimes happens, the moment of leadership is all too brief. The heir apparent, J.T. Macdonald, earned the dubious historic distinction of having chaired for two minutes and nine seconds while Taylor was voted in on a motion by James Short, seconded by Annie Foote.

It was also the opinion of the city solicitor that the other resolutions passed at that special meeting should be reconsidered. This time vice-chairman Macdonald did triumph. He was appointed to a committee along with James Short and Superintendent A.M. Scott, to meet with the city's health board to determine if it would undertake medical inspection in the schools and, thus, assume the cost.[21] Annie Foote was one of those appointed to consult with principals and WCTU officials regarding the offer of the WCTU to give temperance instruction in the schools.

Miss Foote's support of Trustee Short and her preoccupation with stringent economic measures disillusioned Bob Edwards. Although she was not up for election in 1914, he wished she were. Instead he took aim at her cohort, whose term was coming to an end: "If Jimmy Short and Miss Foote were on the board of strategy at the war office, they would advocate arming the British soldiers with bows and arrows." He cited their opposition to Macdonald's "sensible and kindly proposal that free textbooks and scribblers be provided for children whose parents are unable to provide them" as an example of childish collusion against Macdonald and advised voters to remove Short, who had outlived his usefulness.[22] "Man wants but little here below but wants that little Short," was Edwards' pungent advice. Edwards also felt that the LCW's choice of Foote had harmed the women's movement:

> Her appointment not only has proven a fatal mistake, but her work has been sufficiently disappointing to set back the "woman's movement" in Calgary at least five or ten years. The mistake was not in placing a lady on the Board, but in making a choice of Miss Foote. How this otherwise estimable lady will be able to participate in board discussions without getting the high sign from Jimmy, should Jimmy be canned by the electors, as he ought to be, the Lord alone knows.[23]

In late 1914, at civic election time, there was some anticipation that a second woman candidate would try for election to the School Board. The LCW was expected to propose one or even two after Mrs. Jamieson and Mrs. Riley, in a consultation with Mayor Sinnot, had been assured that the Board was being enlarged from five to seven members. Several married women evidently had expressed an interest, but none could meet the mandatory property qualifications at a time when a wife was denied any right to her husband's property. After considering the calibre of that year's male candidates – one of whom was the Reverend George Kerby, Emily Kerby's husband, who became the first minister elected to serve as trustee – the Council decided that another woman was not needed at this time.[24] Nor did they nominate a woman trustee for the 1915 elections.

Annie Foote was persuaded to seek re-election after she received a petition signed by some 50 ladies confident of her ability.

Once again the School Board election focussed on the issue of health of school children and whether the new free medical inspection system should be continued. Two doctors campaigned on different sides, and Annie Foote was not really at the centre of the debate, although early in the year she had been the only one on the Board to vote against investing $10 000 to upgrade Calgary's backward school health services.[25]

She felt that the Board could save money by continuing with part-time services provided by the city medical health officer and his nurse and by relying on the teachers to identify sick children. She had support among the city's taxpayers, some of whom agreed that $10 000 was an unwarranted expenditure.[26]

When questioned about school medical inspection during the election campaign later that year, Miss Foote clarified that she was not against it, but she still felt that it should be the responsibility of the City Health Board. Her make-do response in an era of life-threatening childhood diseases was not enough to persuade voters that she was now a staunch advocate; nor was it enough to give the impression that she was a modern thinker. According to a commentary in the *Western Standard*, she had been a greater success as an "old time" teacher. What the Board needed was women with "modern views," women like Georgina Newhall, or Mrs. Harold Riley and Miss Agnes Waters, both of whom were former teachers. Bob Edwards concurred. Describing Annie Foote as "a most estimable lady," he still thought her to be "too early-Victorian to cope with modern conditions." He threw his support behind a progressive advocate, Dr. William Spankie. [27]

LCW president Alice Jamieson believed school medical inspections were a necessity, not a luxury, and that even in the present civic depression financial stringency should not take precedence over the health of Calgary's school children. In a motivational address to the Mothers' Club of Connaught she urged her audience "to ascertain whether or not the candidates who are to speak at the meeting for women electors are in favour of continuing the medical inspection; and to pin their faith to the man who does favour it."[28]

On election day the voters threw their support behind Dr. Spankie, and Annie Foote placed second behind the popular Archie Nimmo. Voter turnout was low – only 2000 compared to 7000 the year before – but Annie Foote still had solid support. She had the board's confidence as well. At its organizational meeting the Public School Board elected its single lady trustee vice-chairman, a position which she held until her retirement two years later.

Differences notwithstanding, Trustee Foote earned the respect of her colleagues. At the 1917 year-end Board meeting Chairman Davidson paid a glowing tribute to Calgary's first woman trustee saying, "Miss Foote had done more for the advancement of education and was closer associated with education affairs in the public schools than any other citizen in Calgary. The board and the officials appreciated the great work that she had done for Calgary schools. The public would not and could not appreciate it."[29] This last remark may well have been aimed at critics such as Bob Edwards.

When Miss Foote chose not to run again, Mrs. Annie Langford, widow of the Reverend Fred Langford, became Calgary's second woman school trustee. The daughter of a university professor, Reverend John Burwash, and a graduate of Mount Allison University in New Brunswick, Mrs. Langford was felt to be a most suitable candidate. She had long been involved with civic causes and had been commissioner of the juvenile court for several years. The first vice-president of the LCW, she was also active with the church, temperance and social reform. Her successful school trustee candidacy was endorsed unanimously by the LCW, and in 1921 she became the first woman to chair the Public School Board. By 1921 there were also two other influential Local Council women on the School Board, Mrs. Marion Carson and Mrs. Lily Woodhall.

Considering Annie Foote's outstanding electoral victory in 1913, it is puzzling that no woman candidate was proposed for aldermanic office while she served on the School Board. Granted, many civic-minded women were submerged in the war effort during those years, already overworked trying to manage household duties and support the soldiers, particularly through their Red Cross commitments. Local Council's Mrs. Harold Riley affirmed that women's present obligation was to provide comforts to the men fighting in the trenches, to the sick and wounded. It seems highly improbable that not one of Local Council's members knew from the outset that the trustee amendment of the City's Charter would automatically qualify women for City Council candidacy. Aldermen Ross, Tregillus, Frost and Maude Riley's husband, Harold, a recent MLA who was a successful aldermanic candidate in 1913, enjoyed the confidence of politically committed women. Probably these politicians advised a cautious approach, one that would allow male voters the opportunity to get accustomed to the idea of women in office. This was the key to their success. By asking less, women actually gained more. Alice Jamieson, Emily Kerby and other influential LCW leaders also understood that until more women were enfranchised and more voted, their early role would be mainly consciousness raising. The overwhelming support that male voters gave to Annie Foote proved that.

In seeking the office of school trustee, a woman had preceded a minister; in seeking aldermanic office that order was reversed.

It was a cleric who entered the star chamber first. In 1916 Reverend A. MacTaggart, pastor of St. Andrew's Presbyterian Church in east Calgary, a recent arrival from Winnipeg, was nominated by the local Ratepayers'

Association. Two days later the *Calgary News-Telegram* gave approval to his candidacy: "Mr. McTaggart believes in associating the church and its ideals with the city and with the state as well as with the individual and a leaven such as he would introduce into the aldermanic body would be distinctly beneficial." The writer then assured readers, "Mr. McTaggart has no axes to grind: he has no special class to serve; no interests he must consult other than the broad interests of the community."[30] Three and one-half years earlier, in the spring of 1913, when the exclusion of ministers was being debated, Alderman Crichton and his supporters shared the opposite view. Had prejudice abated?

Reverend McTaggart placed fourth among six successful candidates in the December 10, 1916 municipal elections. When the returns were published the following day, the *News-Telegram* felt that, in light of his voter support, there was no longer a bias against ministers becoming aldermen.

Then, the next year, one year before World War I ended, an attractive, intelligent, 40-year-old wife and mother accepted aldermanic nomination from the Women Ratepayers' Association.

Chapter Nine

Canada's First Woman Alderman

Seven months earlier, Annie Gale attended the April founding meeting of the Federation of Ratepayers, where she heard the president, Mr. Williams, warn women that their situation "was the same as that of a minister who went into political life and who must accept the same treatment as the ordinary politician." If they enter politics, he cautioned, "they should not expect because of their sex to be eliminated from the same dealings as that accorded men in public life."[1] These warnings proved particularly prophetic for Canada's first alderwoman, Annie Gale, who won three aldermanic elections, lost one, topped the polls in her only school trustee candidature, but lost her deposit when she stood for election to the Alberta Legislature.

Hannah Elizabeth Gale, née Rolinson, was born December 29, 1876, in Warwickshire, England. The daughter of a merchant grocer, she was privileged enough to be educated at the private Proprietory School for Girls, but responsible enough to go to work in the family store at age 15 upon her father's death.[2] According to one source, she was an honors student at school, one of the few girls in her day to pass the Oxford Entrance Examinations.[3]

In 1901 Annie married William Gale, described as a handsome civil engineer 13 years her senior, and for the next decade they moved around Britain from one engineering assignment to another. They emigrated to Canada with their two young sons, William and Henry, in 1912, having been persuaded by Annie's sister, who had come here earlier, that Calgary was a booming city where opportunities for civil engineers abounded. Upon arriving here, however, the Gales faced two unexpected and costly realities. There were very few houses to rent, so they soon built one, and there were no jobs awaiting civil engineers either, so William Gale was unemployed until he obtained a position in the city's engineering department.[4]

The culture shock that the young Englishwoman felt when they arrived at the height of the 1912 boom is recounted in her 1919 autobiography. "I was struck with what appeared to me the absurdly high price of land in what seemed to me the small town of Calgary," she wrote. "I looked with suspicion on the fever, the gambling spirit of the real estate dealers. . . . I looked around for industries, mills, something stable behind the city and could find very few."[5] People tolerated prohibitive store prices for vegetables of poor quality that were contracted from British Columbia growers. It seemed there was neither incentive nor interest in growing them locally, and without competition, the impoverished families suffered most. The cost of medical and hospital services also deprived the poor of their rightful access to health care. Calgary's seeming tolerance of socioeconomic injustice changed Annie Gale into an activist interested in women's suffrage and in righting community wrongs.

In the late spring of 1913, she joined the Consumers' League, an economic protest movement totally attuned to her sense of outrage over the continuing high cost of living in a city where the economy had begun to crumble a year earlier.[6] Under the presidency of Georgina Newhall and with Mrs. McGregor as interim secretary, the League proponents carried the campaign to other women's groups. They also canvassed small local producers in an effort to convince the dubious ones that interested buyers would now come.

During Local Council's second annual pre-election forum, the city market quickly emerged as the live issue. Euphoric over their leavening role in market regeneration, feisty Consumers' League members in the audience, Annie Gale among them, kept the League's profile high. Former commissioner and city license inspector, William Manarey, now a candidate for the office of city commissioner, fared particulary poorly in the heckling. His claim to equal credit for the market's success were ably trashed by Newhall and Singley (the president and the secretary), while Annie Gale in turn raised another rankling issue. "Tell the women why you so bitterly opposed us in an attempt to keep horses out of the market building." Manarey's lame reply that the horses were few in number resolved nothing. Later, when aldermanic candidate Hallet of the Retail Merchants' Association had the effrontery to criticize the league's most recent lobbying achievement, the reduction of butcher's license fees to one dollar, as opening the gates to vendors of trash meat, "the women almost hissed," whereupon Annie Gale sliced back noting that the meat inspectors were "so busy at the market that the butcher shops are almost free from their visitation."[7] She had been noted and quoted as an able advocate.

The lobby for market expansion and upgrading was long, frustrating and difficult, despite public support and the economic buffer it offered against World War I food profiteering. Annie Gale described the trials of her advocacy role:

> I used to meet the members of our City Board of Health to get regulations eliminated from the Health Act to encourage the small producers, and meet the Aldermen of the Legislative Committee to get By-Laws made and amended. On several of these occasions, when pleading with reactionary business men, I remarked: "Why do we not elect women with vision? We could get there much

quicker." But I never imagined in those days that we should ever dream of doing such an audacious thing.[8]

She did, however, view these municipal market confrontations as a learning experience which toughened her for aldermanic confrontations:

A fighting spirit, which was engendered absolutely by the necessities of this undertaking, remains with me to this day, and gives me courage to dare to oppose a full Council of men when occasion arises.[9]

In the autumn of 1914, she helped launch a different producer-consumer venture, the wartime Vacant Lots Garden Club. Its motto, "Make the Waste Places Fruitful Gardens," motivated residents to cope with food costs and shortages by growing fresh produce on leased empty lots – preparing the ground in the fall and planting it in the spring. The level of industry varied from year to year. Sometimes lots languished unattended, sometimes crops were left unharvested, but during the best years, thousands of lots were brought under cultivation.[10,11]

The unconscionable plight of isolated homestead women dying needlessly in childbirth for want of medical care in a province where veterinary service was provided almost free regardless of distance for livestock births drew her into another pioneer movement. She became Treasurer of the Free Public Hospitals League and a persuasive advocate convinced that, like the public school system, hospitals should be free. In the summer of 1916, Bob Edwards, wholly in favor of the idea, publicized in his *Eye Opener* a petition prepared for presentation to the fall session of the Legislature and named the workers, Annie Gale among them.

What proved to be of more relevant political interest, however, was Annie's presidency of the South Calgary Women Ratepayers' Association, which she had helped found in April 1917. The only one of its kind in Canada, its purpose was to introduce women to civic politics and politicians, so that they would one day be prepared to stand as candidates. Her involvement in this organization also allowed her to take a more active interest in elections than she could in her other position of political influence as President of the recently formed St. Mark's (Anglican) Church Guild, even though churches did influence community issues.

Even though Alberta women now had the provincial franchise, the prospect of a woman being elected at either level seemed remote to Annie Gale: "I have no vision of the women on the floor of the Legislature, nor in the council chamber. I think that the women, by the exercise of the franchise, will use it to place men in the Legislature who will represent the ideals of the women better in the future." She elaborated, "We want men who will embody our ideals in good government, and by good government I mean looking after the weak as well as the strong."[12]

That year, at the end of October, Annie Gale's active interest changed to candidacy when she accepted aldermanic nomination from her

Women Ratepayers' Association. In a rather ambivalent acceptance speech, she told a combined nominating meeting of the Federation – which also endorsed her – that she might not see the contest through, but she would discover for certain how men felt about women entering politics. Nevertheless, her next comment seemed to refute a temporary commitment. "'I do not expect,' she said, 'or want to receive any special treatment other than that which is accorded to men, as I fully realize that when women enter into public life they must be willing to submit to the criticism which is part of the price of public service.'"[13]

Two weeks later, a *News-Telegram* item speculated that other strong public women might run as well, rather than see her go to the polls alone.[14] Nellie McClung's column, "What The Women Of Alberta Are Doing And Saying," in the December edition of the *Woman's Century*, stated that Mrs. Grevette, president of the Next-of-Kin Association, was considering either aldermanic or trustee candidacy. Nonetheless, when nominations closed, Annie Gale was the lone female contestant.

Although her nominating society was in its infancy, and hence not that influential, Annie soon received impressive support. In November the Local Council of Women endorsed her candidacy along with that of the new school trustee candidate Annie Langford. The *Calgary Herald*, never an admirer, noted a difference in fervency. "Mrs. Fred Langford's decision to run for the school board was enthusiastically endorsed, and Mrs. W.J. Gale for the City Council was also approved."[15] The organization's preference for Annie Langford was real, and it resurfaced in ensuing elections. Furthermore, Local Council's executive had decided earlier that as a measure of wartime economy, members of City Council and boards should continue for another term. During the discussion, Mrs. Newhall stated she knew of no "particularly shining lights outside of the present council."[16]

Still, Annie Gale had support among Calgarians of note. Among those signing her nomination form were: R.B. Bennett, KC, M.C. Costello, MP (the successful incumbent mayoralty candidate), Anglican Bishop Cyprian Pinkham, *Calgary Eye Opener* publisher Bob Edwards, Public School Trustee Alexander Ross, Alice Jamieson, W.M. Davidson (Public School Board Chairman and publisher of the *Morning Albertan*), and Miss R.J. Coutts, a school teacher, LCW committee member, and a strong advocate of equal pay for women.[17] Mrs. Gale did not sign Mrs. Langford's trustee nomination form, but she did endorse Margaret Lewis for the Hospital Board.

Calgary's newspapers took note of Annie Gale's aldermanic candidacy. The *Calgary Herald* ran her attractive profile. Her friend Bob Edwards printed the same portrait, then championed her in "manly" western style:

Now then, cast your lamps over this cut and tell us if you can possibly resist voting for the original, who is the only woman running for the Calgary City Council. Mrs. Gale has for several years been active in many public movements of a useful nature and enjoys the distinction of having been the president of the first woman ratepayers' association formed in this city. This lady has all the mental and businesslike qualifications requisite for a seat on Calgary's council board.[18]

And the *News-Telegram* described her as more than competent to address the city's serious financial problems:

Mrs. Annie Gale should get a vote from everybody but herself. She will make the council a more profitable organization for the city and for the citizens. She possesses the invaluable attribute of an analytical mind and she is not afraid to ask questions and to gather information for herself and at the same time for the other citizens. Her marked ability in handling municipal questions has been known to the people of Calgary for several years, and she should have an opportunity to use that knowledge to the best advantage by serving on the council. It will be a mistake to leave Mrs. Gale off this board.[19]

From the outset, Annie Gale ran as an independent candidate unaligned with local factions. "We [women] should be free lances," she stressed, "steering our course by the righteousness and justice of the questions before us. We should be perfectly disinterested, and we could then be of untold benefit in raising the tone of public service, which is generally conceded to be badly in need of such elevation."[20]

She also wanted an arms-length relationship with the civic corporation. In this regard, she told a candidate's forum that her husband was leaving the city engineering department where he had been employed for the last five years so that, if elected, she would have "a free hand."[21] Her exemplary idealism notwithstanding, William Gale may not have resigned.[22]

Annie Gale actively solicited votes as Calgary's first woman aldermanic candidate, asking voters, especially women, to make her their first choice on the new preferential or ranking choice ballot to assure her election on the first count. Her feminist commitment was a determination to do well, but she acknowledged her feminist burden: "If I am elected and fail to make good, I shall consider that I have done the women's cause a great harm."[23]

Voter interest in the December 10, 1917, civic election was overshadowed by the federal election to be held a week later. For the first time, British subjects 21 years of age who were wives, daughters, sisters or mothers of armed service personnel, living or dead, or honorably discharged, would be able to vote. The issues were conscription and a coalition government, and women's exercise of this restrictive ballot was a patriotic obligation. When civic candidates spoke, they spoke to small audiences, and when voters finally voted in surprisingly large numbers

(5118), their main interests were the Wednesday half holiday bylaw, aldermanic pay and appointment of city commissioners.

Although Annie Gale was not among the four candidates elected on the first choice count, she was just two votes behind the fifth place candidate, Albert Mahaffy, a minister. Even though she expressed personal pleasure in placing sixth overall in a field of nine, she had not realized her hope of being elected on the first choice count. Why? At the statistical level, an unusually high number of spoiled ballots could have included votes for Annie Gale. One newspaper did note the number of queries from women voters confused by the new ranking choice system which replaced the old "X" ballot.[24]

Her membership and executive office in the Calgary People's Forum, a vehicle for the Canadian Labour movement, may have cast doubts on her Independent status claim. Although she credited this affiliation as a learning experience that enhanced her social conscience and understanding of union issues, and which later helped her in City Council labor negotiations, her participation implied a pro-labor bias. While replying to questions during the Forum's pre-election "aldermanic Sunday," Annie Gale stated she favored the trade union principle and civic employees organizing for mutual benefit. In the minds of political purists, she was not truly an Independent.

The original sponsoring organization may also have been a determining factor. It was the conservative, broadly-based Local Council of Women that had selected and sponsored Calgary's first woman candidate for public office, Annie Foote. Now, four years later, the new, rather feminist Women Ratepayers' Association nominated Annie Gale.[25] Local Council's more conservative women felt the time had not yet arrived for a woman to be in the limelight of civic office – women, they believed, should put their trust in worthy men – and would not give her their vote, even if LCW had endorsed her. Those who did think the time was right felt that several women were qualified, but Annie Gale was not among them.

There was no overt campaign evidence that Annie Gale had aimed too high, but in all of Canada, it seems, a woman had yet to be elected to a City Council. To conservative voters, women's echelon was the school and hospital board – an appropriate extension of their mothering role. Her City Council candidacy was a singularly feminist gesture for which no comforting precedent existed.

Although the *Morning Albertan* noted that Mrs. Gale was the "First Woman Member Of City Council In The Dominion," none of the city's three dailies mentioned that she had won the seat on her first attempt, a considerable achievement for anyone running for political office. The March 1918 *Woman's Century*, in noting that a woman candidate for Windsor's City Council had been disqualified because of her sex, congratulated Mrs. W.F. Gates [sic] on her election to the position of Calgary alderwoman in a field of 13 candidates. The editorial continued, "Old Ontario must 'sit up' and have legislation during the coming session which will enable her to keep pace with her sister province of the west."[26]

At the 1918 City Council organizational meeting, Annie Gale was not offered a chairmanship, but she was appointed to two standing committees. She was Mayor Costello's choice on Assessment and the aldermen's choice on Railways, Power, Development and New Industries. Despite its impressive name, the latter committee was said to be one that, "under the present circumstances, does not have much to do." Her board appointments for her first term of office included the VON and the Library Board, on which Mrs. Newhall joined her as a citizen appointee. The two women were also named to the High Cost of Living Committee.

In her second year she was once again appointed to the High Cost of Living Committee, as well as to the Receptions Committee and the Board of the VON. In the summer of 1919, she was also appointed acting mayor for three months, adding a unique political laurel to her first-woman-aldermanic crown. These distinctions attracted national attention, and *Maclean's* asked her to prepare her own story – an account of her commitments and philosophy – for publication in September.

In late November of that year, she stood for re-election, having served her two-year term as the only alderman with a record of perfect attendance at council meetings – family holidays excepted. Her 1919 campaign motto was "No governing body is complete without a woman's interest," and she stood on her record. Her accomplishments were cited in an *Albertan* article in defense of women entering public life:

> As yet only one woman has seen fit to offer her services to the city council, and no one can deny that her services have been valuable. She was the first member of the council to take a serious interest in health problems, and the result of her painstaking investigations has been improved hospital service in some ways, cleaner police cells, an increased supply of fresh unpasteurized milk from inspected cattle, and a more humane treatment of the insane who hitherto have been housed in the police cells like filthy cattle, while awaiting examination and commitment to the asylum. Ald. Gale has not accomplished everything she sought to do. She must have a greater amount of support from progressive thinking women before she can do this, but she has done good work in exposing many vile conditions and letting in the flood of light which inevitably awakes the public conscience.[27]

Her nomination was again endorsed by R.B. Bennett, Alexander Ross, Bob Edwards, W.M. Davidson, Mrs. Fenkell, president of the LCW, and others. Edwards had endorsed her earlier without reservation in mid-September:

> Whoever else may run for the City Council this fall, we must all see to it that Ald. Mrs. Gale is re-elected. This lady has proved herself one of the most

*valuable members on the council and, judged alone by her work, has more horse
sense than all the rest of the bunch put together. She gets down to earth and
makes a specialty of tackling matters which intimately concern the ordinary
folks of this city – and she has no fads. Blessed, thrice blessed be such a woman.*[28]

The low attendance at early election meetings presaged voter apathy,
until two local factions, business and labor, took action. Their vested
interest was to have their "men" on City Council. In the manoeuvering,
Annie Gale and Mrs. Langford unwittingly became embroiled in a ladies'
tempest in a political teapot. Rumor took precedence over substance,
machinations were described in minutest detail, and the nasty word
"cabal" was used.

On the civic scene, an embryonic Citizens' Committee formed on
December first "to stir up interest" – and that it did, when it immediately
endorsed a slate of civic candidates. James Ryan, the new Citizens'
Committee chairman, guaranteed the organization's integrity, "Calgary
people interested in good civic government, and in no way connected,
either directly or indirectly, with business concerns." "Everyone" was
invited to join.[29] Although Mrs. Fred Langford made the slate for school
trustee, Annie Gale was not chosen for alderman.

Her exclusion caused immediate repercussions. Rumor had it that a
group of nine women was planning a counter-attack committee to rally
forces for Mrs. Gale. Press coverage was immediate and partisan. Both
Mrs. Gale and Mrs. Langford issued public statements in their own
defense, and the reason for Annie Gale's exclusion surfaced in a depre-
cating news item that described the origin of the rumored women's
counter-attack committee, using as its source "information provided by
a member of the Citizens' Committee":

> *Mrs. S.G. Corse, Mrs. A. Grevette, and Ald. Mrs. A. Gale are alleged to
> have been the three chief promoters of a meeting attended by some nine local
> women on Wednesday to start a counter-attack on the Citizens' Committee.
> As one phase of their effort, the little gathering of women are said to have
> endeavoured to get Mrs. A. Langford, candidate for school trustee, who has
> received the endorsement of the Citizens' Committee, to withdraw from that
> endorsement and accept one from the new organization, which has apparently
> a semi-political flavour, as most of the women in it were noted for their activity
> on behalf of the provincial liberal government.*[30]

The *Herald*, which had backed the Citizens' Committee and Mrs.
Langford from the outset, described the meeting as one of secession by
the rebuffed. "Mrs. Grevette and others of those attending it had previously signed up promptly on the rolls of the Citizens' Committee, but
when they discovered that they were not in a position to dictate to the
large membership, with equal promptness, they withdrew to organize
their own following." The one they organized, the so called "counter-attack" committee, became the Woman's Civic Committee, with Mrs. A.

Grevette as acting chairman, Mrs. S.G. Corse as secretary, Miss E.P. McKinney as treasurer and Mrs. F.A. Davis as publicity chairman.[31]

The *Morning Albertan*, which supported Mrs. Gale as a woman alderman with a worthy record of civic service, offered a different explanation: the "several prominent women," who included the four mentioned in the *Herald* along with Mrs. Parkyn, had withdrawn from the Citizens' Committee upon discovering that their names would be used to endorse the aldermanic slate which did not include Mrs. Annie Gale. Among these prominent women, Mrs. Corse was quite prominent indeed, particularly in the Labor movement. "We are concerned in good city government as well as others," the women are quoted as saying, "and are willing to work in any campaign to forward good government, but we are not endorsing these particular candidates, and did not intend to be tricked into doing so."[32]

The next day, December 5, 1919, the *Herald* published Mrs. Langford's official denial of two rumors: that she had been asked to withdraw from the Citizens' Committee, and that she had refused to be endorsed by the Women's Civic Committee. Mrs. Parkyn provided a different version of what had really happened, and she put a fine point on it. She stated that Mrs. Langford did not enter the room of the local newspaper office where the women's committee was meeting. Instead, she knocked at the door and called out Mrs. Grevette to tell her she did not want the women's committee endorsement, but she would be glad to address any of their meetings. Mrs. Parkyn then needled: Mrs. Langford had not been endorsed.

Annie Gale's repudiation was published by the *Herald* on December eighth. She assured the *Herald* and its readers that she attended the aforementioned women's committee solely upon an invitation to explain her platform, which she did, and then left. She also denied any opposition to the Citizens' Committee and said she would welcome the vote of all its members on her behalf.

Why was Annie Gale not included on the Citizens' Committee's aldermanic slate? According to R.J. Deachman, a Labor candidate, the origins, membership and purpose of the Citizens' Committee served "capitalistic interests." There was no intent to include either a woman or a labor representative on the slate.

If Mr. Deachman was right, then Annie Gale lost on both counts. She had received the support of the Women's Labor League after Mrs. Corse had pointed out the deterrent effect of a certain element of the local population on potential women candidates. "The meeting felt that the women of the city should stand behind the women candidates in every way and a motion was passed expressing the appreciation of the league of Mrs. Gale's efforts on behalf of the city since she had been on city council."[33] During a forum held on the Sunday before the election, Annie

Gale commented wryly on her political image: "it had been reported to her by some of her canvassers that she was too partial to labor. Her stand had always been for fair wages and conditions, and she had never dreamt this would reflect on her in any way."[34] If she had unintentionally acquired Labor's political stripe, it was not one that was widely viewed. Labor forces fared poorly in the election, but Annie Gale fared well.

Voter turnout was the heaviest ever, 7000, and Annie Gale was the third alderman to be declared elected on the first choice ballot. She came in 163 votes behind the second place candidate, Alderman Broach. Calgary voters had strongly endorsed their first woman alderman for a second term. Then, in the summer of 1921, six months before the end of her second term, she decided to run in the July 18th provincial election as an independent candidate. Her timing could have been better: in this election she could neither campaign as the only Independent nor as the only woman.

There were five other Independents in that election, one of whom was Bob Edwards. His intermittent satirical weekly, the *Eye Opener*, was the most eagerly read in town and wherever it was mailed in Canada or overseas, and the one time he spoke during the summer campaign, to a veterans' rally, he received an overwhelming ovation. Edwards' telling cartoons, lampoons of pecksnifferism and tidbits of local gossip had been their morale raiser overseas, and the returned men had not forgotten.

Mrs. Fred Langford had also accepted an invitation to run for the incumbent Liberals led by Premier Stewart, considering it her moral right and duty to accept this opportunity. Mrs. Langford did not have Annie Gale's municipal government experience, but she benefitted from the endorsement of party candidates and leaders during political rallies. Just three days before the election, Mrs. Ralph Smith, identified as "the only woman in the world to hold a cabinet position and the only woman in the British Columbia Legislature," spoke on her behalf to a Liberal women's rally held at Crescent Heights School in northwest Calgary.[35] The Alberta Liberals welcomed the presence of this high-profile BC Minister who praised her long-time acquaintance Mrs. Langford as a woman well-known in Canada, an educated intelligent, refined person deserving of, "the support of all women who have the best interests of their sex and of humanity at heart."[36]

BC's Minister Without Portfolio also had strong Council of Women connections. In June of 1920, Mrs. Mary Ellen Smith represented Vancouver, New Westminster, Victoria and Nanaimo at the 1920 NCWC Annual Meeting held in St. John, New Brunswick. The next year she was a Calgary Local Council of Women nominee for the office of NCW vice-president. At that mid-July 1921 pre-election Liberal rally in Calgary, Mrs. P.S. Woodhall, then Local Council president, also urged support for Mrs. Langford, clarifying that she was speaking not as LCW president but as an individual. Nevertheless, her disclaimer certainly must have telegraphed a message.

Although the Honorable Mrs. Mary Ellen Smith's "special plea" was for Mrs. Langford, the BC Cabinet minister may have had more in common with Calgary's other woman candidate. Like Annie Gale, she had campaigned as an Independent on her first try for the Legislature, and she, too, believed very strongly that women should hold public office. "Whether men want women in public life or not, men have realized that women are citizens and must be reckoned with as such. The woman has just as much right to go out into the legislature, the house of the province, and clean it up as she has to stay home and clean her own house."[37] This statement echoed an earlier comment of Annie Gale's campaign, "I have always felt that the mission of women in political life was to clean up politics."[38]

Both Annie Gale and Annie Langford were forthright in declaring their conviction that women should seek legislative office, and both staunchly supported continued prohibition, a contentious political issue in the election. The WCTU, which had endorsed Mrs. Langford, was most concerned about the status of prohibition. The Prohibition Act was proving difficult to enforce, and anti-abstemious forces (the liquor interests and the Moderation League) posed a potentially powerful lobby for watered down amendments to the Act.

Annie Gale and Mrs. Langford were invited by the WCTU to explain their stand at a July eighth afternoon meeting. Mrs. Langford, who had suffered a fall, did not attend, but she sent a letter affirming she would work for complete suppression of the liquor traffic. In her view, alcohol was a beverage to be removed from the face of Alberta's earth. Annie Gale assured her audience that the Prohibition Act could not be moderated without another provincial plebiscite. She felt prohibition would be upheld if such a plebiscite were held, because the vote for it had been so strong. Meanwhile, she urged the women to work for enforcement of the Act: "Don't be discouraged, your work is not yet over. If women are true to their higher instinct, they will do as I have done and support prohibition. A nation that is temperate will achieve much greater things than a nation that is intemperate."[39]

An erroneous report that Annie Gale was endorsed by the Local Council of Women caused unfortunate and needless embarrassment during the campaign. Two disclaimers followed. The *Morning Albertan* explained, "in the report of H.B. Adshead's meeting . . . published in the Albertan Saturday morning, it was stated that Mrs. Gale 'disposed of the liquor question by stating she had been endorsed by the Local Council of Women on this issue and had always been strongly in support of prohibition.' What Mrs. Gale said was that she had attended a meeting of the WCTU that afternoon and had made her position quite clear," the Albertan stressed. "No reference was made by her of being endorsed by any organization."[40] LCW's terse clarification appeared at the bottom of the same page under the signature of LCW's president, Mrs. Lily C. Woodhall. All doubt was thus removed.

Annie Gale campaigned on her aldermanic achievements, among them successful charter amendment negotiations with the provincial government for increased local autonomy. Her nine-point platform attested to her breadth of knowledge and experience in civic matters: the division of fiscal responsibilities between the cities and the province, social welfare, unemployment, and industrial and agricultural development.

To publicize the policies of candidates, the *Morning Albertan* ran a political series printing the candidate's photograph each time and the issues addressed. In the July eleventh notice, "Direct Appeal to Women Voters in Calgary Riding," Annie Gale invoked the support of the Local Council, then subtly elevated her own political integrity above that of her colleague, Mrs. Langford, with the reminder that women should be non-partisan: "I feel that I am running true to the tenets of the Local Council of Women, and that members of its affiliated societies will support me. Women have always advocated independence of all party ties in their women candidates. I am conducting my own campaign, paying my own expenses, and this fact should plead for me and will, I am sure, enlist your support."[41] This appeal for Local Council support happened to coincide with the erroneous report and may have focused Mrs. Woodhall's official disclaimer of LCW's endorsement.

An informative but somewhat biased campaign analysis of the 1921 provincial campaign and its predicted outcome appeared in the July 13th edition of the *Western Farmer and Weekly Albertan*. Its author, William Irvine, identified a swing away from the traditional parties – the Liberals and Conservatives – to two newer ones based upon economic interests: the rural-based United Farmers of Alberta (UFA) and the urban-based Labour party, which he espoused.[42] He considered people who ran as independents to be anomalies, a disparate group without common ground and interest who thought they knew "what the people ought to want." Mr. Irvine correctly forecast a UFA victory overall but erred in his prediction that Calgary's six independent candidates, because they all appealed to the same middle class, were likely to be defeated. In the end, two won: Bob Edwards placed second and Col Pearson fifth among a field of 20 Calgary hopefuls. The other three Calgary seats were taken by two labor and one government candidate.

Neither woman was elected, but Mrs. Langford fared better. She polled less than half of the number of votes of the winning candidate, while Annie Gale received less than one-third and lost her deposit. In their post-election commentaries, both candidates spoke gently of their passage into the provincial night. "The people have had their way," commented Mrs. Langford to the Albertan soon after the returns were in, "so that is quite all right with me. We must abide by their will." Annie Gale was more analytical. "Men have not supported the women candidates in the provincial field as they did in the municipal contests. . . . This is a new field for women and it is only natural that the public should be very cautious. The women who enter the political field at this period must do so in a spirit of adventure and be prepared to accept gracefully the verdict, whatever it may be." Concluding on a patient note, she said: "There is plenty of time ahead and I am not discouraged for the future of independent women candidates."[43] In the *Herald* report, she stated that she "should have liked to have been elected so that every independent woman might be encouraged to run simply on the woman's platform."

Upset over the competition provided by Annie Langford, Annie Gale's strong supporter, Mrs. John Drummond, was less genteel in her Herald interview. "If the women of Calgary had been equally loyal to what has always been the dominant note in the woman's platform, to keep clear of party affiliations, our woman candidate who followed these ideals would not have had the unnecessary handicap of running alongside of a woman backed by a party organization." She lashed out, "If the contribution of women to politics is only to revivify and accentuate party lines, I think it would be in the interest of the community if they remained at their domestic duties where they would be less likely to retard the wheels of progress."[44]

Mrs. Sidney Houlton, district president of the WCTU, just blamed women voters generally:

> *From the Women's viewpoint, it is a matter of great regret that neither of the women candidates in Calgary was elected to the Legislature. The women of this city were strong enough to have returned at least one of their sex if they had used their ballot to the full extent of their voting power which they should certainly have done if they ever expect to take their part in the control of public affairs in this province.*[45]

But the news for women voters was not all bad. Three members of the later "Famous Five" ran in the same election, and two of them – Nellie McClung (Liberal) and Irene Parlby (UFA) – became members of the provincial Legislature. The third, Louise McKinney, lost. In 1917 she had been the first woman elected to the Alberta Legislature as a candidate for the Non-Partisan League. Four years later, she had won the UFA nomination in Claresholm only after a hard fight stemming from her "definite and courageous stand on the liquor question." The possibility of her losing the election was real even before voting day.

Undaunted, Annie Gale faced the 1921 civic election. She was still the only woman in a field of 15 aspirants for the six vacant council seats. Again she claimed to be independent of the two major civic factions – the Civic Government Association (CGA) and Labor – but the Women's Labor League did endorse her as a candidate known to be in sympathy with the labor movement.

Toward the campaign's end she became a target of the CGA, caught again in the partisan paper war between the *Herald* and the *Albertan*. Two days before the election, in an attempt to discredit her claim to independent status, the *Calgary Herald* attacked her for voting against a City Council proposal to allow stores to remain open throughout the week before Christmas. This would oblige store clerks to work all day the Wednesday before Christmas and take their half-day holiday the following week. Although two labor aldermen as well as Annie Gale voted against the store opening proposal, it was her motives that the *Herald* impugned:

"With Mrs. Gale it was a straight case of bidding for Labor's support on the eve of an election," then admonished "If Mrs. Gale would be a Labor alderman, let her secure the endorsation of the Labor men of the city. And if she is to be a Labor alderman, let Labor elect her." Those voters "who may have had any inclination to vote for Mrs. Gale" were asked to remember her "outstanding exhibition of bad judgment."[46]

The same day as the *Herald*'s attack, at the final civic candidates forum, Annie Gale defended her opposition to stores remaining open on the basis that the clerks, the people most affected, had not been consulted beforehand and she had always held that view in relation to working hours. She wryly noted, "such articles as appeared in the *Herald* did not make it easier for women to offer themselves for civic service."[47]

The *Albertan*, Annie Gale's press champion, reminded its readers of her value on Calgary's council.

1. *She has wider experience than any other candidate for the council board.*

2. *She belongs to neither group, neither the Citizens' Committee group, with its pessimism and its Hugill tax,[48] nor the Labor group, with its uncompromising attitude on municipal affairs.*

3. *She has been a competent, courageous and public-spirited representative.*

4. *She is a woman, the only woman with any experience in the city council and the only woman seeking election for wither city council or public school board.[49]*

Electors must have harkened more to the *Albertan*'s campaign. That year, 1921, saw the largest voter turnout in Calgary's history. On the final count Annie Gale placed third. The loyal *Albertan* commented proudly,

Mrs. Gale's election was a notable victory. She secured votes from nearly every candidate as the counts proceeded, and her first choices put her well up toward the top. Had the 1 000 or more women who found themselves disenfranchised through failure to register or otherwise voted, Mrs. Gale would have undoubledly . . . headed the poll.[50]

In terms of voter support, it was the summit of her aldermanic career. She had proved her mettle and risen above campaign attacks. When it came time for the 1923 election, her opponents used another tactic. The Lishman biography tells how her opponents engineered William Gale's resignation before the election, and describes the deterrent effect on his wife:

> *Several powerful men who could exert control when and where they chose approached Mr. Chapman, the city engineer and Mr. Gale's boss. They convinced Mr. Chapman that he should ask for William Gale's resignation and that, if he refused, that they should fire him. Mr. Gale had no choice but to comply.*[51] *. . . How could she continue on City Council when her husband had been forced to resign? Alderman Mrs. Annie Gale announced her intention not to be a candidate for re-election in the December 1923 elections.*[52]

Then, when it appeared that no woman candidate was forthcoming for public office, she reconsidered. Rather than allow those civic forces who wanted women out of public office to prevail, she promised her League of Women Voters that, as a matter of principle, she would now stand. When the League's president, Mrs. John Drummond, later volunteered to be a School Board candidate, a still reluctant Annie Gale asked to be allowed to withdraw. Instead of consenting, the members unanimously refused and warmly promised support. But when the two women approached the Local Council of Women for endorsement, a storm of controversy ensued. Although the LCW had supported Annie Foote, Mrs. Margaret Lewis, Annie Gale and Mrs. Fred Langford in their first (and successful) attempts to achieve public office, the organization had now decided to reverse its policy. The reason given was that ambitious women of lesser merit expected Local Council's influential endorsement just because they were women standing for public office. Unwilling to endorse women per se, Local Council had extricated itself from this delicate situation by passing a resolution prohibiting any further role in civic elections. By 1923, however, times had changed and some felt that Local Council should rescind that motion and return to its initial policy.

The issue was debated at LCW's executive meeting on November 16th, despite some concern that a return to endorsement could involve the Council of Women in provincial or federal elections and, thus, in party politics. The president, Mrs. Glass, reassured the executive that official approval of capable women candidates would conform with National's precept of furthering "the interests of good citizenship in every way possible." Such endorsement also demonstrated an affirmative commitment to adequate representation of women on public boards. Annie Gale, who was now Local Council's Convenor of Taxation, convinced the executive that the Council, with its machinery, should take this "wonderful opportunity for putting women into public office." The executive obliged. After rescinding its non-endorsement policy, the executive nominated Mrs. Annie Gale for alderman and Mrs. John Drummond for trustee. But a potential for conflict of interest existed. Once again the CGA's slate included Mrs. Annie Langford for school trustee, and Mrs. Langford was held in the highest regard by the executive. By comparison, Mrs. Drummond was the newcomer. With the gates to endorsement re-opened, other candidates also awaited without. The CGA wanted its all-male slate of aldermanic candidates endorsed, and Emily Kerby was the CGA's vice-president.

The controversy smouldered for two weeks until it erupted at the December sixth executive meeting. LCW's handwritten minutes provide the actual account of the dissension caused by the executive's seizure of that "wonderful opportunity to put women in office." The final solution provides an good example of strategic withdrawal.

> A letter from O.H. Patrick, Secy. Civic Government Association, asking the endorsation of the six candidates brought out by them was read. This letter called forth a great deal of discussion, Mrs. Briney and Mrs. Edwards being strongly in favor of endorsing the Civic Government candidates. Mrs. Woodhall wanted to know where all this would lead to. Mrs. Kerby stated endorsing candidates did not mean we were in duty bound to vote for them, it simply meant we considered them fit and proper persons to be members of the City Council or School board. Mrs. R. Smith rose to a Point of Order, asking if we were acting as individuals, – we could not as a Council Executive deal with these questions. Mrs. Riley and other members spoke of keeping friction out of the Council. The motion moved by Mrs. Birney and seconded by Mrs. Edwards –"That we, the executive of the Local council of women endorse the names brought for by the Civic Government Association" was not put to the meeting.

> Mrs. Drummond moved, Mrs. Annie Gale seconding, "That we do not endorse any candidates for Civic offices and that the former motion allowing the endorsation of candidates be rescinded." Cd.

> Mrs. Gale & Mrs. Drummond were commended upon their attitude in this matter.[53]

With the election campaign underway, Annie Gale once again found her credibility as an independent candidate attacked in *Calgary Herald*. This time a particularly persuasive editorial was directed to women voters:

> The women voters of Calgary have no objection to a woman being a member of the City Council, provided she displays the standard of judgment that is desirable in aldermen and does not play politics. The women of this city have been electing Mrs. Gale on her plea that she should be returned as an independent to look after the interests of the women and children. Once her election was assured, she reverted to voting consistently with the Labour aldermen.[54]

As election day drew nearer, she countered that she had stood by her principles in voting for social benefits such as the minimum wage, the factory act, pre-natal clinics, school clinics, and free hospitals and other services which bettered the lot of women and children.[55] When the votes were in, Annie Gale lost by a narrow margin, edged out on the eighth ballot count. Her friend, Mrs. Drummond, also lost, but Annie Langford won.

There is probably no overriding reason why Annie Gale finally lost a civic election. The *Albertan,* which still supported her claim to Independent status, pointed out that City Council was now a two-group government where the only successful aldermanic candidates stood for either the CGA or Labor. Reverend Alex McTaggart, an Independent with Labor leanings, had been defeated the year before, and now Annie Gale was gone. The *Albertan's* view was that Independent candidates had finally lost out because a vote cast by them was judged to support either CGA or Labor, rather than being a vote on principle. It stated that there was no doubt that Annie Gale was ideologically a socialist, and the faction which shared her commitments to improved working conditions, health services and bettering the lot of the poor was Labor.

Did she also lose because too few women voted, or because women did not vote for her? The latter appears to have been the case. The total male vote in the aldermanic contest was 6582 compared to 4240 ballots cast by women. As a *Herald* analyst pointed out: "had the women of Calgary been determined on a representative of their own sex in the council, they could easily have elected two members with their first choices."[56] The women's ballot now accounted for 39 percent of the aldermanic vote, but Annie Gale was not their candidate of choice.

The possibility that other women were envious cannot be discounted either. Annie Gale was a self-made woman who did not fit the mold. She was a doer, a leader ahead of her times in socio-economic reforms. She possessed an analytical mind, a fearless style of questioning, dogged perseverance and unwavering commitment. She was also a community activist who worked against the status quo. In public debates and association meetings her manner could be confrontational, and to hear her described as the power broker on City Council must have galled some.[57]

By contrast, Annie Langford enjoyed the general approbation of other women. She belonged to the establishment – her background and breeding were impeccable and references to her personality suggest that she was of gentle and harmonious disposition. She also "belonged" to important women's societies. Belonged in the sense of being 1912 president of the Central WCTU, being chosen to succeed Mrs. Price as president of the Woman's Canadian Club in 1913, and being nominated along with Mrs. Kerby to succeed Alice Jamieson as president of the Calgary Local Council of Women in 1917. Her style was not confrontational; more importantly, her civic aspirations did not extend beyond the level mentored by Local Council. That LCW bias was undoubtedly a factor in the embarrassing disputes over endorsement.

It is quite probable, too, that the earlier support of wives of city businessmen fell away. A *Herald* editorial pointed out the paradox of such women supporting Annie Gale:

While the husbands of these women have been working to get good business administrators for the city council, their wives have been electing Mrs. Gale, and she has regularly used her vote against the vote of aldermen elected by the efforts of men seeking good business administration. A genuine independent would, from time to time, at any rate, find opportunities to work with the business element in the council.[58]

Throughout her aldermanic career, Annie Gale had made enemies of the establishment. During her early council years, her well-publicized censorious City Market Advisor reports identified unsatisfactory procedures and officials, causing offense in the process. In the eyes of retail merchants, her stand favoring continued taxpayer subsidization of the market amounted to an unfair trade practice. Her crusade for the municipalization (sale by the city) of all food commodities brought her into conflict with city officials, her colleagues on City Council and tax-paying businessmen. Her argument that since a great deal of the money for unemployment relief came from the city, City Council rather than the Board of Public Welfare should have jurisdiction over the organization, so infuriated one of the community icons, Reverend D.A. McKillop, the superintendent of relief on the Board, that he threatened a libel suit.[59] Her controversial stand favoring taxation of churches not used entirely for spiritual purposes offended many in the religious community, inspiring a malicious letter to the editor which ended:

It seems too bad that we have in civic offices people who have no appreciation of the better and finer things of life. Aside from the service rendered to the city by these buildings, is it nothing to Alderman Gale that these same people who erected these churches dipped deeply into their pockets? Is it nothing that these churches contain fine organs which are also an asset to the community? Has Alderman Gale no sense of the value of good music to our city? It is surprising that one should be so absolutely ignorant of the real meaning of "a church."[60]

It was a vitriolic attack on the first president and founding member of St. Mark's Women's Guild, who was herself an accomplished musician.

Annie Gale was a feminist who campaigned on the principle that a woman alderman was a necessary ingredient for good civic government. This premise appealed more to the male voters' sense of fairness than it did to the enfranchised women who were not strong feminists. No woman candidate followed immediately in Annie Gale's footsteps, and it was four years before another woman entered Calgary's court of the star chamber. In conservative Calgary, a woman's proper civic office seemed still to be the School Board or the Hospital Board.

Her greatest electoral triumph occurred after her aldermanic career was over, when she became a Labor candidate for school trustee and worked overtly for the Party during the 1924 election. In keeping with her socialist commitments, she supported the long-debated expenditure of $10 000 for improved health services. Whichever side voters took on issues, they acknowledged her municipal background and outstanding abilities. In her final victory she led the polls, her election assured on the first choice ballot.

Throughout Annie Gale's years in public life, she enjoyed the loyal, proud support of her own family. She was a devoted wife and mother in a close-knit family whose members must have been scarred by the treatment meted out to her and her husband. When William was offered a good position on the West Coast, they decided to accept the opportunity to start again and live where the climate was better suited to his asthmatic condition.

The day before her departure, the leaders of 12 women's organizations, the Council of Women among them, and many personal friends gathered at a farewell tea in her honor. Nellie McClung paid her this tribute:

> *Women haven't had an easy time in public life, and Mrs. Gale has played her part courageously and intelligently. Mrs. Gale could always be depended upon to take a sane, forward, dependable view. Her tact and charming personality have carried her through many difficulties. Women haven't had an easy time in public life but they count the cost before they enter. Mrs. Gale has always upheld the standards of womanhood and we cherish the hope that she will come back to us again.*[61]

Annie Gale's own parting words were profoundly simple and charitable: "The work is its own reward because it develops you. I dearly loved my work here."

One wonders, however, just how pervasive charitable feelings were Both the Albertan and the Herald account of of those present at the farewell tea named over 70 women. For whatever good reason, Mrs. Kerby, Mrs. Woodhall, Mrs. Langford, Mrs. Newhall, Mrs. Jamieson and Mrs. Harold Riley weren't among them.

Chapter Ten

This Highest Office Yet Achieved by Woman

ᴄᴈ ᴄᴈ ᴄᴈ ᴄᴈ

A first of national importance occurred with the announcement in January of 1914 that Alice Jamieson was about to be appointed the first woman judge of a juvenile court in Alberta, indeed in all of Canada and the British Empire. The trumpet may have sounded, but the magisterial wall remained unbreached for more than a year.

By 1913 Alberta had established juvenile courts in its larger centres for the hearing of law and morals charges against juvenile offenders (those under 18 years of age).[1] The Rev. A.D. McDonald, Superintendent of the Children's Aid Society in Calgary, explained the approach taken: "wherever possible, mercy and leniency are shown and none but persistent offenders are severely punished. The idea of the court is to save the children, show them the folly of their ways and point out the disgrace and humiliation which will visit them if they persist in wrong doing."[2] Children so saved were counted as "rescued."

Juvenile court judges held appointments from both the provincial and federal governments, and their duty was to administer the Alberta Children's Protection Act and the Dominion Children's Act. The Alberta Children's Protection Act was modelled on the Ontario legislation, but the definitions were expanded to include practically all forms of neglect and delinquency in children under the age of 18. A roster of men chosen from among the pillars of the community – ministers, civic officials, church and youth leaders – served as magistrates.

Whenever possible, miscreants willing to mend their ways were returned to the support of their own families. But other children could not be repatriated. They included the victims of family breakdown, children at risk in their own homes, or the abandoned. The illegitimate child and pregnant adolescent girls who "went wrong" presented special problems. A constant concern was the shortage of suitable adults who would provide a wholesome, stable home atmosphere and some instruction in religion and morals, and who would not exploit the children as a source of free labor. In the interim, youngsters awaiting acceptance in foster homes, a return to their own homes, or a transfer to industrial schools were accommodated in the Children's Shelter managed by the Children's Aid Society.[3] The Society had a lofty mission indeed:

The Children's Aid Society stands for the cause of neglected, delinquent and homeless children. Its doors are open to all without regard to age, creed or nationality. Believing in the principle of equality and opportunity, it aims to give every unfortunate or dependent child a chance in the struggle of life. It regards the delinquent child as a victim of circumstances rather than a criminal, and seeks to win the wayward one to a love of what is right and true. It aims at making good citizens, and prevents the filling of prisons by reforming the boy and girl outside of the reformatory. In a word, the society aims to find homes for the homeless, to be a friend to the friendless, and to care for and protect the weak and erring.[4]

This was no light undertaking. The statistics contained in the Society's annual report for the year ending October 31, 1913, showed an average of 42 children cared for each month at the shelter. That year, 100 were returned to their parents and 56 were placed in foster homes.[5]

In Calgary's juvenile court, the Commissioners dealt with several hundred cases each year. In 1913, 92 sessions were held and 475 cases processed, 316 of which dealt with delinquency. In this large category, the majority of the delinquents were young girls, and 98 percent of their cases involved sex crimes. In testimony involving morals charges, the Provincial Superintendent of Neglected Children held that girls' credibility was at risk because their testimony was not given before a magistrate of their own sex. To address this inequity, the provincial government decided in 1914 to appoint women magistrates, beginning with Mrs. Jamieson.

The precedent-setting news of her appointment by the Attorney-General was not broken by local papers. Instead, it first appeared in the *Edmonton Journal* on January 22, 1914, two days before the *Calgary Herald* informed its front page readers: "Mrs. R.R. Jamieson Is First Woman Judge Of Juvenile Court." And it was the *Vancouver Sun,* not the local papers, which reported four days later: "First Woman Judge In Canada To Rule At Calgary." The *Winnipeg Free Press* item "Woman Head of Juvenile Court" overlooked the precedent altogether, noting instead her former charitable work there. The notices in these leading western newspapers were generally brief and factual, and none elaborated upon this precedent, even though it was an international one.

Calgary's *Morning Albertan* did include an enthusiastic commentary on the widespread reaction to the announcement: "Interest all over the country is being manifested in the appointment of Mrs. Jamieson. Eastern papers have commented on it freely, stating that the result of the appointment will be watched with interest, and prophesying that women magistrates will quite generally be appointed throughout the country in children's courts."[6] A Calgary *News-Telegram* editorial, published on the same day as Mrs. Jamieson's anticipated debut on the bench, concurred. "As an experiment in this country, the effect of the appointment upon offenders will be watched with much interest, and if the sequel justifies the trial, lady magistrates will become the rule in juvenile courts in other provinces than Alberta."[7]

A few months later, the eastern magazine *Everywoman's World* featured Alice Jamieson's appointment in its "Prominent Women" section under the heading "A Judge." By then, Alice Jamieson had even been likened in wisdom to "a twentieth century Portia" – a slight exaggeration of her advocacy role. The writer attributed the appointment to her involvement with the Children's Aid Society, where she had served as second vice-president since its beginning:

> *An influx of foreigners one year [1909] . . . brought with it the need on the part of the city to provide for the care of scores of neglected children. A Children's Aid and Shelter was formed, Mrs. Jamieson serving on the board. And doubtless it was her unfaltering service in this . . . connection which inspired Mr. Chadwick, Superintendent of Homes for Delinquent and Dependent Children of Alberta, to bring her appointment as magistrate to pass.*[8]

A letter to the editor of the *Women's Century*, the official organ of the National Council of Women of Canada, provided a more immediate reason:

> *During the autumn of 1913, a great deal of dissatisfaction was evidenced among the women of our city in various assault cases, where it seemed almost impossible to get a just verdict. The women expressed themselves very freely through the press in regard to it, which we believe led the men to realize that something must be done. . . .*
>
> *So through Mr. Chadwick, the children's probation officer, Mrs. Jamieson was offered the position which we are sure she will accept, as she is without doubt, the woman best adapted for the office at this time. It links up the whole womanhood of Calgary with a leader who is true and just, and whose one and only aim in life is service to her country. Again and again she has proven to us her worth, and so she passes up to this highest office yet achieved by woman, with the hearty support and best wishes of 3,000 women behind her of the council, as well as thousands of others not so connected.*

The letter, signed "Alberta," concluded on a note of local pride: "we are proud to figure in Canadian history as having our own Mrs. R.R. Jamieson for the first woman judge in Canada. And it came as a tribute to womanhood totally unasked."[9]

The cases referred to in the *Women's Century* were those where a minor's account of an assault was discredited by men sitting in judgment who favored the account of an adult male witness. Accounts of the notorious ones that occurred in 1913 and the reaction they provoked are excerpted from three local newspapers, the *Calgary News-Telegram*, the *Calgary Eye Opener* and the *Morning Albertan*.

The most inflammatory case involved a white child and an oriental male. In mid-summer of 1913, a member of the LCW Social Service Committee reported that a young Polish girl had been enticed, drugged and sexually violated by a Chinese storekeeper as she walked to and from St. Mary's School. Afraid to tell her parents, she had endured his perversion for over a year, until she finally confided in a policeman who understood Polish. The fear and outrage engendered by her story prompted the Local Council of Women to call for the appointment of women police officers.

Four months later, the accused, Tai Loy, appeared before the criminal assize of the Supreme Court, charged with criminally assaulting a girl of 14. The trial lasted all day, with the jury returning a verdict of not guilty because the members did not find the evidence very convincing. A week later, an editorial entitled "Was This A Miscarriage of Justice?" appeared in the *News-Telegram*:

> *Tai Loy, a Chinese resident of Calgary, who was indicted for outraging a girl of tender years, was tried at Calgary a few days ago and acquitted. The details were of a revolting character, and the jury must have had considerable difficulty in arriving at their verdict, for they occupied an hour and a half in deliberating. It has transpired that the evidence of the child was not convincing enough, and in the absence of corroborative testimony, they gave the accused the benefit of the doubt.[10]*

The writer offered an excuse – "The difficulty in all these cases is that a child gets confused in cross-examination, and a capable barrister can nearly always get the evidence so mixed up that acquittal usually follows." – but Bob Edwards did not. He saw corroborative testimony as nothing more than a dodge. This case and a similar one prompted him to write a scathing article condemning the court system. Using blunt, racist language that would shock modern sensibilities, Edwards wrote:

> *Some extraordinary verdicts and sentences are being pulled off in Calgary these days.*
>
> *A Chinaman running a store on First street west enticed a 14-year-old school girl into his store and debauched her. Having done this, he produced a revolver and threatened the child with death if she told and ordered her to come back again. The terrorized girl returned and was used for the Chinaman's vile purposes again and again, until, driven to distraction, she finally summoned up enough courage to tell her mother.*
>
> *The Chinaman was duly arrested and naturally denied the charge. It was unlikely he would admit it.*
>
> *The jury decided the Chink was not guilty on the ground that there was not enough corroborative testimony![11]*

He continued, "Every one knows that this is the commonest and most favourite and most successful trick . . . inveigling young girls into their stores with gifts of candy and perhaps a little pocket money, for the purpose of debauching them." Edward's described the mistrust given to evidence from a girl bold enough to tell her story, "a complacent judge and jury say the white child-girl is lying and that the bestial Chinaman is telling the truth, and the brute is honourably acquitted."

Edwards wrote hauntingly of the aftermath. "The girl and her poor mother walk sadly home from the court house, the girl with her disgrace, the mother with a ruined child to rear in a dishonoured home. The judge steps over to his club and the jury scatter to their various homes, laughing and joking over the events of the day."[12]

In a similar case, he made another sardonic observation noting that the accused Chinese man was given "the very heavy sentence of two months" whereas a two-year penitentiary term was meted out to two men who stole $28 from a comrade. Such civic and judicial attitudes aroused Edward's moral indignation. "The ruin of a child seems to be regarded in this city with appalling callousness by the citizens and by the bench. No wonder the mothers of Calgary are up in arms over the sublime indifference manifested by those in civic and judicial authority over the fate of their little girls."[13]

In addition to calling for the immediate appointment of women police officers, Local Council of Women's Social Service Committee proposed a far-reaching solution to the problem of how courts treated debauched women and young girls. On November 28th, the Committee, after listening to social service workers tell of similar frustrations with the courts, unanimously passed a resolution to petition the Alberta Legislature to grant the franchise to all women. "It was decided to ask for enfranchisement, not for equal rights with men, but as the only means affording protection for young women and girls."[14] All women, whether or not they belonged to the Local Council, were invited to join the franchise movement.

Six months later, the Reverend McDonald commented upon the ineffectual way in which the courts dealt with the sexual assaults on young girls by men whom he labelled "moral lepers":

> An outstanding feature of the month's work was the number of girl cases dealt with, the ages of girls ranging from 14 to 17 years. These girls were beginning to mingle with the votaries of folly, and coming under influences which, if unchecked, meant lasting shame and ruin. Action was taken in the police court against the four men, three of whom were married. Three of these cases were dismissed on the grounds of insufficient evidence. . . . In the cases referred to, the corroborative evidence was not considered strong enough to warrant conviction."[15]

That spring, when there was still no woman magistrate to address the "girl problem," Bob Edwards suspected bureaucratic stonewalling. Three months after the original January announcement, he expressed his irritation:

> The Attorney-General's department in Edmonton should get a move on and send along the commission for the lady-judgeship in Calgary's juvenile court.

The selection of Mrs. R.R. Jamieson for this office has met with universal approbation and citizens would like to see this very capable lady take her seat on the bench without further delay.[16]

In May the executive of the Calgary Local Council sent on a congratulatory resolution which also served as a gentle reminder to that dilatory authority:

Resolved that we, the executive of the Local Council of Women, have heard with pleasure of the intention of the provincial government to appoint women judges in connection with the administration of the juvenile delinquent act, and we desire in this connection to express our hearty approval and endorsation at the appointment of our president, Mrs. R. Jamieson, as the first woman in the capacity indicated.[17]

And in a further show of solidarity, both Mrs. Langford and Mrs. Kerby were quoted as having resented the current report that they were candidates. Although Mrs. Kerby dismissed her name as press rumor, Mrs. Langford did admit that she had been approached "regarding a position as commissioner, but understood it to be only as an assistant to Mrs. Jamieson." The *News-Telegram* reporter commented, "It is unfortunate that politics should enter into an appointment such as this. While there are many able women in club circles in Calgary, Mrs. R.R. Jamieson is one of the most thoroughly equipped women in the province for this position."[18] In spite of denied reports of other candidatures, by intriguing coincidence, Mrs. Langford did become the second woman juvenile court judge in Calgary, and she was appointed at the same time as Alice Jamieson. The reason surfaced later.

Near the end of 1914, with Mrs. Jamieson still not on the bench, the Provincial Superintendent expressed his disappointment to the annual meeting of the Calgary Children's Aid Society. The idea of a woman commissioner had not yet been officially endorsed, but R.B. Chadwick wanted women magistrates appointed throughout Alberta's juvenile court system, and he held the provincial Children's Aid accountable for the delay. Frustrated, he emphasized the urgency:

It is absolutely impossible for the ordinary man to understand the girl problem. The problem of a boy is a simple one in comparison to that of the girl. It has also been the experience in the past year that there have not been sufficient good homes open to girls dealt with by the juvenile courts. Otherwise kindly intentioned people seem disposed to let the girls go their own course. As a result, many girls who would not, find their way into police court. We cannot spend too much money and time on this work.[19]

The year 1914 ended with no woman magistrate on the bench. Finally, on April 15, 1915, Superintendent Chadwick's fondest hope was realized. By order-in-council, Alice Jane Jamieson and Annie Elizabeth Langford of Calgary were appointed Justices of the Peace in and for the Province of Alberta, and members of the Commission of the Peace to administer

Alberta's 1909 Act for the Protection of Neglected and Dependent Children.[20] Only one newspaper, *The Western Standard*, anticipated the confirmation. Other than that, Alberta's first women juvenile court judges began their duties without fanfare.

The *Western Standard* also revealed why Alice Jamieson and Annie Langford were appointed at the same time. Simply put, the office was a political appointment attendant upon the advice of the Liberal patronage committee in Calgary. Mrs. Langford spoke the truth when she said she was approached regarding the position, but it was not very likely as Mrs. Jamieson's assistant. The Liberals were in power in Alberta and Annie Langford was a staunch Liberal – she ran under that party's banner in Calgary in the summer of 1921. According to the *Standard*, Annie Langford was offered the office of juvenile court magistrate first, but declined. Mrs. Jamieson was subsequently approached and accepted. After the attendant laudatory publicity, either Mrs. Langford had second thoughts or the Liberals still really wanted one of their own in that office. At this juncture, however, it would have been most unseemly to deny Mrs. Jamieson's candidature, so they arranged the appointment of Mrs. Langford in the same capacity.

These negotiations took time, but a remarkable compromise it was when only one precedent-setting appointment had been intended. Equality prevailed. The *Standard* described the two women as sharing the same qualifications: "Both . . . have taken an active interest in the matters which make for the good of the city, social, moral and otherwise, and both should be well qualified for the position for which it was originally intended to make one appointment."[21]

In December of 1915, during the annual meeting of the Children's Aid Society, both Mrs. Jamieson and Mrs. Langford were commended for the large amount of time, thought and effort given during their juvenile court sessions. By the end of that year, the number of cases had dropped from 439 to 267 and the number of court sessions totalled 62.[22]

By 1919 the appointment of female magistrates as proposed by Superintendent Chadwick had proved an unqualified success:

> It is the opinion of the department that the experiment made a year or two ago in the appointment of women commissioners for the juvenile court has demonstrated its value. The advantage of having girls tried before a commissioner and officers who are sympathetic members of their own sex is so valuable that it is a wonder that the system was not initiated years ago.[23, 24]

Less than two years after her 1915 precedent-setting commission, Alice Jamieson received a further distinction. Effective January 1, 1917, she was appointed Police Magistrate for the Province of Alberta, with jurisdiction in and for the City of Calgary. In being so named, she became the second woman police magistrate in the Dominion of Canada; the honor of being the first went to Emily Murphy in Edmonton. When the two women were elevated to the bench in 1917, it was on a trial basis, even though this innovation was a logical extension of the earlier decision to appoint women juvenile court judges.

For Alice Jamieson, the new judicial role proved a much more difficult one. It meant dispensing justice before the police court to women charged with criminal code offenses. It meant dealing with "thieves, drunkards, drug addicts, prostitutes, and victims of insanity, as well as the usual types of lawbreakers coming before the general police court."[25] It also meant dealing with women who were down on their luck or the victims of circumstance. Until now, women giving testimony before all-male courts had been denied the benefit of a woman's judicial interpretation of their particular cases. Would a woman magistrate be better able to make this distinction?

Three years after her elevation to the women's police court, Mrs. Jamieson's opinion was that the experiment had proven to be sound: "the idea of employing a woman magistrate, which was tried out for the purpose of ascertaining whether a woman could not better understand women offenders than men could, is no longer an innovation."[26] However, some of Calgary's legal community viewed the appointment of a woman police magistrate not as an inequity addressed, but rather as an ineffectual, even illegal, female intrusion.

[Local legal wiseacres] concurred in the belief that a woman could never step out of her female personality and entirely abandon her alleged prejudices and partialities. They argued that it would be useless to plead a case before a woman, for her mind would be made up from the time she read the newspaper report of the alleged crime. They pulled strings and they spun red tape until they finally gained a hearing before the Supreme Court, which, after considerable deliberation, upheld the legality of Mrs. Jamieson's appointment.[27]

Within a few months of Mrs. Jamieson's appointment, McKinley Cameron, a Calgary legal eagle well-known for soaring with lost judgments to the higher court, appealed Mrs. Jamieson's judicial authority on the grounds that the province had no jurisdiction to appoint a woman magistrate, and therefore the court over which a woman magistrate presided was not properly constituted. McKinley Cameron's *modus operandi*: at the outset of each trial he challenged Mrs. Jamieson's legitimacy to act as judge, and then, when judgment was passed, he appealed her decision.

Rex versus Cyr became Cameron's celebrated case in point. On May 18, 1917, the *Calgary Herald* reported "a passage at arms" between Magistrate Jamieson and McKinley Cameron, whose client, Lizzie Waters, alias Cyr, was charged with vagrancy. At the outset, Mr. Cameron challenged Mrs. Jamieson's authority, contending that the section of the 1916 statute "An Act Respecting Police Magistrates and Justices of the Peace," under which she was appointed, had "been wrongly interpreted to mean that every man and woman in the province of Alberta has the same rights and can be given the same public appointments."

Mrs. Jamieson said that her jurisdiction had been disputed before, but she had no time to argue the matter out in court, and that Mr. Cameron would have to take it up to the Attorney-General's Department.

"No indeed I won't. I am going to take it up right here," retorted the lawyer.

"Well, I won't listen to it," ejaculated the magistrate. "Call the first witness for the prosecution."

After having temporarily mollified the advocate by having his objection noted, Mrs. Jamieson affirmed her determination to preside until notified otherwise by the Attorney-General's Department. Ruled by a personal compulsion to have the last word, Cameron rebutted, "Well, that's all right, you can go ahead, but I shall do my very best to stop you."

In hearing this case, Mrs. Jamieson passed sentence of six months imprisonment with hard labor without giving the accused an opportunity to present a defense. Mr. Cameron immediately protested her legal error. Magistrate Jamieson, who stood corrected, offered to withdraw her conviction and rule after hearing the defence evidence, but McKinley Cameron posed a technical impediment which enabled him to use her oversight as another ground for appeal. Her adversary counselled, "once a prisoner is sentenced and the conviction recorded by the stenographer, no further proceedings can be taken until the conviction is quashed in the Supreme Court. And I shall see that your decision is overruled."

Undeterred, Magistrate Jamieson proceeded and the accused was fined and convicted under the Vagrant Act. McKinley Cameron appealed to have the conviction quashed immediately.[28]

A month after the mid-May "passage at arms," Mr. Justice Scott of Alberta's Supreme Court dismissed McKinley Cameron's application to quash Magistrate Jamieson's conviction of Lizzie Waters alias Cyr. Calgary's legal eagle soared to the next height. In November the Court of Appeal upheld Mr. Scott's conviction, expressly deciding, in doing so, that sex was not a ground of legal disqualification from holding public office. In other words, the fact that Magistrate Jamieson was a woman did not disqualify her from public office. That decision confirmed Emily Murphy's appointment as well.

Almost two and one-half years later, Alice Jamieson reflected on those early years on the bench:

Well, being the first woman magistrate was no position to excite envy, I assure you. I had to fight down a good deal of prejudice on the part of certain members of the legal profession and the police department. When I first assumed my duties in the police court with cold shoulders greeting me on every hand, I said to myself, "I don't know why I ever came here – I don't have to do this," and then I drew myself up and said, "well I'm here and I'm here to stay."[29]

She stayed for 15 years. An impression of the diminutive Magistrate Jamieson dispensing justice is included in the 1920 *Calgary Herald* retrospective:

> *The voice in which she questions prisoners is clear and low and finely cultivated. Her strong regular features lend an element of clarity and force to her countenance that is seldom seen in women; but for all her professional coolness and legal acumen, there is something in the whole of her makeup that never ceases to betray to the observant the fact that her woman's heart often throbs with sympathy, which has to be concealed, for the unfortunate ones before her. To offset this and to help her conserve her sanity and her faith in womankind in such unpleasant surroundings, there is always at the back of her serious expression a threatening glint of humour quick to spring into life when the situation grows comic.*[30]

One of these situations occurred in December of 1917, when Magistrate Jamieson sentenced a woman vagrant, Bertha Muldenhauer, to four months in jail to protect her from freezing to death in the streets. Upon hearing the sheltering sentence, the vagrant was less than appreciative: "she told the magistrate in language not used in polite society, just what she thought of her."[31, 32]

For those optimists who anticipated the appointment of women police magistrates across Canada, the wait was long. By 1924, only one other woman besides Emily Murphy and Alice Jamieson served on the bench, and that was in the East. Some even feared there was an intent to remove those already appointed. A National Council of Women resolution addressed this concern, asking its members to fight "a wide movement to remove women magistrates from the bench." Magistrate Emily Murphy, however, disagreed that there was an intent to remove women magistrates in Alberta. "No movement looking to our removal," she stated, "other than as it pertained to jurisdiction, has ever taken place in this province; we have been accorded an equal approbation and courtesy with the male magistrate."[33] In fact, Magistrate Murphy's opinion was that women magistrates enjoyed an advantage – they received extra recognition for rehabilitating wayward women and stabilizing homes. However, when one considers that well over a year elapsed before Alice Jamieson received official confirmation as a juvenile court judge; that her police court jurisdiction was appealed to Alberta's Supreme Court; and that seven years later, there were only three police court magistrates in all of Canada, women warmed the magisterial bench at a glacial pace.

While presiding as a juvenile court judge, Alice Jamieson also served as president of the Calgary Local Council of Women, an onerous commitment because LCW was, if anything, over-achieving in its early years. Concerned that her new judgeship might interfere with her role in Local Council, she subsequently declined the 1917 presidency to which she had been elected unanimously. The *Morning Albertan* acknowledged her leadership of the organization:

Mrs. Jamieson has proven a most interested officer of the council and has given the advancement of better conditions, not only for the women and children of the city, her ablest support, but has always aided any movement which bespoke the interest of citizens generally, whether philanthropic, patriotic or charitable, and whether civic, provincial or federal.[34]

Chapter Eleven

Wanted? A Woman Policeman

ᘓ ᘓ ᘓ ᘓ

I am firmly of the opinion that the woman who would be suitable for the position has yet to be born. It would be necessary to apply eugenics and special educational facilities before we would have a woman eligible for the position. I certainly have never yet seen the woman who would be of any use on a police force.

Police Chief Alfred Cuddy, April 1914

Immortal words, those, worthy of inscription in a chauvinist's hall of fame.

The Calgary Local Council of Women's first effort to have women appointed to the city's all-male police force proved as elusive as catching a will-o-the-wisp. Police Chief Cuddy's opposition fell just short of "over-my-dead-body." The wavering commissioners and City Council were of two minds. Literate local wits and wags trivialized the Council's proposal. In a backlash of misunderstandings, Alderman Frost faced the prospect of recall, and the press solicited explanations from Local Council's advocates, Alice Jamieson and Maude Riley. Mrs. Riley chose to remain silent. In the end, the women's cause suffered a setback. Chief Cuddy prevailed, and ranks of the thin blue line remained a male bastion for three more decades.

As pressure increased to reduce prostitution, "the social evil," Local Council was drawn into a Ministerial Association lobby which was backed by church groups determined to persuade the provincial government to establish a detention home for immoral women. A stalling Premier Sifton promised "earnest consideration." Well aware that actions speak louder than words, reforming forces undertook other ways of dealing with the social problem. Two petitions were prepared for presentation to City Council: one asked for the appointment of a police matron, the other for the appointment of women to the police force. Neither seemed contentious until the prospect of a policewoman became real.

In the spring of 1913, the West End WCTU sent a petition to the Council of Women requesting that a police matron be appointed to attend women prisoners. Local Council's aggregate membership, estimated at over 3000 women, supported it. But Calgary's Police Chief Alfred Cuddy strongly disagreed – in his view the present services provided by Calgary's finest were just fine. The city already had access to a police matron who could be called upon when required to deal with female prisoners. To him, she represented a sufficiency of female authority, properly diluted.

Whether palpable to local police authorities or not, kernels of information concerning the introduction of women police in American and Canadian cities fell on fertile soil in the spring of 1913. Los Angeles earned the distinction of having the first woman police officer in America, Alice Stebbin Wills. Albeit prematurely, Ottawa and its Local Council of Women claimed the honor of having Canada's first policewoman, Miss Flora Campbell. Calgary's reform-minded women hoped their western city would be next, ahead of Toronto. Alfred Cuddy, however, was not anxious at all. With all of his brave heart, he hoped that honor would pass his city by.

An optimistic editorial writer for the *News-Telegram* pointed out that if the City Council wanted a policewoman then, "as the servant, and not the master of the civic corporation, Mr. Cuddy will have to change his attitude; and there is reason to believe that before long, the example set by Ottawa and other cities in this respect will be followed here."[1] The writer felt such an appointment did not threaten the existing bastion of male authority because the policewoman's role would be different – she would be protecting women only.

Rescue workers from Calgary's social services, the traveller's aid and church groups who met, guided and sheltered those at risk from dire circumstance or the fell clutch of pestering males complained that they were "powerless to act except through the police." The constabulary's less-than-prompt responses often allowed criminals to escape, thus avoiding arrest. "The police, being men, are never closely in touch with the girls, and consequently are not in a position to obtain facts in a great number of cases, as would women police and women detectives."[2] It appeared that Calgary's finest did not provide much back-up.

On August fifth, the *News-Telegram* endorsed the Local Council's women police petition as a move which would do much good. A case in point (possibly overstated): Toronto's innovative appointment of two women police officers six months earlier had proven so successful that the Chief of Police there was thinking of adding a dozen more. The argument followed that if women police officers were thought so important to Toronto, they would be doubly so in a western city like Calgary.[3]

However, there is evidence that not only Police Chief Cuddy but also his men had reservations. Their reactions to the news that the Women's Press Club of Calgary recommended the addition of two women police officers elicited different opinions, ranging from apprehension to anticipation. "Some of the uniformed men thought it would be a good idea while others were of the opinion that life would be unbearable should the ambitious blue skirts succeed in obtaining promotion to the rank of sergeant."[4] One married man confided that he was opposed because a woman boss would be intolerable – tyrannical to the point that a man would either be fired or have to quit for picayune lapses. On the other hand, three single detectives looked forward to the innovation, anticipating that the "lady coppers" would be of favorable age and appearance.

In mid-October, Local Council's president, Alice Jamieson, and its Convenor of Laws, Maude Riley, met city commissioners Samis and Graves on behalf of Local Council's 53 federated societies. Their purpose was to request the appointment of two women police officers. The *Morning Albertan* reported:

> The ladies made it quite clear that they are not asking for brass button, uniformed policewomen, but that they want to have two women given the powers and authority of police officers. They may be called probation officers or styled anything it suits the council to call them, so long as they are made qualified members of the police department.[5]

Local Council's advocates argued that women officers would prove most effective in dealing with "correction of incorrigible children and young girls, and in dealing with cases in which women figure either as petty offenders or young criminals." Insofar as that interview was concerned, the delegation received a sympathetic hearing but when asked later, the person most involved, Police Chief Cuddy, turned a deaf ear: "The ladies are all right in their place, but their place is not on the police force. I don't see how or where we could use women police to any good advantage." He was willing to oblige to the extent of acquiring a police matron when the new station was ready next summer. Right now, quarters were too cramped. But, if need be, he would bow to his superior authority, the commissioners and City Council, if they so ruled for a policewoman. The odds favored the Chief.

Belfast-born Alfred Cuddy emigrated to Toronto as a young man and joined the police force. He served there for 30 years, 20 of them as a police officer and the remaining ten as an inspector. A fine figure of a man – over six feet tall and 46 inches around the chest – Cuddy arrived in Calgary on March 14, 1912, in the prime of his manhood. Calgary's officials considered themselves very fortunate in acquiring one of Canada's widely known policemen.

The new Chief's mandate was to bring order out of chaos and to mold the Calgary force into one of the best on the continent. The police authority promised him a free hand, and he pledged to do his best. Cuddy's plans included enlarging the force, implementing a state of the art identification system, and constructing a new police station and two new outlying substations.[6]

Calgary's new Chief addressed the social problem from the outset. Three weeks after taking office, he and his men assisted Children's Aid authorities in an opium raid on Chinatown. In early June, during the opening ceremonies of the new Presbyterian home for girls, Cuddy was praised as being "widely known for his splendid work" in civic moral reforms. In a July *Eye Opener* issue, Bob Edwards credited him with having removed, without fanfare, an entrenched, notorious white slaver from the city scene.

By late fall, dance crazes of the time fell also under Cuddy's scrutiny. The Police Chief promised to do all within his authority (and more if given power) to curtail bunny hugs, turkey trots and Salome writhes – seductive dances which brought couples temptingly close. He classed these preoccupations as "the high schools of vice from which many girls graduate as street walkers or undesirables." As a custodian of public morals, he emphasized, "We do not want any Barbary coast reels in Calgary. The city, with all its transients from different parts of the world, is difficult to police now without officially encouraging immoral dances."[7,8]

If anything, Cuddy may just have been a tad overzealous. Because of this, he did not always enjoy favorable reviews in the newspapers. For example, in the summer of 1915, when rumors circulated that he might be leaving, he was criticized for being overly strict.[9] Even his great admirer, Bob Edwards, complained in the May 22nd *Eye Opener* that the Police Chief was "too prone to force the virtues of Toronto down our throats." In a police raid a few weeks before, several reputable young men had been arrested for playing poker on the Sabbath. An upset Edwards felt local moral monitoring had just gone too far, thanks to the influence of narrow-minded church leaders who had succeeded in making Calgary Sundays "the one and only miserable day of the week." By inference, Cuddy was on Salvation's side.

Meanwhile, encouraged by their mid-October 1913 meeting with the Commissioners, Mrs. Jamieson and Mrs. Riley resolved to press their case for women police officers before their strongest opponent, Chief Cuddy. The crucial meeting occurred on November seventh. After listening to persuasive argument, a more pliable but still sceptical Police Chief proposed a compromise. He offered two appointments: a policewoman to act as probation officer only, and a police station matron. This compromise fell short of the expectations of feminists who wanted women appointed to the police force in the same capacity as men. It also failed to meet the expectations of others who were aware that the city's plan for a new jail included two rooms for two future female police officers, to be assigned patrol duty along Calgary's major streets. The next day's *News-Telegram* carried separate photos of Mrs. Riley and Mrs. Jamieson, each captioned "reformer," with the words "persuaded" and "converted" used to describe their successful advocacy. But Police Chief Cuddy's reactions – "not any too anxious" and "not thoroughly in favour of the scheme" should have sounded a caution.

Newspapers carried a comic cartoon or two. Whether based on fact or fiction, the *Morning Albertan* item reported Chief Cuddy's uncomfortable interview with an ingenue who

> *blushingly asked to be sworn in as a full-fledged, 'flat foot' with a nice blue uniform trimmed with red and a pretty silver badge, and a big club with which to beat the 'nasty' men should her duties require her to adopt such strenuous measures.*

According to this account, the Chief then terminated the interview by telling the applicant there was no such opening. The article continued:

> *After chivalrously bowing the applicant out of his office and thanking his stars that he got off without any arguments or suffragistic talks, the Chief drew a long breath and silently prayed to heaven to delay the day when women police officers would be added to the strength of the local department.*[10]

Bob Edwards, who endorsed the idea of women police as "in strict conformity with modern requirements," playfully pondered the mode of address: "'Coppess' and 'coppette' do not seem to hit the mark, and 'bulless' is obviously absurd."[11]

One day after the New Year, the warning whistle blew. "Woman Cop May Not Be Appointed" headlined the *News-Telegram*. Chief Cuddy now claimed that in his November seventh meeting he had agreed only to the appointment of a matron assigned to the police station to search and supervise women prisoners in the cells. He had not agreed that a woman police officer would be appointed to the force. Mrs. Jamieson and Mrs. Riley had assumed too much from their discussions. However, it is unlikely that Alice Jamieson and Maude Riley both misunderstood. It is more likely that the "not any too anxious" Police Chief had second thoughts.

By now, Cuddy had statistics on his side. Figures released in the January 1914 *Annual Report of the Chief of Police* showed "remarkable improvement." Crime was on the decrease. Seventy-two percent of stolen property had been recovered; a large number of disorderly houses had been closed; dives serving alcohol had been targeted; and street walkers were now a rarity. Arrests, 6868 of them, were down 323 from the year before. Ninety-five percent of those arrested and charged were men. Although drunkenness accounted for 35 percent overall, other social problem categories were low – only 12 percent for vagrancy; 7.5 percent for theft; 2 percent for running disorderly houses; 1 percent for frequenting them; 0.8 percent for opium drug act infractions; and 0.1 percent for living off the avails of prostitution. That year, 1913, three manslaughter and two murder charges were laid.[12]

If one combined the percentages for disorderly houses, frequenting them and living off the avails, then prostitution ranked fourth, at 3.1 percent. The Chief of Police asked for ten more staff including a police matron, not a police woman, to be added when the new quarters opened.

Newspapers complimented the Chief and his 101-man force for doing a very good job of improving the city's moral condition. The citizenry seemed satisfied. It was hardly the opportune time for the Council of Women to press for an innovation so strongly opposed by the man-of-the-hour and captain of Calgary's constabulary.

In the third week of April, when the City Council approved salary estimates for the coming year, there was no provision for a policewoman. In noting the absence, Maude Riley's husband, Harold, moved that this item now be included. During the discussion it became apparent that Alderman Tappy Frost had joined the Police Chief's ranks. When Alderman Harold Riley reminded him that his wife (LCW's Laws Convenor) understood a woman police officer would be appointed, Alderman Frost said there must be some mistake. One matron only would suffice because Mrs. Bagnall, who was attached to the juvenile court, also acted as a probation officer.[13]

At this juncture, Mr. Frost did not volunteer the relevant information that Mrs. Bagnall was a provincial, not a civic employee. Because Mr. Frost also served as a juvenile court magistrate, he was well aware of that fact. His reticence was suspect. At the time of Mrs. Bagnall's appointment as matron, an article in the *Calgary Herald* stressed that her duties were not comparable to those of a policeman. She was to serve as a friend and adviser for newly arrived strange girls, to help them find accommodation and employment, and to attend under-age females called before the juvenile court.

The April 21st motion for a policewoman's salary was defeated by one vote, and a vindicated Chief Cuddy later reiterated, "I didn't ask for one and I never will. One might be a fine ornament, but I cannot see where there would be very much use for one."[14]

"All that the local council of women has done with a view to having a policewoman appointed here came to naught," lamented the *News-Telegram* reporter.[15] But the cause was not abandoned. A matter of principle was involved. A matter of entitlement. Because 57 societies representing thousands of Calgary women had unanimously supported the petition, their unqualified endorsement justified the appointment of a woman on the city's police force. Also as a matter of principle, Ald. Frost should have clarified the status of Mrs. Bagnall to the less well-informed aldermen before they voted. His lack of principle had misled some.

No time was lost in correcting Alderman Frost publicly in the local papers regarding Mrs. Bagnall's duties. All seven of them were listed in the *News-Telegram*, and it was clear that her matron's authority extended neither to girls 16 and over wandering the streets, nor to the men pursuing them. The Council of Women's petition applied there. Although Mr. Frost wasn't accused of mendacity, a very angry, prominent Local Council officer fumed, "We are highly incensed at the way this matter was railroaded through the council meeting the other night by Alderman Frost, and the matter is not going to be dropped by us."[16] The categorical correction of his statements in the press so personally upset the alderman that he threatened to "call for the retraction of any further vicious references of this kind."[17]

By now, the commissioners had become the power brokers. They negotiated a ceasefire in the war of words. Because three aldermen were absent when the matter was decided at the salary estimates special meeting, the commissioners advised that the matter had not received sufficient consideration and that it should come before all 12 aldermen. The commissioners also recommended that a female detective be appointed at a salary of $75 a month. In the presence of a Local Council contingent, the mayor and aldermen reconsidered the appointment on the 27th of April. Opponents lost the motion to refer the matter back to the commissioners, and the vote was on. "Under the fire of a battery of a dozen pairs of feminine eyes," wrote the *Albertan* reporter, "the aldermen executed the right about-turn . . . when the matter of appointing a 'lady detective' to the city police force came up again."[18] The vote was six to four in favor of an amended motion which read: "In accordance with the wishes of a large number of citizens, and particularly the Women's Council, your commissioners would recommend that a woman detective be placed on the police force of the city, with quarters in the police building."[19] Salary to be left in abeyance. Nine hundred dollars per annum warranted reconsideration.

At this point, some members of the Local Council of Women were considering applying the principle of recall to their once knight in shining armor. Alderman Frost had twice disappointed them. This former Baptist minister, now a custodian of civic coffers, had earlier prioritized revenue over religion and voted against tax exemption of church properties. With that disappointment a recent memory, others recalled his promise of support for the women's cause in the 1912 and 1913 civic election campaigns. Those women gifted with a memory for specifics narrowed the pledge down to women police. Armor now tarnished, Thomas Alfred Presswood Frost's sword of moral reform, earlier brandished aloft, moved downwards on church exemption, and now lay at rest, handle pointing toward the thin blue line.

The press picked up on the recall threat – where it originated, how the recall and referendum process worked, and the fascinating prospect of a national precedent being set in Calgary. Heady stuff. The *Calgary Herald* reported that Local Council's Social Services Committee and its Suppression of Objectionable Literature Committee (the watchdog that included the total executive) had met to discuss recall of "the verbose little alderman." In the absence of their president, members recounted in detail Alderman Frost's sins of omission and commission to date, and then decided:

in view of Mr. Frost's off-handed disregard of his promises, and direct
antagonism to the work they have undertaken in the past, it would be unsafe
to allow him to continue in office.[20]

Although the proposed action was not discussed beyond the committee level, rumors persisted that a petition was underway.

At this time, recall was a feasible exercise and the press calculated. Calgary's City Charter had recently been amended to put in place a very simple procedure. Now the number of signatures required on the petition was a mere 25 percent of the total mayoralty votes cast in the last civic election. Based upon the mayoralty figure of 5210 votes at the December 1913 municipal election, a mere 1303 signatures qualified. If removed from office, the unseated alderman could still enter as a candidate in the resulting by-election.

This ominous turn of events boomeranged. It actually generated sympathy for the alderman, and begged an official statement from the Council of Women. Alice Jamieson apologized:

I regret very much that this groundless rumour gained circulation. The
council is not responsible for the individual opinion of any member of the
organization, but as a body it has never gone on record as favoring the recall
of Alderman Frost. Mr. Frost was honest in his opposition to the appointment
of the woman police officer and is certainly entitled to his views.

The circulation of reports in both the local and outside press . . . will
prejudice the women's cause in Calgary.[21]

In the end, Police Chief Cuddy won. Promised a free hand if he came to Calgary, he had no intention of extending it to welcome a policewoman. So set was he against the innovation that he threatened to resign if his wishes were not respected. In a ground swell of support, two of the three daily papers – the *Herald* and *The Albertan* – moved onside, stating that the Chief was doing a good job and should not be interfered with. The *Herald* censured city commissioners and City Council so severely for reversing the initial vote that it proposed placing the police department under a permanent, independent commission. In a lighter vein, a poem attributed to Cuddy envisioned the Chief's intransigence if his superiors appointed a woman:

P'raps the hand that rocks the cradle is the hand that rules the world,
But with women on the police force, my banner will be furled.
They may name one as detective and her standing job will be
If any trace of emerald in my optics she can see.
This latest female fancy is a foolish waste of "chink"
They may lead this horse to water, but they can't make me drink.[22]

When asked to comment upon Cuddy's threatened resignation, Alice Jamieson's comment, as might be expected, was tactful. "The matter is one that must be arranged between the Chief and the city commissioners and the city council. Personally, I would regret to see the Chief resign, as I have a high opinion of him as a police official."[23]

Mrs. Harold Riley's response? It was quite out of character for this "prominent member of the executive": "When asked . . . if her attitude toward the appointment of the woman detective had changed by reason of Chief Cuddy's continued opposition and owing to the criticism being offered by citizens and the press," she replied that she "would not discuss the matter at all."[24] It was not like Maude Riley to remain silent.

The more astute leaders in the Women's Council had learned two lessons the hard way. Firstly, the press could be manipulative, even mischievous, and therefore, matters of an inflammatory nature discussed only at the committee level should not receive coverage. Secondly, petitions, resolutions and delegations are advisory instruments only. They are not official commands.

Why did the leadership of Calgary's finest so strongly resist the inclusion of women? The best evidence indicates that out west in Calgary, where men were men, policing was considered a man's job. Chief Cuddy's ally, Alderman Frost, explained why a woman police detective (ergo, a respectable woman) would prove inadequate to the task: "strictest . . . surveillance must be kept on these women by men who know them and their ways, and who have spent years studying conditions in the underworld."

Gifted with a penchant for hyperbole, he credited Calgary's plainclothesmen as having, through their persistence and expertise, made Calgary "the cleanest city of its size on the continent." Now, "streetwalkers, gamblers and other scum . . . regard Calgary as one of the most dangerous places imaginable to be in."[25]

This lack of confidence in a woman's ability to cope showed in two other incidents. When asked how women police were faring in other cities, the Chief felt vindicated. Toronto's Chief Stark would be glad to get rid of theirs because they had proved of no practical value. He denigrated the status of Edmonton and Vancouver's women police – saying that they were probably just police matrons, not detectives or policewomen in the true sense.

Calgary's Chief of Police was not the only one who felt that a woman couldn't do the job. An *Albertan* reporter passed on the tidbit that, while chatting with the Chief in his office, a woman had phoned in her support for the Chief's stand. Cuddy must have relished repeating her comment. She said that if a woman policeman was appointed, then a second policewoman would be required to look after her. Two written applications allegedly signed by Mrs. Mary Beers and Kate Knowles – both well-known and disreputable *habitués* of the police court – had been placed on the Chief's desk that same morning. Page one of the usually straight-laced *Calgary Herald* listed their qualifications: "their familiarity with the Calgary underworld, their expert knowledge of police methods, and their intimate acquaintance with the psychology of the criminal classes, to say nothing of their need of a good position at once congenial and remunerative."[26] This prank caused further merriment.

A clever *Albertan* send-up, "Chief Smart Wants A Firewoman," parodied the idea as a promotional opportunity. Not wishing to be outdone by the police, the article read, the fire department now wanted a firewoman of its own for an ornament. The author's satire barbed moral reformers and suffragists:

> Everything would come our way. When manufacturers thinking of locating sites here started asking questions about the size and prospects of the city, all we would have to do would be to proudly point to the firewoman. She would indicate how up-to-date and progressive we were. When showing distinguished visitors and members of Sunday school conventions how far in advance of any place of our size on the continent we were, all we would have to do would be to point to the firewoman. If Mrs. Pankhurst invaded the city with her anarchistic equipment, all we would have to do would be to point to the firewoman and tell her the appointment of the lady in blue was as sure an indication that Calgarians favoured equal suffrage as a robin redbreast is that spring is here. If Carrie Nation came with her hatchet to chop the bay window out of the Palliser hotel, all we would have to do to dissuade her would be to point to the firewoman on the water wagon and talk provincial prohibition.[27]

The message was that a policewoman was a token appointment – a political gesture to pressure-groups – and Calgary had no real need for one.

The news that Canada's first policewoman, Miss Flora Campbell, was sworn in as an Ottawa policewoman on March 10, 1913, was premature. Nor was she truly "sworn in" as a police constable in August, as reported. This former superintendent of the Women's Hostel and Traveller's Aid Worker acted first as a probation officer until the third of January, 1914, when she finally joined the ranks officially. Only at this juncture were her duties "similar to those of other policemen." Six months later, the nature of her work was described in a feature profile in the magazine *Everywoman's World*. Her duties included accompanying women and girls who came before the courts; straightening out family problems involving children and juveniles; removing under-age children from movie houses; and searching for missing females. The number of arrests she had made to date was two – both girls. Canada's first woman policeman wore no uniform, but she could make arrests, when advisable. Her main work was preventive.

Women police were not appointed in Calgary until three decades later, during World War II. Even then, they were appointed cautiously, temporarily and with carefully rationed wartime authority. "The long arm of the law is to be shorter and sweeter in Calgary," announced the opening sentence of a February sixth *Herald* news item. Two women would be attached to the police morality squad to "check dance halls and morality matters." Shortly thereafter, two older married women, Mrs. Bell and Mrs. Mowatt, were indeed appointed but on a temporary basis. Neither long-term commitments nor pensions were involved because of their age and the fact that they were married. In those days, only single women received permanent positions with the city. The choice was a discriminating one.

Well before these actual appointments, civic authorities had given the proposal due – bordering on *overdue* – consideration. Beginning in the autumn of 1942, Mrs. Harold Riley brought the request for women police to the city's legislative committee. She must have experienced a strong sense of *déjà vu* as she assured the city's legislative committee that "U.S. cities had found women police officers valuable in the work of crime prevention." But Police Chief Patterson felt the move was premature and could wait until the need arose, which it did a few months later, in January of 1943, when Calgary's all-male ranks found themselves short six constables and nine officers, with little prospect of replacement during wartime. A cautious Mayor Andrew Davidson checked with Edmonton's mayor and found the two women police recently appointed there were proving satisfactory. Thus reassured, the police commission recommended to City Council that two policewomen be appointed to the morality squad to check dance halls and morality matters. Upon being informed of the decision, Mrs. Riley (surely with tongue restrained in cheek) congratulated the commission for being so alive to the situation and in seeing the need in Calgary. She thanked the commission on behalf of the Alberta Council of Child and Family Welfare, not the Local Council of Women. Members of the latter expressed gratification at the appointments a few days later, while noting that their own Local Council had endeavored since 1931 to have women on the police force. Actually, they had tried since 1913, but that earlier date was lost in the mists of memory.

Calgary's finest finally embraced women symbolically on a permanent basis, one at a time, in the form of three World War II armed services "girls." The city's first three were Vera Russell, appointed in December of 1945; Margaret Sadler in February of 1946; and Cubby Stanton in October of the same year.[28]

Chapter Twelve

Marketing – The Women's Toy

ꙮ ꙮ ꙮ ꙮ

The introduction of copper coinage was a simple matter compared to the protracted city market revitalization campaign "managed" by Georgina Newhall's Consumer's League with one end in view – to bring down Calgary's cost of living. The price exacted proved to be eternal vigilance.

A languishing city market did exist in 1913 but the city council, under the influence of established tax-paying storeowners, gave it lukewarm support, as did consumers – but for different reasons – prices were high, and the indifferently-maintained, poorly-located site lacked a direct rail link. Led by Georgina Newhall, LCW's 15-member Home Economics Committee organized a largely attended April 29th housewives' meeting in the public library. There the women questioned wholesalers already under contract, and more importantly, listened to their own members tell of effective countermeasures elsewhere, particularly in the United States. Under the encouragement of Mr. Fee, a commission agent for the Vernon Fruit company, housewives were assured that a wholesale market could cut down transportation costs by offering goods directly on site to the retailer. If women themselves ceased charging and offered their retail grocers cash instead, they could expect a discount of as much as 20 percent. Understandably, that kind of publicity alarmed the retailers and prompted a clarification on the cash discount saving, now referred to as 10 percent. The saving would accrue from "a succession of cash payments to the retailer, the wholesaler, the jobber, and the producer."[1] Like pie in the sky.

A week later, on May 14th, LCW's home economics committee sponsored a follow-up meeting intended to bring the producer and consumer together on a "level playing field" as it were.[2] Representatives of United Farmers of Alberta and the Farmer's League of Strathmore came, as well as the mayor and city aldermen, most of the latter with ears attuned to business interests. Market pros and cons were thoroughly aired, the city's objection being historic – that neither housewives nor farmers had patronized the existing market so they couldn't be counted upon to support the proposed one. Mr. George Wells, a well-known local market gardener, spoke for local producers saying that with proof of buyer support and good trackage they would grow more produce. In this catch-22 situation, Alderman Tregillus adopted a conciliatory stance. If both consumer and producer patronized each other, Calgary's high cost of living would be reduced by the savings in middlemen costs. Mr. Woodbridge, secretary of the United Farmers of Alberta, estimated producers would be satisfied with a 5 or 10 percent profit margin and that amount, of itself, would reduce the cost of living in Calgary. Theories acknowledged, the most practical step taken at that meeting occurred when the Home Economics committee merged into a Consumers' League. Georgina Newhall became president and Mrs. McGregor, secretary.

The metamorphosis had been Georgina Newhall's intention all along. She wanted to form a broadly-based Consumers' League – similar to the Housewives' Leagues in the United States – to coordinate the campaign against Calgary's high cost of living. Ontario-born Georgina Fraser, who may have been the first woman stenographer in Canada, was a woman of impressive literary talents and organizing ability with a honed interest in economics and food conservation. After pursuing a very successful secretarial career in a Toronto law firm, she married an American, E.P. Newhall, and moved to the United States, living at one period in Toledo, Ohio, where she belonged to the Women's Civic League. When Calgary's American Woman's Club formed in 1912, Georgina Newhall, who had lived for 28 years in the United States before arriving here, joined. Later that year when city women were debating whether to form a Civic League or a Local Council, she recounted how successfully Toledo's League, backed by 50 women's groups, had tackled the problem of uncovered meat and foods offered for sale, as well as the high prices charged by food combines. Georgina Newhall know whereof she spoke because she was credited with founding that League.[3]

Membership in the new Calgary Consumers' League was not restricted to Local Council women. Any interested men could join, and some did. Unlike the Local Council, the League could raise funds for advertising and license fees. Its constitution, adopted at the end of May, had three stated aims:

(a) To investigate the increasing cost of living and to counteract the same by any legitimate means within their power.

(b) To study and teach the principles of co-operation in connection with home economics.

(c) To watch, influence, and promote civic legislation in connection with either of the foregoing clauses.[4]

Whether intended or not, the last of these presaged adversarial roles in any relationship with City Hall.

League leaders met with Mayor Sinnot at 11 o'clock the morning after the organizational meeting to press for an improved location for the market, preferably one with a direct rail link. The city was asked to use its influence to persuade the CPR to build wholesale market sheds along a spur so that city retailers could buy fresh produce directly there, thus saving time and draying costs. The city itself was to provide the more centrally-located old power house on Ninth Avenue, between Fourth and Fifth Streets West, to house its existing public market. Proponents and opponents both understood the significance of a prime and not-so-prime location. Both crafted their strategy accordingly.

The idea of the market, and of the Consumers' League involvement in it, was enthusiastically received. On May 29th, the *Albertan* headed an upbeat news item on the front page "Organization of Consumers' League Attracts Widespread Attention – Is First In Canada." Beginning with a touch of local pride, the account read, "The Consumers' League . . . has excited widespread curiosity in other western cities, and the mayor has been the recipient of numerous inquiries from the women of Victoria, Vancouver, and other cities, for information as to the modus operandi of the organization."[5] Also included was an encouraging item on the city hall request: "At the meeting of the city council on Monday night the mayor expressed his personal interest in the matter and the city appointed Ald. Tregillus to confer with Mr. Woods, on a proposition advanced by the latter, to utilize the former city power station on the line of the C.P.R. for this purpose." The Tregillus plan received the approval of the League, the Local Council of Women, the Vernon Fruit Company and the United Farmers of Alberta. Championed by Tregillus, the women asked for the appointment of a "capable market master . . . familiar with the conditions and resources of the provinces." City fathers were also asked to allocate roughly $1000 to construct a street railway spur to the proposed new market.[6]

Official approval was not forthcoming. In truth, these innovative proposals were met with as much enthusiasm as had earlier been shown to curfew appeals. Frustrated by civic inaction, an aroused Consumers' League womanhood threatened to go it alone by bringing in a carload of fruit and vegetables, selling them in a tent if need be, and acting as the clerks. That embarrassing tent threat probably goaded both parties into reconsidering the existing shelter. The city assigned the League the spacious central area, but did not allow the 10 percent member discount on purchases. At the last minute, City Council's Market Committee piously pointed out that there could be no such discrimination because "the market was built for the public by public money." It was a strategic coup which undercut the League's early membership drive.

Changes notwithstanding, the hard work paid off. Well before opening day, market converts had carried their campaign to other women's groups and canvassed small local producers in an effort to convince the dubious ones that interested buyers would now come. Newspapers published the market prices, competing storeowners published theirs, shoppers compared, and an estimated 5000 came in droves to a highly successful June 21st opening. League members who had brought in a carload of fresh vegetables from BC also waited on the public. Shoppers were delighted with the bargains, and farmers, who got good prices for their produce, promised to return. Temporary market manager, George Wells, spoke optimistically of a biweekly public market and of being able to upgrade the old building without incurring too much expense.

But not all was sweetness and light. On Monday a few negative remarks trickled out. Some discerning ladies observed that George Wells had been drinking. Other female olfactory nerves had been assaulted by the presence of incontinent drayhorses which were used to move goods into the building then left to stand about, creating an indoor atmosphere of "danger and filth." Women working in the rather shabby market stalls complained that they were gloomy and that they had too much wood-work and too little glass. League members prepared a petition suggesting eight items for improvement and presented it for the approval of City Council at its June 23rd meeting. In the meantime, the civic fathers had already taken the advice of their own authorities, and the Council shelved the League's recommendations. Instead it designated two extra streetcars with awkward route connections which entailed more transfers for market shoppers, and elevated the now less than exemplary Market Master George Wells to permanent status, his salary set at $100 per month. Disappointed League representatives accused the City Council of blundering in its location in the first place, but Alderman Carscallen reminded the women that the revitalization project was their idea. He warned the market would soon fail unless League women were prepared to "put their shoulders to the wheel" and run the stalls. An *Albertan* account describes the eloquent penny-wise rebuttal telegraphed by Georgina Newhall's body language: "Mrs. Newhall was not militant in her attitude. She addressed the Council with an air of gentle persuasiveness, and she carried her purse full of housekeeping money in her left hand just conspicuously enough to impress married aldermen."

The effect was immediate. "'I think we will support the women,' said Ald. Tregillus hastily, and Ald. Ross hastily seconded it." Under that impetus, the main sceptic, Alderman Carscallen, turned gallant and added his endorsement. It was a safe shift. The "in principle" motion did not contain the specifics that had been requested: a woman superintendent responsible for cleanliness and sanitation standards, a freshly painted interior, a shelter outside. The ladies were assured by Alderman Garden that "these 'little details' would be worked out as time went on."[7] The expression "little details" spoke volumes about the level of support. At that June meeting, astute League members sensed that City Council could afford to make haste slowly because the League was not growing by leaps and bounds. Major management details like prime market location, ongoing contact with a range of suppliers, and efficient access routes did not have to be promptly addressed by city authorities.

From the League's perspective, there was one gratifying outcome of the appointment of Mr. Wells which suggests that the women of teetotalling sensibility won out: the market master was dismissed within six weeks. At its October 13th meeting, City Council appointed Mr. D.G. McKenzie as market superintendent. The next day's *Albertan* described how George Wells defended, with pen and spoken word, his record of service and the charge of intoxication.

> *In his letter to the council the former Market Master pointed out that so far as he was aware there had never been any complaint against his administration of the market except on the first market day, when he was accused of being intoxicated, but in vindication of himself he said:*
>
> *"I only had one drink of whiskey on that date and that was paid for by Mr. Manarey."*[8]

No one volunteered the charitable defense that the stress of opening morn may have justified a launching stiffener.

Although three months lapsed before the Consumers' League took the obvious step of broadening its lobby base by joining the Local Council, this delay was not due to ill feelings. From its founding Local Council officers worked within the League, and there was no press report of opposition to the changeover, so evidence suggests that the League was intended to undergo a trial period. Two press tidbits provide corroboration. On May 22nd the *Albertan* informed readers that the League committee preparing the new constitution would also recommend that when the organization was formally completed, the League should, "sever all connections with the local council of women and work out its own salvation."[9] The other item was nestled within a succinct League write up which appeared a month later in the *News-Telegram*. There readers learned that the League was operating on a trial basis, until September, "to see whether its parent, the local council of women, will support its efforts to bring down the cost of living."[10]

The trial period ended on September 19th, when the League affiliated with the Local Council. By then the Consumers' League could attest to the clear success of its market venture throughout the summer, although it still needed to increase membership, which now numbered in the low hundreds, to at least 2000 in order to persuade reluctant city officials to carry out improvements.

One of the League's major problems was its image. There was a prevailing misconception that its mission was to fight established retail and wholesale grocers and jobbers rather than to reduce the high cost of living by cutting out food distribution costs for the benefit of all. When the League's secretary, Mrs. Singely, asked Local Council's permission to explain the work of the Consumers' League to each member society, that permission was unanimously given.

On the other hand, bonding under pressure, not mutual trust, described the relationship between the City Council and the Consumers' League. One example which the *Albertan* referred to as "the closing chapter of the agitation, for this year at least, in behalf of business at the public market" occurred during the vote on a League-initiated bylaw to reduce the cost of a retail butcher license. Intended to bring down meat costs by reducing the license fee drastically from $50 to $1, the bylaw would mean a loss of $1000 to city coffers and would undoubtedly lead to resentment among retail grocers who received no such reduction. The *Albertan* writer provided the tense vote monitoring scenario: "a delegation of ladies, members of the executive of the Consumers' League, occupied conspicuous seats in the council chamber and fixed the aldermen with their glittering eyes when City Clerk Miller read out the bylaw." No last minute fortuitous mischance would be tolerated, "the ladies . . . did not intend that the bylaw by any untoward accident should slip under the table or be eaten by the caretaker's cat."[11] The bylaw passed.

Along with Georgina Newhall, League members Mrs. Singley, Annie Gale, Mrs. Wade, Mrs. Davidson, Mrs. Simons and others worked very hard during the first fall and winter to include fresh produce so that it did not turn into a meat market as sceptics had predicted. Patronage held so well that a market addition was proposed in the spring of 1914, and an April 30th ratepayers plebiscite clearly endorsed the expenditure of $20 000 for the extension. The League strove for higher standards in other areas. It forced the problem of customers being cheated by shorted weights and measures onto the City Council agenda, with the result that the City Charter was amended to permit the customer legal redress. Calgary's City Council also agreed to send to England for special equipment to be used by its standardized short weights and measures inspector. Complaints regarding meat inspection standards resulted in the appointment of a qualified meat inspector.

Not surprisingly, morale was very high among the members who attended the League's April 23rd annual meeting, and they re-elected Georgina Newhall unanimously. Encouraged by their "monumental success in the rehabilitation of the retail market," the League resolved to go "still further afield in their warfare on that arch fiend, the high cost of living" and begin a wholesale market. An article in the *Albertan* recounted Newhall's clever reminder concerning possible neglect of household duties, "Mrs. Newhall, . . . asked pathetically whether it would be needful to go through the same siege as last year, leaving a trail of undarned socks and burned dinners in their wake in order to overcome the inertia of the public and especially the commercial organizations in regard to the project."[12]

By 1915 the League's City Council and public market monitoring role was modified, at the League's request, by the appointment of an official city Market Advisory Board composed of three women and two men responsible for monitoring market management. The League's three appointees were Georgina Newhall, Mrs. Fryling and Mrs. Simons. This new authority would free the League to undertake a more comprehensive wartime role, "a systematic educational campaign in Production and Thrift." Patriotic plans included raising consumer awareness through public lectures on such topics as "Food Values and the Balanced Ration," "Correct Buying," "The Care of Foodstuffs In the Home," "Home Canning" and "What Factors Combine to Cause High Prices."

A year later the League seemed to have won its greatest marketing victory – a City Charter amendment (referred to as the "socialist clause") which allowed the city authority to sell agricultural produce at its own stall directly to consumers. Soon, however, the market's new aspect was undermined by an April third City Council decision to forbid the sale of groceries at the city market and to offer all perishable produce for public auction after 4:30 each afternoon. The former meant that women couldn't buy flour, sugar and other staples at lower prices; the latter meant a reduced profit for farmers, who would soon take their products elsewhere. Although the League women in attendance at that April meeting expressed their disapproval immediately and audibly, they could not intimidate on the spot.

Over the years, the League's remarkable record of well-publicized coping adaptations in the war on living costs exacted its toll in personal energy and interpersonal relationships. Citing the need to devote more time to her family, Georgina Newhall resigned the presidency in the fall of 1914, but dissension within the executive was later suggested as the underlying reason. Mrs. Singley succeeded her for a very brief period, then she too resigned, to be succeeded in turn by Mrs. Fryling, who agreed to take the office for one year. Having soon found "the duties and responsibilities of the position . . . of a straining and exacting nature," she tendered her resignation within six months but was persuaded to stay on until the annual meeting. With each change in the presidency, other officers changed, and gradually a power struggle, dissension and instability threatened.

By the spring of 1916 internal problems became a matter of public knowledge and concern. Under a March 22nd *News-Telegram* heading "Insurrection In The Ranks Of Consumers' League Reported," readers learned that there were two opposing factions: one wanting the return of Mrs. Newhall to the presidency; the other siding with "two other members who have been particularly active in the affairs of the League of late." The next day's follow up, "War Rumours In Consumers' League Camp," pointed out one "peculiar situation." None of the League's three representatives on the Market Advisory Board – Mrs. Newhall, Mrs. Simons, Mrs. Fryling – now held office in the League itself. None of the women who tendered her resignation would comment, but the *Herald* did report a strong difference of opinion between Mrs. Newhall and Mrs. Davidson over whether a separate trade agent should be appointed to the city market. It surfaced during the March 29th City Council Legislative Committee meeting.

In anticipation of the annual meeting of the League on April 27th, a petition calling for Georgina Newhall to assume the presidency again received some 800 signatures, but in spite of this ground-swell of support she staunchly declined. Mrs. Fryling also refused. However, as happens in organizations after flare-ups, matters seemed to settle down. The annual meeting proved unexpectedly peaceful, but with only fifty of the 114 members in attendance, clearly the ranks had thinned. To its credit, the nominating committee brought in a full slate, with the exception of the presidency. When nominated from the floor, Mrs. Davidson declined, saying she had never aspired to the office. Mr. W.T.D. Lathwell also refused, stating that he believed the office should be filled by a woman. He did agree, however, to stay on as legal advisor. When Georgina Newhall also declined to continue as honorary president, that distinction was offered to Annie Gale, who accepted an honor well-earned. She had served as corresponding secretary almost since the League's inception.

Although peace seemed to have returned, the *Herald* still believed that peace could be short-lived. Two days after the annual meeting, an editorial writer stated that discord still existed among the executive members and that if personal differences were not settled in the interest of public good, the League was doomed.[13]

By December of that year a market investigation inquiry called for by Lathwell revealed that such an atmosphere of mistrust prevailed between the market management and certain League members that Market Master McKenzie admitted erasing names from his books to discourage the women, Mrs. Simons in particular, "from coming down to pick flaws in the books." He justified this precaution because, in his view, "what she didn't know wouldn't hurt her." What she and others wanted to know was just who might be getting preferential treatment.[14]

In wartime, in spite of some outstanding successes, it was very difficult to sustain market support. Consumer energies were redirected to many patriotic obligations other than the practice of thrift, and civic officials were indifferent. When attendance fell in 1916 and 1917, market relocation, deficits and subsidies provided vulnerable targets for critics, much to the frustration of Georgina Newhall, who truly believed that a public market was essential, a kind of public utility that provided "the only balance which the common people have against the rapacity of private interests."[15] City authorities did not agree. On the contrary, they viewed the market as "the women's toy," and felt its problems did not warrant serious attention.[16] In 1920 criticisms of the poor location, cleanliness standards and indifferent customer support echoed those of 1913 and 1917.

Encouraged by the early success of Calgary's revitalized public market and the founding of Canada's first Consumer's League, Georgina Newhall had envisaged a national movement.[17] But her plans to go national were thwarted at first by the National Council of Women itself. As early as May of 1914, NCW's Household Economics Convenor had asked Calgary's organization to change its name and join the Householders' League movement favored by eastern cities.[18]

By 1917 Georgina Newhall had accepted the limitations of her circumscribed League, which never attracted the large membership necessary to wield buying and lobby power. She now decided that an umbrella-type consumer protection association modelled on the Manufacturers' Association would be more effective. As the convenor of the National Council's Household Economics Committee herself, she was now in a good position to promote such a new organization nationally. She began in Calgary, mentored by Local Council's leading women. The transformation took place when Mrs. Harold Riley made the motion to found the Associated Consumers at a well-attended meeting in the Public Library on February seventh. The provisional executive included Alice Jamieson, second vice-president, Emily Kerby, third vice-president, Mrs. Fryling, treasurer, and Maude Riley became convenor of the Constitution and Laws Committee. The new Association must have functioned harmoniously, because that provisional executive was re-elected at the first annual meeting in January of 1918.[19]

With the formation of the Associated Consumers, Georgina Newhall again dreamed on a grand scale. It would link all consumer and co-operative organizations in Canada and have provincial associations as well. In her capacity as convenor of the Household Economics Committee, she also ardently urged the practice of thrift at every level of Canadian living – by individuals, households, industry and governments. As had happened before, though, Newhall's energetic admonitions and motivational suggestions did not reap the harvest she anticipated. Her 1919 NCW Household Economics Convenor's report was uncompromisingly pessimistic. It had been a year "almost devoid of any record of accomplishment." She had found that the national committee which she convened was more structure than substance. From the twenty-four letters sent to members of her committee, she received only two replies. As president of the Associated Consumers of Calgary she had written all the Housewives' Leagues, Thrift Societies and Consumers' Leagues across the country explaining the new Association's aims and soliciting memberships. Only one replied.

The scales of illusion had fallen from this visionary's eyes. Georgina Newhall attributed this almost negligible support to "the great diversity of interests occupying the attention of women . . . the overlapping of objectives and methods of attack which the possession of the franchise has brought upon the women of Canada . . . the hope of the housewife that the Government would at last do something worth while in reference to Household Economics." The bottom line was "the undoubted apathy of women," who filled the air with "groans and complaints" but expended little if any energy.[20] Her one hope was that the adoption of the Woman's Platform would "properly" direct women's energies.

Sometimes it is interesting to read how a woman like her is remembered. When Georgina Newhall died in November of 1932, the tribute which appeared in the *Calgary Herald* revealed the contributions of this remarkable woman as a thinker and writer on economics and food conservation, as convener of the LCW's Committee on Economics, as the planner and organizer of many schemes for the production and conservation of foods during the war. One of the first writers to edit a woman's page (in the *Mall and Empire*), she also contributed regularly to *Saturday Night*, advocated her causes persuasively in the *Woman's Century*, the official publication of the National Council of Women, and applied her creative talents to a special literary interest, poems and articles on the Scottish bards. She was always keenly interested in conditions affecting the home, in laws and problems relating to women and children, as well as in child welfare work. She was, the *Herald* wrote, "A woman of lofty ideals and high character, absolutely devoid of self-seeking, devoted to her home and family."[21] It was a fitting epitaph for her and for other "women workers" of her time.

Chapter Thirteen

Railroading Laid Bare

ဢ ဢ ဢ ဢ

Local Council of Women's *cause célèbre* during the '60s was its opposition to the CPR's proposal to build a new set of railway tracks along the south bank of the Bow River as part of the City-CPR Downtown Redevelopment Plan. The Council of Women's chief protagonist was undoubtedly its Convenor of Laws, Ruth Gorman, who conducted a dual campaign. As chairman of the Special Study Committee struck to monitor the CPR issue, she co-ordinated LCW's opposition in the form of resolutions and public meetings; as Ruth Gorman, Lawyer, she wrote letters to the editor and spoke to interested groups.

Beginning in the early spring of 1963, press coverage of the City-CPR Plan issue lasted for over a year, providing an opportunity to document public actions taken by the LCW and by Ruth Gorman in particular. In retrospect, she personally ranked this confrontation as, "the most lasting and effective move for Calgary in the legal field of LCW's efforts."

Ruth's initial motivation to fight was her anger over the City's seeming abandonment of a commitment to Local Council's proposal for a park along the river. Although she originally entered the fray as LCW's Convenor of Laws, an office she had held for 20 years, she later took a personal stand, realizing that the City-CPR Agreement and its implications were not being revealed to the citizens of Calgary. When I asked her if as one of the key figures in a highly contentious issue she was ever threatened or very frightened, she replied:

No, but I must admit there were two occasions when I was truly shocked. One occurred when I was walking unrecognized down 9th Avenue and I had a pamphlet titled, "Yes, Ruth Gorman, There Is A Santa Claus" shoved at me. (I had been pointing out that the CPR was not playing Santa Claus to Calgary citizens.) Seeing my name glaring forth so unexpectedly impacted like a physical blow. The other occasion was when my views were referred to as "Ruth Gorman's lies" before a packed audience. I'll just never forget hearing myself called a liar before 500 people.

At that time, she explained, City Council consisted of aldermanic and mayoralty candidates nominated by one of two groups – the Civic Government Association (CGA) and Labour – with the division of votes usually approximating two-thirds for the CGA and one-third for Labour. The mayor was Harry Hays, a rancher, auctioneer and dairy farmer whose land had become a part of Calgary's southwest expansion. He had been elected in October of 1959, backed by a majority of CGA aldermen. Ruth noted:

> *Mayor Hays had in his term proposed that Calgary have a master plan for integrated downtown redevelopment. The LCW member delegated to attend City Council meetings relayed this information back to our women, but, unfortunately no copies were released to the public. Sketches were merely flashed before City Council because the planning process was managed by city planners, the commissioner and the land department.*

Railway interest in riverbank locations went back a long way in Calgary. Historically speaking, it was the CPR railway which established Calgary, and by tradition, its wishes were respected. What was good for the railway companies was generally good for Calgary, with a few minor exceptions. A case in point occurred in mid-December of 1912, when a *Morning Albertan* editorial writer protested the prospect of the Interurban Railway Company acquiring two blocks of Bow riverbank for its shunting yard "as a free gift" if electors passed the required bylaw. The author reminded readers that, over the years, short-sighted conversions of riverbank strips to commercial use had vandalized the waterfront, depriving Calgary's citizenry of its use and beauty. He cautioned electors who might support the pending bylaw: "If we are ever to have a city beautiful, it will revolve around our water front."[1]

Four decades later, during the 1950s, the Calgary Local Council of Women lobbied City Hall to preserve areas along the Bow River for public enjoyment. Background readings of LCW records confirm that as early as 1955 City Council adopted in principle the women's concept of a green strip that would extend from Fourteenth Street to the Cushing Bridge. Then, in 1958, it approved in principle LCW's proposal for a plan to designate the strip of land along the south bank of the Bow between the Louise and Langevin bridges as a park.[2]

It should be noted, however, that "approval in principle" is sometimes a misinterpreted term. It is by definition a procedural motion permitting detailed discussion; it does not mean that the specifics of a recommendation or plan have been adopted. Hence, Local Council's concern was whether the aforementioned master plan would still reserve the downtown banks of the Bow for public enjoyment. For years the area had been a site for slum properties and for businesses which used the river, among them laundries, abattoirs and vinegar works.

On March 13, 1963, Mayor Hays hinted that a mystery project worth between $12 and $25 million would be announced within 90 days. The mayor's profile was unusually high at the time because he was also running as a federal Liberal candidate for Calgary South against one of his Aldermen, Jack Leslie, a Conservative. Election day, April ninth, was fast approaching. On April fifth – sooner than anticipated but propitiously for Mayor Hays – the City and the CPR unveiled a $35 million project. It was identified as the CPR Relocation Plan, and as Ruth explained it was launched, "not in City Council but at a very fine party hosted by the CPR at the Palliser Hotel to which prominent businessmen and aldermen were invited, but to my recollection, representation from LCW was not solicited."

Three photos graced the front-page of the *Herald* that day: exterior and interior views of the new 5000-seat, $3 million, dish-shaped international-calibre convention centre crowned the headline "35 Million Face-Lift For Calgary Revealed." "The largest of its kind in Canada," it would be erected on the east side of CP's Palliser Hotel, be paid for by the City, and would potentially increase tourism fivefold over the next five years. Below the headlines, VIPs were shown viewing a model of CP's first ten-acre right-of-way proposed for redevelopment. Readers learned the $10 million rail relocation would remove existing subways and would free 102 downtown acres (the existing rail right-of-way) for commercial development. Over the next two decades, an estimated city tax yield of $90 million could accrue from ensuing development. A transportation centre adjacent to the convention complex would be paid for by the prospective users: Greyhound, Calgary Transit and all airlines. Canadian Pacific and Canadian National would relocate to the banks of the Bow, sharing a new union station near the site of old Fort Calgary. An eight-lane parkway was to parallel CP's east-west tracks when they were shifted to the south bank of the Bow. CP was to buy the land it needed along the south bank from the city.

When asked if the proposal to run a parkway (arterial highway) along the riverbank would be opposed, Mayor Hays replied, "The benefits so outnumber the liabilities that any thinking Calgarian will go along with it."[3] Nevertheless, Works Commissioner John Steel, in anticipation of public protest, shored his defence. He gave the assurance that landscaping with grass belts, trees, shrubs and a wide median would actually accelerate the river bank beautification. To placate those who were apprehensive, the Commissioner provided an innocuous definition of a parkway: "the equivalent of a road going through a park."[4] Almost without exception, the paper's coverage was euphoric. The visionary City-CPR project would transform Calgary into a brand new city unrecognizable in 20 years. Million dollar signs tantalized, and the *Calgary Herald* was all for it!

The *Morning Albertan's* April sixth photograph, which appeared under the caption "Your Slip is Showing, Mr. Mayor!" was less convention-minded. It might have been serendipity, but the photo implied that all was not being revealed. It showed Harry Hays grasping a corner of the city map to prevent a portion of CP's downtown plans from being seen.

Beside him stood CP vice-president Ian Sinclair, laughing at the Mayor's discombobulation.[5] Time and again throughout the next 15 months, as problems emerged, they did so as revelations. Sometimes a picture *is* worth a thousand words.

Generally speaking, the project was welcomed, as it offered prospects of millions being spent in Calgary, much needed employment opportunities, provincial grants and the removal of the downtown trackage that was always a source of tax and traffic complaints. The press and prominent businessmen sensed that Calgary was headed for a boom, and developers were waiting in the wings. From a planning point of view, however, much had changed. The glittering City-CPR project had preempted the more mundane but prerequisite downtown master plan.

CPR officials had greater knowledge of the project's history than did City Hall. Although Mayor Hays (by this time also Honorable Harry Hays, Federal Minister of Agriculture) and certain city commissioners had been involved in the CPR negotiations which began a year earlier, the reality was that most aldermen and some commissioners were not privy to the same level of information. More significantly, although Calgary's chief solicitor had worked on the plan, he was removed from the project when he became lukewarm to it. Truth to tell, the agreement had been finely crafted by the CPR's legal department.

Two weeks after the unveiling, at the April 21st Council meeting, a concerned Alderman Jack Leslie successfully initiated a request for a separate city economic impact study by outside consultants. With reference to LCW's concern, Leslie noted previous plans had called for river beautification, not railway track relocation. To him the two terms were not synonymous.

Ruth Gorman stressed that although the women in Calgary's LCW welcomed the predictions of prosperity, their main concern was still what the effect would be on their earlier proposal for a public green strip along the river, if the railway ran there. That April, at her suggestion, LCW formed an embryonic watchdog committee comprising Grace Stonewall (ex officio), Laura McCullough, Aileen Fish, Lilian MacLennan, and later, Alberta Clark. Committee members were charged with studying the City-CPR agreement and regularly attending City Council meetings. This core group was referred to in the press as the Special Study Committee. Also based on Ruth's advice, LCW passed a motion requesting, "the City planners to provide for a green strip at least a city block width, with access, along the south side of the Bow River; and that the railroad tracks and roadway be placed south of this green strip, thus confining a beauty spot for use of the downtown Calgary citizens."[6] Supported by this endorsement, Ruth was promptly sent back to City Council to get a confirmation that they would respect LCW's earlier proposal.

At the May 23rd special City Council meeting, the City-CPR project was approved in principle. Ruth recalled, "I was allowed to speak on the subject of our proposed green strip, and to my surprise Council instructed the commissioners to investigate but, I noted, did not adopt our suggestion for river beautification." The commissioners subsequently hired a Montreal firm, van Ginkel and Associates, to prepare an independent report on "the alleged spoliation of the Bow River frontage and the loss of amenities pertaining thereto."[7]

"Why did City Council not adopt outright our proposal for a green strip?" Ruth wondered. She sought an explanation.

I decided to read carefully the proposed city contract with CPR, and to see the actual plan by spending a day in the Planning department as a private citizen studying documents although no copying was allowed. I was shocked at what I found.

The old tracks weren't going, there would just be a second set of railway tracks in downtown Calgary, and the new set would run right on the edge of the river, marked in places running right in the river, with long range plans for a traffic bridge over the lovely but undeveloped Prince's Island. Furthermore, the City in effect would be paying for all the land and, through rent, paying for the new station. As well, its whole downtown area would be destroyed by elevated ramps and bridges necessary to run over the new rail line.

As might be anticipated, the van Ginkel Report endorsed the City-CPR plan. In the consultant's view, relocation of the downtown railway tracks meant, "one hundred acres in the heart of a healthy downtown area are freed for development and the railway track will occupy only 10 acres of (riverbank) land which is at present worthless." The firm encouraged a further opportunity, "The relocation of the C.P.R. right of way along the South bank of the Bow River gives the city a golden opportunity to project a parkway along the river, facilitating the traffic movement across town in an east-west direction." Later in the report the consultants waxed eloquent, "The new parkway will give the river back to the city."[8]

The potential cost of the development to city taxpayers, along with the prospect of expropriation of private property, begged the question of a plebiscite. To his credit, Alderman Grant MacEwan did try to obtain confirmation at the June tenth Council meeting that a plebiscite would be held. He was unsuccessful, but eight days later Council appointed a three-man committee to promote the plan to citizens. Then, on June 27th, the Council supported a money bylaw resolution. Bolstered by the prestige of his new federal position, the Honorable Harry Hays, whom Council had persuaded to continue as Mayor until the October civic elections, pressed his advocacy of the City-CPR scheme.

In due time Hays' candidate of choice, Grant MacEwan, won the election with CGA support. Though the new mayor also endorsed the project, he was not so privy as Hays was to the City-CPR contract details. Unfortunately for him, it was a time when a clear understanding of the documentation was prerequisite to stewarding the City's interests. Furthermore, MacEwan had come from the halls of academe. The former Dean of Agriculture at the University of Manitoba played by the rules of cricket, whereas the game out here was hardball. The case for a plebiscite was reinforced in mid-November, when costs to the City were quoted at $6.6 million, still a large amount.

In anticipation of a spring plebiscite, several lobby groups formed by early 1964 to enlighten the 300 000 citizenry. The first group, Calgarians for Progress (CFP), co-chaired by prominent Calgary oilman Carl Nickle, was a high profile pressure group dedicated to promoting the CPR Plan. Although it was composed predominantly of businessmen, one noteworthy exception was Mrs. Wilma Hansen, an LCW member who, in recognition of her election as a public school trustee, had been designated an honorary vice-president of Local Council. With its uniformly pro-Plan membership, CFP enjoyed the amenity of a donated downtown office from which it distributed promotional propaganda one of which, Ruth remembers, was the "Yes, Ruth Gorman, There is a Santa Claus" pamphlet. By February of 1964, Calgarians For Progress was perceived as City Hall's anointed promoter of the City-CPR redevelopment scheme.The more broadly based Calgary Development Committee (CDC) formed later, with members coming from the Chamber of Commerce, the Real Estate Board, and the Downtown Business Association. Carl Nickle also headed this catalyst lobby, which tried to act as a credible mediator between the City and the CPR when their differences threatened to destroy the project.

"Neutral striving but negative tending" groups, as the *Albertan* described them, included the Calgary Regional Branch of the Community Planning Association of Canada and its later offshoot, the Citizens for Community Development (CCD), which formed in early January of 1964. The latter's diverse membership encompassed architects, lawyers, professional planners from the university and the private sector as well as LCW members. From a planning perspective, it held the view that a downtown master plan was prerequisite to agreement on the City-CPR scheme. The most intimately involved opponent was definitely the South Bank Bow River Property Owners' Association. This vocal group focused on the negative aspects of expropriation, compensation to persons living in the area, and tax exemptions to the CPR. They later hired a lawyer, Hugh John MacDonald, to act on their behalf and present their brief to the Provincial Hearings in early March.

But what about testing general public support? This plan which could potentially cost Calgary's taxpayers millions had neither been publicly presented nor voted upon. Ruth remembered her sense of frustration:

When I expressed my concerns early on to LCW, the press was absent from our meetings. Neither of the two prominent newspapers would publish the details I had discovered regarding financial implications of the plan and loopholes regarding the extra track removal. I then went to Roy Farran who published the weekly North Hill News. His paper, with its motto, "Without Fear Or Favour" finally published my views. At first he was reluctant for fear he would be sued. However I prevailed upon him to phone his lawyer Bill McGillivray (later Chief Justice of Alberta), who, after seeing the contract, informed him what I was saying was legally true. My submission subsequently appeared but relegated to the back of his weekly.

By January 25th. I did get a letter, "Time to Call Spade a Spade," published in the Albertan. Three days later it printed Carl Nickle's rebuttal, "CP Plan Will Benefit Taxpayers." Later these two exchanges were reprinted and distributed as part of the Citizens For Progress propaganda campaign.

One ameliorating factor was that problems in the City-CPR contract surfaced beginning as early as May of 1963, when the City's share of costs was estimated at $8 787 000. By early January of 1964 the citizenry had, at various times, learned that estimated costs to the City varied between $6.6 and $8.8 million; the CPR was becoming intractable in negotiations on a Second Street West crossing; the CNR (whose officials had not attended the official launching ceremonies) would not release its land for a parallel city parkway along the south banks of the Bow. When the CPR threatened for a third time to pull out, negotiators prepared a draft agreement which was approved January 22nd by a Council vote of eight to three. Alderman Dave Russell, an architect by profession, voted against it, describing the Plan as being about as dynamic as "a wet noodle."

With further reference to the draft agreement, the letter of intent was amended to include the proviso that before the City-CPR agreement became binding on either party, it must be approved by a majority of the proprietary electors. Because certain sections of the agreement were at variance with the City Charter, the City agreed to petition the Legislature for an act (enabling statute) which would "relieve the City from any liability arising out of the Municipalities Assessment and Equalization Act . . . ; authorize the City to borrow needed monies, without a bylaw; empower the city to expropriate land for the parkway and new right-of-way and transfer to CPR land needed for the right-of-way as specified in the agreement; without a bylaw."[9] Approval of proprietary electors notwithstanding, critics must have viewed the exercise as an "empowerment trip" to Edmonton.

Legislature hearings, the pre-requisite to the enabling statute, opened in Edmonton on March third, and 13 briefs were heard. One of these, presented by lawyer William Morrow on behalf of a group of 50 Calgary businessmen, called for a royal commission to investigate the City-CPR plan. In this brief the government was advised to, "appoint a five-man commission, headed by a judge, and including an engineer, economist, town planner and a private citizen." The 64 MLAs in attendance were cautioned that they were also stakeholders, "If anything goes wrong with this project, both the CPR and the aldermen of Calgary will pass the buck to the present [provincial] government."[9]

Ruth recollects that she prevailed upon two of her law school friends to include Local Council's material in their briefs. With further reference to these hearings she revealed,

> I did send a personal wire to Premier Manning pointing out that Calgary citizens should have the option of hearing the city solicitor on this contract, but I can assure you neither I nor Local Council had ever discussed the agreement with the city solicitor. When Premier Manning suspended the hearings pending the arrival of Calgary's city solicitor to testify under oath, we women on the Special Study Committee who were monitoring the hearings sat with fingers crossed hoping for forthright statements. We were not disappointed.[10]

Albertan staff writer Peter Thurling's editorial comment on the three-day Legislature hearings was tamely titled "The City's Performance," but the added word "Failed" would have provided appropriate piquancy. Thurling described how, in his attempt to summarize the city's 59-page brief, Mayor MacEwan omitted the contractual obligations involving the Alberta legislature itself; how, in attempting to answer questions from the floor both the Mayor and Chief Commissioner Steel revealed how little, not how much, they understood the terms of agreement. It was CPR lawyer Sinclair who provided the crucial clarification and saved the day. But not for long. Two days later, one of Calgary's most able opponents, lawyer Robert Barron, so effectively damaged the city's case in his "sharp, restrained, witty" attack on the proposed transportation centre[11] that Premier Manning then seconded the chief city solicitor from Calgary to comment on Barron's brief. During that hearing Carson MacWilliams' most shocking revelation was probably that his department had never been asked by City Council for its opinion! MacWilliams also said he generally agreed with Barron's brief and assessed the agreement as, "the most one-sided he has ever seen."[12] And he meant one-sided in favor of the CPR.

The local press soon took sides. An editorial in the March seventh Calgary Herald, "Out Of Order," ruled the city solicitor's expression of a personal opinion to be contrary to his obligation as a civil servant to inform and advise the mayor and commissioners on legal matters. Period. As a matter of conscience, the Herald felt, he should now resign. But not according to the North Hill News. On the contrary, a later reaction in Roy Farran's weekly showed a clear tone of respect and admiration for the opposition of "brave city solicitor" Carson MacWilliams, who "showed complete honesty and integrity under question by the Premier."[12] Despite denials from the Mayor, there was a sense of apprehension that MacWilliams' outspoken opinions would result in the 67-year-old chief solicitor's decision to "retire." He didn't, but chief commissioner Steel eventually did.

LCW forces felt that the proprietary electors in Calgary needed a special public debate where the agreement's content and omissions would be presented objectively. Such an undertaking was judged to be an appropriate local application of the organization's common national goal of community betterment; so the Calgary LCW scheduled the debate for March ninth and chose three participants for each side. Invitations were sent out on February 28th, and those invited to argue in favor of the City-CPR plan were Rod Sykes, CPR's land development project manager, the Mayor, and the citizen's committee of Calgarians For Progress. It was decided that Robert Barron, QC, a prominent city lawyer, Professor Mike Coulson, a University of Calgary urban geographer, and Ruth were to debate the cons, but each speaking as individuals not as group representatives. This was done in order to avoid a platform opportunity for organized opposition lobbies. Aileen Fish of the LCW's Special Study Committee agreed to moderate the debate. At that time Aileen enjoyed a high civic profile, being on the Canadian Club's travelling speaker roster as well as a popular guest on local media panels.

Not everyone viewed Council of Women's invitation as a privileged opportunity to seed truth. On the day of the forum, a hand-delivered letter addressed to Mrs. Kay [sic] MacLennan, LCW's president, from Rod Sykes, explained that their letter and telegram had arrived too late; he was occupied that day on business in Edmonton. As CP's Manager of the Calgary Land Project, Sykes negated the need for a meeting "to obtain facts and clear up confusion about the Calgary development plan" because these facts were already available from both the City and CP. He listed independent consultants hired by the city and specific organizations who, "believe it to be good for Calgary," then tacked to a more paternal approach:

> If your organization cannot accept the findings and recommendations of these groups representing wide and varied interests in the community and made up of leaders of the community, then we would offer the suggestion that you do as they have done – appoint a committee to make a thorough study of the whole plan.

Rod Sykes offered full assistance as well as his personal assurance that CP did not intend to "sell" an unwanted plan to Calgarians. The next sentence proved a sound prophecy: "The case for the plan must stand or fall on its own merits." He then philosophized, "It is always easier to destroy than to build and to criticize rather than to contribute constructively."[13] In their March tenth editions, both the *Herald* and *Albertan* printed excerpts from this letter, along with Sykes' additional comments.

Calgarians for Progress chose to remain unsullied. Joint chairman, Carl Nickle had his group decline on the anticipation that proper rules for debate, discussion and maintenance of order would not be followed. Mayor MacEwan did attend and filled the debate vacancies with two Aldermen, Ted Duncan and Ernie Starr, who came at his invitation. Nonetheless, this now meant that the City was left to defend the agreement alone, abandoned by its partner, the CPR, and by the project's strongest advocate, the CFP. For them, the fickle finger of fate now pointed clearly in the wrong direction.

Five hundred of the citizenry came. Their preference was to bury the CPR rather than to praise it. In what was described as a "searing attack," Ruth opened debate, urging citizens to discover document loopholes themselves. One of the most glaring allowed the CPR two sets of tracks: a new one along the south bank of the Bow for passenger service, and the existing ones. She warned that the CPR could retain these old tracks indefinitely for freight operation, and such use would exempt it from paying right-of-way tax to the City.

Mayor MacEwan had neither recent history nor the audience on his side. According to the *Albertan*, "the catcalling" began before the Mayor stood up. Finding himself in somewhat the same position as a dove in an eagle's nest, he optimistically ignored the derisive greeting claiming, "the crowd was a good omen as to the amount of interest citizens had in the plan." The Mayor persevered, citing the City's equitable cost-sharing agreements on land for the parkway and new right-of-way along the Bow as well as for related utility costs.

Robert Barron countered that the CPR's $10 million development commitment was "not worth the paper it was written on." Moreover, its special status under the Planning Act now enabled CPR to acquire 25 acres of valuable downtown land which the city should have had for streets and parks.

Quite unexpectedly, Mayor MacEwan discovered he did not have Alderman Ernie Starr in his firmament. Starr's words, "The trouble we are in today in this city is due to a pressure group brought in by CP – I'm talking about the Calgarians for Progress; they've been sending out literature Council has never seen," delighted the wrong side. Alderman Ted Duncan loyally persevered despite constant booing and heckling, especially from the vocal South Bank Ratepayers' Association. He insisted the agreement was no giveaway to CP. "No one on council has any love for CP," he said.

Professor Coulson spoke last. Referring to the trend in certain other cities to remove, depress or build over railways, he asserted, "I am opposed to destruction of [a] natural resource – the south bank of the Bow River," then charged that the parkway was a City strategy dreamed up to rationalize the CP right-of-way along the river bank.[15]

The meeting lasted two hours and twenty minutes. To put it delicately, moderator Aileen Fish experienced great difficulty in restricting questions and answers to the factual content of the agreement itself. Subjective questioning cast aspersions on the City's competence throughout CPR negotiations, and one of Alderman Duncan's remarks, "If you want to believe Ruth Gorman's lies," cast aspersions on her honesty.[16]

The next day the *Herald* headlined, "Mayor, Alderman Booed, Hissed at Noisy City-CP Project Forum," and the *Albertan's* front-page read "Debate Stacked, Duncan Claims." The LCW Executive met, their sensibilities offended by the press coverage, which gave the impression the meeting was not well-conducted. In part because Mayor MacEwan had that night congratulated several members on the meeting's high calibre and in part because LCW did not want to jeopardize its "happy relationship" with City Council, Ruth was instructed to write a letter to City Council refuting newspaper accounts and objecting to Alderman Duncan's breach of decorum. The executive even struck a committee comprising the President (Lilian MacLennan), Grace Stonewall and Ruth to prepare the contents. LCW files contain a one-page letter countering in point form Alderman Duncan's charge that the debate was stacked. As would be expected, it was typed on official stationery, addressed to the Mayor and signed by the President, but an unexpected "cancelled" is written across the top. This indicates some internal disagreement on how the matter should be dealt with. One recollection was that the letter was delivered, retrieved, then delivered again.

Mayor MacEwan's afterthoughts regarding the absence of the CPR and Calgarians for Progress was an exemplary understatement, "I was hoping both would have been there last night, their support would have been most helpful." He then allowed, "But I can understand why a group would not want to appear at a meeting where such indifference to getting both sides of the story existed."[17]

It may have been coincidence, but beginning after the LCW-sponsored debate, Ruth did receive press coverage when she accepted invitations to speak to city organizations. Among them was the Alberta Old Age Pensioners' Society, where all panelists concurred that the City-CPR agreement was not worth the paper it was written on.[18] When the press covered Ruth's speech to the Janey Canuck Toastmistress Club, the headline was "Listening to Calgary Council Suggested as Murder Penalty." Here she told the 50 members, "After the last council meeting we have eliminated hanging for murder. The guilty party should have to sit for the rest of his days and listen to City Council."[19] She was referring to the chaos that resulted in City Council following the "bombshell" news of the multi-million dollar cost to gain a right-of-way across the CN property. During this same address, Ruth estimated that City costs of the CPR project were now at least $15 500 000.

That June eighth City Council meeting was chaotic indeed. Moving and seconding of crisis-oriented proposals provided no escape route. "Seven motions were defeated in a confusion-packed three-hour debate, during which three aldermen spoke of resigning." Alderman Roy Deyell – who no doubt asked himself "Why just three?" – spoke up, "inasmuch as we have lost the ability to govern the city, the mayor and all twelve aldermen should resign."[20]

Other humorous reprieves besides Ruth's death penalty suggestion did occur during stressful speaking occasions. Ruth recalled one delightful entrapment during a panel discussion which included CFP co-chairman, Carl Nickle. This important meeting was arranged by the politically powerful Calgary Labour Council, who sponsored candidates during civic elections to ensure strong representation at the aldermanic level. When Ruth asked Carl Nickle why the CPR could not at least put its central tracks underground so the remaining set of tracks could be moved further back from the river edge, he replied it was impossible for CPR to go underground because of Calgary's high water table. At this juncture a little old lady in the audience stood up to say she had only one question and it was addressed to Mr. Nickle. The lady prefaced her query by noting Mr. Nickle had said that a large transport section would be built under the present CPR station for the use of city buses. Bearing in mind his reference to Calgary's high water table, she asked, "What was his intent? Was he planning that the transport section would be in a swimming pool?" Tensions broke as the meeting dissolved in laughter. Such an exchange re-enforced Ruth's credibility because it proved Mr. Nickle's argument was superfluous – the city intended to keep two sets of tracks.

But it was a headline story in both dailies on May 21st which brought the LCW to the fore. That morning, based on a phone tip, the *Albertan* broke the news that Alderman Dave Russell's employer had "transferred" him out of Calgary to open a Kelowna branch of Rule, Wynne and Rule Associates. The reason given by the firm's senior partner was pressure from clients who favored the CPR plan. When Russell refused the move, which would mean resigning his position as alderman, he was dismissed. Ruth recalled, "When this information leaked into the newspapers, citizens, especially the women in our organization, were shocked."

At her suggestion, LCW notified City Council that its "16,000 strong group" was considering asking for a royal commission inquiry into the CP plan. During the June seventh meeting, the City Council tabled the matter for two weeks along with a letter from the Calgary Labour Council, "deploring 'the dismissal of Alderman David Russell from his employment with Rule, Wynne and Rule because of his stand on the City-CP plan.'"[21]

Council of Women once again moved into the public arena, hosting an open meeting on June tenth at Central High School to investigate whether democratic and moral principles had been compromised. Leaders of Calgary's religious denominations were invited to speak out on how they felt about business interfering with our democratic process. Under the chairmanship of University of Calgary Chaplain Reverend John Paterson and with well over 150 in attendance, including Aldermen Dave Russell, Walter Boote, Ernie Starr and Jack Leslie – all of whom opposed the CPR project – the meeting voted to ask for an impartial judicial inquiry into influence exerted on civic employees and elected officials. The meeting also discussed the moral implications of whether Chief City Solicitor Carson MacWilliams was excluded from Plan negotiations as a result of his stated opposition to the scheme. With reference to biased reporting, a motion to censure the *Calgary Herald* was carried, while one to reprove the *Albertan* was not.

Media interest was uncommonly high. Both dailies and the *North Hill News* carried detailed advance notices of this meeting, covered it, then reported on ensuing decisions. An editorial in the June 12th *Albertan*,"Put Up Or Shut Up" sarcastically identified LCW and speakers at the Wednesday meeting as being privy to information which they should have the courage to reveal in a straightforward manner rather than by innuendo.

Back in the '60s, money was money, even at the civic level, and escalating costs put the Plan out of its misery. The city's dollar commitment was shockingly increased by the revelation that relocating the Bay Warehouse west of 14 Street to allow for the parkway would cost $250 000. A later disclosure revealed that acquiring a right-of-way link across CN property could cost a stupendous $5 million or more. In both instances, Calgary's Council delegated committees to negotiate cost-sharing with the railways, but negotiators for the CPR and CN were no give-away greenhorns about to share high costs. Finally, when Calgary's five-man committee composed of the mayor, three aldermen, and the chief city commissioner returned from Montreal, their unanimous recommendation was that the agreement be dropped. On June 22nd, City Council supported them by a vote of ten-to-three. That same day, Council returned to the downtown master plan.

Post-mortems followed. The *Herald's* editorial, "Death Blow," spared few. CP was censured for not revealing its position on its own property. City commissioners were blamed for not divulging to Council their knowledge of major impediments. City Council was also culpable: it failed to require an identification of major impediments and to ask probing questions about the right-of-way. Plan opponents "who tried to murder the over-all concept" never revealed implied alternatives. In the final analysis, the City was faulted for belatedly testing a fundamental assumption:

> *The whole program of negotiations was predicated on one assumption namely, that land could be acquired in the sense of practicability along the south bank of the Bow for a new rail route and a new city throughway. In the end it turned out that this assumption was judged fallacious.*[22]

From the perspective of Local Council's commitment to a park-like river bank for public enjoyment, the city's refusal of the $5 million right-of-way cost might be viewed as having greened LCW's cause. Ironically, the rejected dollars (green paper bills in those days) had rejuvenated the concept of a green south bank. The same City Council meeting that voted to abandon the Plan considered letters from Council of Women and the Calgary Labour Council urging an inquiry but decided instead to support a resolution deploring the pressure that was put on elected officials. One reason for this softening was that the person most affected, Alderman Dave Russell, was now placated by the city's rejection of the CP Agreement and by censorship of the press. "I don't need an investigation to find out what happened to me," he remarked. No good would come from investigating a rejected Plan now.

But an *Albertan* editorial writer disagreed. A matter of principle was involved: "Surely, if there was wrong-doing it ought to be investigated and the wrong-doers punished, regardless of the fate of the re-development scheme. That would seem essential for the maintenance of justice and the prevention of further wrong-doing."[23]

Calgary's Local Council of Women, who held the same view, proved tenacious. When the press contacted Ruth to learn LCW's position on City Council's action, she informed them the matter was not over. Ruth was quoted as saying, "I think it is an issue which could be a serious threat in the future, no matter what has happened to the CP plan." Council of Women would contact its affiliates when they reconvened in the fall, she said, at which time the decision on an enquiry would be made. If it was endorsed, then it would become a combined effort of both women and men. Ruth stated, "it was important that women had taken the initiative and shown such a deep interest in a civic matter."[24]

The October eighth LCW executive minutes contained follow-up information. With specific reference to the downtown master plan, Ruth asked for and received permission to solicit affiliate support for her letter asking all aldermanic candidates to state their position on retaining a green strip. A petition that originated from an earlier citizens-at-large meeting was also accepted for mailing. It asked the provincial government for, "an amendment to the City Act to prevent recurrence of alleged intimidation in connection with recent CPR negotiations, and a judicial enquiry into Calgary's civic administration."[25]

The interim report for the Downtown Master Plan, released in September of 1966, contained this river land use proposal:

> *Riverbank Development, though mentioned last, is by no means the least important of the major proposals. Together with the headland bluffs, the riverbanks should be an attractive backdrop to Downtown, a recreational area for the use of Downtown and city-wide residents, an attraction to visitors and a feature that, above all else, is unique to Calgary.*

Epilogue

At the end of his term, Mayor McEwan began his new career as Lieutenant Governor of Alberta, and Jack Leslie, the alderman who first opposed the plan, was elected as Calgary's new mayor. Alderman Russell joined Peter Lougheed's new provincial Conservative party, was elected, and later became a cabinet minister and Deputy Premier.

In Calgary's centennial year, the Alderman who rose phoenix-like from the still-smouldering ashes of that civic conflagration to become mayor reminisced about the "year-long fight with the CPR to keep the railroad off the banks of the Bow River."

> *The end result wasn't exactly what we wanted, but it was certainly a lot better than what the CPR proposed – to have tracks along the river bank, through where Fort Calgary is now. We do have the development of the CPR tracks; but we also have beautiful pathways and parks along the river and Prince's Island. It sure beats a dusty railroad track along the edge of the Bow.*[25]

Chapter Fourteen

Justice Should Be Seen to Be Done

ᖍ ᖍ ᖍ ᖍ

[A] long line of cases shows that it is not merely of some importance but is of fundamental importance that justice should not only be done, but should manifestly and undoubtedly be seen to be done.

Lord Hewart

When the Calgary Local Council of Women initiated the Irene Murdoch Fund in March of 1974, Mrs. Murdoch's action against her husband for an equal share of his property had failed. The decision had come down five months earlier in a controversial dismissal by the Supreme Court of Canada. A chapter of feminist history was in the making. Widely publicized excerpts from the majority ruling of Justice Roland Martland and from the minority decision of Justice Bora Laskin reinforced the perception that justice had not been served. Irene Murdoch's peers and activists committed to matrimonial property reform felt that the law as applied was outmoded and unjust.

Irene Murdoch had begun two actions in the Supreme Court of Alberta, Trial Division. One asked for judicial separation and the other for a declaration of partnership with her husband in the farm lands and other related property owned and used by him in the farming operation. She testified in the Alberta court that her work on the family properties included, "Haying, raking, swathing, mowing, driving trucks and tractors and teams, quietening horses, taking cattle back and forth to the reserve, dehorning, vaccinating, branding, anything that was to be done."[1] Furthermore, she was responsible for running the 480-acre farm, also referred to as a ranch, during the five months of the year when her husband worked for a stock-grazing operation. Asking for a declaration of partnership based upon her personal labors and contributions with no records or contractual agreement put the issue before the court.

On February 24, 1971, the judicial separation decree, including $200 a month maintenance, was granted, but the partnership action was dismissed. The property action was dismissed because the evidence failed to establish that Mrs. Murdoch had made any direct financial contribution of any substantial nature to her husband's acquisition of his farm property. In handing down his decision Alberta Trial Court Justice Mr. Hugh John MacDonald said, in part:

> I feel . . . that were I to declare that Mrs. Murdoch had an equitable interest in the farm lands and farm assets it would be tantamount to establishing a precedent that would give any farm or ranch wife a claim in partnership. I have read nothing and nothing has been referred to me that suggests this is either public policy or the intention of any legislation that exists.[2]

He was correct. Judgments are based upon precedent and existing legislation. It was the partnership action which continued to be appealed after the judicial separation. When the property action was appealed to Alberta's Appellate Court, it was dismissed for technical reasons unconnected with the substantial issues in the action.

Irene Murdoch appealed to the Supreme Court of Canada. Her case was argued on the basis that there was a trust in her favor resulting from her labor contributions to the farming operation over the many years of married life. The Supreme Court dismissed the case for three basic reasons:

1. There were no financial contributions by her.
2. Her labor was nothing more than the work done by any farm or ranch wife.
3. There was no common intention that the property was not to belong solely to her husband.

Two opinions cited from the October 2, 1974, Supreme Court of Canada's four to one decision on the Murdoch case moved the dismissal into the realm of controversy. Both excerpts became rallying words for other farm women in similar circumstances and for those working for matrimonial property reform. The first quote came from Judge Roland Martland, who held that Irene Murdoch had made "only the normal contribution to the farm that most farm or ranch wives make." In light of the vivid imagery evoked when Irene Murdoch detailed her labors, this assessment seemed chauvinistic and reactionary. In its majority decision the Supreme Court applied existing law, which meant that in the absence of a direct financial contribution – for example, mortgage, bill of sale, land held in joint tenancy by husband and wife – the wife had no right to a partial or whole interest in the property. From the majority perspective, justice was done; however, the interpretation of dissenting Justice, Mr. Justice Bora Laskin, contained the kernels of truth:

> In making the substantial contribution of physical labour, as well as a financial contribution, to the acquisition of successive properties . . . the wife has, in my view, established a right to an interest which it would be inequitable to deny. If denied it would result in the unjust enrichment of her husband.[3]

To the two vested interest groups, farm women at risk and matrimonial property activists, Justice Laskin's dissenting view that the wife had "established a right to an interest which it would be inequitable to deny" seemed fair and contemporary. From their perspective the Supreme Court of Canada did not seem to have ruled justly.

The Irene Murdoch Fund originated five months later, on March 27, 1974, as a last minute request of Patricia Krasinski, Local Council's Citizenship Chairperson, during the general meeting. Quite by coincidence the panel topic for that day was "The Status of Women." In moving from the general to the specific during the question period, Patricia detailed a case in point: Irene Murdoch, the southern Alberta farm wife, 25 years married, who was fighting through expensive, lengthy judicial separation proceedings for a half-interest in the family farming operation. Her legal fees and court costs had amounted to around $3000 already, and she still hoped to appeal the Supreme Court decision. As well, there were $2000 in uninsured medical bills which had accrued from the treatment of facial injuries inflicted by her husband.

Patricia told listeners she had become involved after reading a recent *Time* magazine article on Canadian Law which referred to the Murdoch versus Murdoch case as a "troubling precedent." Acting immediately, Patricia phoned her friend, Dorothy Groves, Local Council's publicity convenor, with the direct query, "What is the Council of Women going to do about Irene Murdoch?" Dorothy then read the *Time* article. To allay a personal concern that the facts as presented should be verified, Dorothy proposed and Patricia agreed that a visit with Irene Murdoch was in order. On a winter's day the two women drove out to Turner Valley and located Irene Murdoch. During their impromptu visit the women also perused copies of court documents.

Patricia then briefed the March meeting on the background of the case:

> We found out why Mrs. Murdoch filed for a separation and not a divorce. Mr. Murdoch wanted to sell the farm and buy another one in a remote area far away from schools and club facilities for their son. Under Alberta law the Dower Act gives the wife a life interest in the homestead. Mrs. Murdoch refused the sale of the property. Mr. Murdoch reacted by physically abusing his wife to such an extent that her collar bone and jaw were broken, and six years later she still has to take physiotherapy for her facial muscles. By separation, Mrs. Murdoch still has her Dower rights; by divorcing she would lose even this.[4]

Patricia then observed, "As this case exemplifies, one realizes how redundant the whole Alberta Dower Act is."

With reference to Mrs. Murdoch's farm work and financial contribution claims, Patricia explained,

> at an earlier stage of their married lives, Mr. and Mrs. Murdoch were hired as a couple to work on various farms. Due to their joint efforts they were able to save enough money to buy their first piece of land, helped further by a gift of Mrs. Murdoch's mother which Mrs. Murdoch deposited in her own account and later used towards buying of land and cattle. The Supreme Court of Canada made no consideration of this hiring as a couple and her money contribution,

but came to the extraordinary conclusion "that she made only the normal contribution to the farm that most farm or ranch wives make," in spite of the fact that for five months of every year she ran the farm single-handed.[5]

Patricia then asked, "Is a farm wife considered as slave labour?" And answered, "It seems so."

Although she was optimistic that, "the blatant injustice of this case has caused such a furore that it may spark, more than anything, long needed reforms on matrimonial property laws," she felt that a Supreme Court decision was almost impossible to reverse, and the matrimonial property reform would be difficult to achieve because the vast majority of legislators were male. She concluded by urging the women of Local Council to participate actively by initiating a fund to pay Mrs. Murdoch's legal costs. Patricia's cogent argument:

> *it relieves her of an unjust debt; it thanks Mrs. Murdoch for her courage and tenacity for insisting on her rights, and thus for the rights of all Canadian women. . . . and lastly it is a public gesture, a token of disapproval of the way the law has been interpreted by the Supreme Court of Canada.*[6]

The women of Local Council voted then and there to establish a fund to help pay legal fees incurred by Irene Murdoch. This decision was not precipitous. It was, in fact, a practical application of recently adopted policy. Two years earlier, in 1972, the LCW Annual Meeting passed a pertinent resolution submitted by the Calgary Presbyterial United Church Women. It called on the provincial government to enact legislation requiring equal division of assets, except those acquired through gift or inheritance, upon divorce or legal separation.[7]

The letter sent to Irene Murdoch was also quoted in a *Herald* write-up which read:

> *The Local Council of Women has decided to help you in a practical manner. To do this we have set up a fund to help you pay your legal fees. This is a small but practical token of our support for you and your valiant fight against the odds.*[8]

The first indication of Irene Murdoch's reaction to publicity surfaced a week later in Linda Curtis' column in the *Albertan*. She reported, "This move [setting up the fund] came as a great surprise to Irene who was rather reluctant to become further involved in publicity."[9] Irene Murdoch's reluctance to become involved in any further publicity was something she felt very strongly about, but few bore that in mind during the ensuing notoriety.

President Joni Chorny, Patricia and Dorothy Groves arranged local and national publicity for the fund. At the national level, the project was endorsed by the Advisory Council on the Status of Women on the basis that Irene Murdoch had, "become a symbol of the inequalities of Canadian matrimonial property laws."[10] NCWC also pledged its support. When National President Mrs. Kay Armstrong attended Calgary Local

Council's 1974 Annual Meeting on April 29th, she commended the members for their practical commitment to an issue affecting women's rights. Their exemplary project had, she felt, enhanced the Council's movement across Canada.

Existing Irene Murdoch Fund financial statements and donors' letters indicate that donations ranged from $1 to $50 and that most subscriptions were received within a year. The amount grew quickly, for one month after inception President Joni Chorny reported that approximately 200 hundred donors had contributed a total of over $1200. One unusual contribution came from Patricia Krasinski herself who gave the $38 she received when *Ms* magazine published her account of the Murdoch case. In October of 1974 the accrued sum of $1647.75 was transferred from LCW's general account to the Irene Murdoch Fund account in order to gain higher interest. Audited financial statements scheduled to coincide with annual meetings show the trust at $1854.47 on April 30, 1975 and $1974.83 on March 31, 1976. The only recorded withdrawal was $425 paid in May of 1976 to G.A. Leslie and Co. for an appraisal of the Murdoch land.[11]

Joni, Patricia and Dorothy along with Ruth Gorman, who at that time was a member of the Alberta Committee on the Status of Women, served on the Irene Murdoch Trust Fund until its termination. They proved to be tenacious stewards. With the exception of one appraisal cost withdrawal, the monies were held in trust for five and one-half years until the ongoing three-member committee voted unanimously "that the sums of money collected from across Canada be given to Irene Florence Murdoch."[12] In October of 1979, Patricia Krasinski, Dorothy Groves and Joni Chorny drove out to Irene Murdoch's Turner Valley home, where they presented her with a cheque for $1805.91. By now the women were her friends; they had attended court with her, visited the lawyers with her and tendered advice. Irene Murdoch, who was facing surgery, was advised not to attempt to thank donors individually, but to write instead a general acknowledgement in the *Calgary Women's Newspaper*.

Why did so many years elapse when the announced purpose at the time of the Fund's inception was to pay Irene Murdoch's legal fees estimated then at $3000? One reason was that the funds were held in trust to be released after, and only after, there was no possibility of further court action through an appeal. A letter dated February 19, 1975, now in the Krasinski file in the Glenbow Archives, supports this. It reads in part:

When I mentioned the Murdoch Fund, she thought, as her lawyer Mr. Schymka has also implied to Dorothy Groves, that this would not be the appropriate time to hand it over or do anything much about it. Her divorce proceedings are still going on. Mr. Schymka is rather for hurrying things up, but her other lawyer, working with Mr. Schymka, Mr. Stevenson of Edmonton, who is one of the lawyers responsible for the working paper on Matrimonial

Property Law, wishes to postpone the divorce as long as possible. It seems that he is really hopeful the law may change in her favour.[13]

In more than one progress report on the fund Joni Chorny noted that messages of support and donations came from women all across the country, from men and from married couples. She stressed that there was not one negative response. The following letters from Alberta women affirm the perception that the scales of justice weighed in favor of men. The first, addressed to Joni Chorny, is a representative example:

After reading your comments re Mrs. Murdoch (Lethbridge Herald) I enclose my cheque. I believe all women, including those on the farm, were outraged by the treatment Mrs. Murdoch received in court. I hope we aren't going to forget it. I hope it is a lesson by which we learn to fight for our rights.

Please – let's do something about it. Your organization can do a lot to help change the laws of this country regarding women.[14]

The second of these, a personal account from a Calgary resident, presaged the Murdoch case:

As another woman going through a painful and prolonged divorce, I am appalled at Canada's legal system – its unfair and biased laws and its costly (in money, time, and emotions) procedures, to say nothing of our expensive and uncaring and unethical lawyers!

My divorce will have taken over 4 years and over $3000. A separation agreement, which was all I asked for, should have taken a few weeks and 3 or 4 hundred!

I have heard many heartbreaking stories from women and seen how the laws are not intended to work for women.

Yes, I am bitter.

Keep up your good work![15]

The third alludes to the Irene Murdoch case, then proposes all-encompassing legislation:

Everyone who deplores this miscarriage of justice will be anxious to devise a way to prevent further cases of this sort. I certainly am. But I fear we might introduce legislation which would not ensure that anyone – not only a wife – whose work – is not paid for – gains some suitable equity in property which their efforts sustain and enrich. . . . We must separate the equity which comes from affinal or kinship connection with the owner of property from that earned by the (unpaid for) contributions made to the preservation and growth of the property.[16]

By the spring of 1974, Justice Laskin's dissenting view that the property should be divided equally on the basis of contributed labor had a political impact. In the Alberta Legislature, Mr. Gordon Taylor, MLA for Drumheller, introduced a private member's bill to protect women's rights, and in April another MLA, Stettler lawyer Graham Harle, introduced a backbencher's resolution urging updated legislation which would require the courts to consider during divorce or separation the spousal contribution made in dollars and effort when ruling on property division. Debate did not occur. The motion was held over till the fall.[17] Also in April of 1974, the four-month-old Alberta Human Rights Commission, which agreed with Justice Laskin's minority decision, asked for a reassessment. The Commission called on Parliament to ask the court to "determine whether or not the judgment was inequitable." Meanwhile, Alex Murdoch had already filed for divorce in November of 1973.

However, there were those who held that the high court decided correctly. Mary McCormick Hetherington, a Calgary lawyer who later became a judge, was one of them. She expressed her professional opinion as a guest speaker during a mid-May legal forum held in the Jubilee Auditorium. In response to an audience question about a woman's rights to property in a separation, she was quoted as saying, "I can't understand the publicity that has been given the Murdoch case. . . . What the public has failed to understand is that Irene Florence Murdoch only lost a case based on an application for half ownership in the farm, on which she worked with her husband for 25 years."[18] Mrs. Hetherington explained the farm wife still had recourse to the courts through exercise of the divorce settlement option. At this juncture she could be awarded a lump sum settlement even if the property was registered in her husband's name.

Patricia Krasinski reacted quickly, this time on behalf of the Calgary Status of Women Steering Committee, an affiliate member of Local Council. Her decision to prepare a press release was not an over-reaction, considering that 1100 people had attended the forum. In it she cautioned that in a divorce settlement, there was no assurance that Irene Murdoch would get a lump settlement. Krasinski warned, "Present laws are far from equitable and do not reflect any concept of marriage as a partnership to which both spouses contribute."[19]

It was a widely-read local newspaper columnist, not a member of the legal profession, who charged full tilt to the defence of the courts, rudely jostling feminists aside en route. John Schmidt, agriculture columnist for the *Calgary Herald*, prepared a substantive four-part series on Murdoch versus Murdoch, published in mid-July of 1974, in which he vehemently defended the case for Irene's husband, Alex. Bearing in mind that Mr. Schmidt's vested interest was farming viability, his concern for the splitting of farms and their assets was a valid one. It was his view that the farm should remain an intact inheritance for heirs who intended to continue farming, as he believed that small farm units were less viable. However, his provocative references to those who supported Irene Murdoch's cause were couched in the disparaging terms traditionally used when referring to the women's rights movement. Previously coined descriptors such as "militant women's pressure groups and activists," "female anarchists" and "radical feminists" provided a sense of *déjà vu*.

Under the sub-title "Campaign Became Hysterical," Mr. Schmidt's emotive style provided piquant reading for both sides.

In the following excerpt he refers to the swell of support for Irene Murdoch following the Supreme Court's four to one dismissal of her case in October of 1973, and the backlash it engendered:

> In addition to political motives, the professional females used the case to seek status by mounting a vicious campaign against everything male. It was a campaign based on emotion, mass hysteria and character assassination. It was motivated largely by self-pity and revenge.
>
> The women went about the land wailing imprecations against the Supreme Court of Canada majority judgment.[20]

The establishment of the Irene Murdoch Fund by Calgary Local Council Women was described as a "grandstand gesture" next day under the prediction, "Mr. Murdoch will collect:"

> There is a bit of irony about this grand-standing gesture. In losing her action, Mrs. Murdoch became responsible for the court costs of the Supreme Court of Canada hearing in Ottawa. This meant she was liable for all Mr. Murdoch's costs.[21]

The columnist then pointed out that Mr. Murdoch had, in fact, paid his own court costs, making no subsequent effort to collect the amount levied against his spouse. In theory, he reasoned, Alex Murdoch's court costs came from ranch assets. Then Mr. Schmidt concluded ironically: "the money from the Local Council of Women in Mrs. Murdoch's hands will eventually reach Mr. Murdoch!"

Protagonists within the LCW felt a response was definitely in order. By July 24, the *Calgary Herald* published Patricia Krasinski's letter. In a dismissive reference to Mr. Schmidt, she stated, "his hysterical and abusive language about 'militant feminists' 'professional females' and 'vicious campaigns' has made any serious discussion of the problem with him impossible." On today's scene, this columnist was in her opinion 70 years out of date.[22] Patricia also wrote to Irene Murdoch's lawyer, Mr. Shymka, at Irene's request and with Council of Women concurrence, to express the concern that Schmidt's series of articles might prove prejudicial to her case during divorce proceedings. At the end of July, Patricia proposed to Joni Chorny that the *Herald* should act responsibly and address the four-part series in an editorial. Said Krasinski succinctly, "I think the *Herald* should take some responsibility for publishing Schmidt's crap."[23]

It is very likely that Patricia Krasinski, the British-born granddaughter of a "militant" suffragette, would have undertaken the advocacy of Irene Murdoch even without the backing of Local Council, because she was dedicated to the cause of matrimonial property reform. This science graduate of London University, mother of four daughters, had worked as a researcher and high school teacher for twenty years in Argentina before coming to Calgary, where her husband joined the Department of Mechanical Engineering at the university. An intense awareness of the violation of human rights under a dictatorship in that country was what motivated the family to emigrate. Once here, it wasn't long before Patricia identified discrimination and inequality as issues facing the women of Canada. In a brief autobiographical note, she credits the 1968 *Report of the Royal Commission on the Status of Women in Canada* with directing her towards women's issues. By the time Patricia became involved with the Irene Murdoch Fund she had begun,"studying law from a layperson's point of [view]." As a forceful member of the Status of Women Action Committee, she spent the two years between 1974 and 1976 lobbying MLAs, writing and talking to groups on the Institute of Law Research and Reform's green paper on matrimonial reform, and later on Bill 102, the Matrimonial Property Act.

Not infrequently the Murdoch case is identified as a precedent, prefixed on occasion by the words "troubling" or "dangerous." Such distinctions were appropriate, because the ruling in favor of Irene Murdoch's husband did not bode well for other farm women making similar undocumented matrimonial property claims during judicial separation. A majority of justices had remained unconvinced by her testimony of unremitting farm labor and undocumented financial contributions, believing instead the husband's testimony – that there was no partnership intent. However, there was a positive side to all of this. Especially throughout western Canada, those on the distaff side awaiting matrimonial property reform were now very aware of the critical need to have matrimonial property registered jointly.

There is another optimistic view of how the Murdoch case became precedent-setting. Justice Bora Laskin's minority interpretation provided proof that existing legislation could be interpreted in a wider context. It was possible that courts might look instead to his opinion. By March of 1975, the Law Reform Commission of Canada had espoused the principle of equal sharing of property acquired during marriage upon termination of the union. Furthermore, it deplored the results of "recent, celebrated court cases in which female spouses have been deemed, under existing law, to be entitled to far less than an equitable interest in land and assets despite large contributions of labour and money."[24]

Subsequent newspaper reports and studies of cases where the wife claimed an interest in property in her husband's name contain references to Murdoch which suggest the ruling was viewed both as a nadir and a benchmark. One careful analysis of ten matrimonial property decisions, three of which involved prairie farm women, appeared in the September/October 1976 edition of the magazine *Branching Out* under the title "Matrimonial Property: What has Happened since Murdoch?" Its author, Stella Bailey, was a second-year law student at the University of Alberta and Director of the Women's Project, Student Legal Services. By the time

Katie Kawalchuk of Oakburn, Manitoba, received undivided half interest in the farm and machinery and Barbara Ann Fiedler, of Sundre, received property rights to one and three-quarter sections of farmland, the courts were seen as beginning to recognize a wife's substantial contribution to the family farm. Although both decisions were appealed, Kawalchuk was upheld.

The Matrimonial Property Act came into effect in Alberta on January 1, 1979, too late to benefit Irene Murdoch, who in the 1976 divorce settlement got $65 000, one-third of her husband's net assets. This new legislation governed distribution of matrimonial property on the basis of certain rules set out in the Act, the dominant principle being that a distribution shall be equal in value. However, other principles in the Act relating to exemptions allow the court to give either spouse more or less than a 50 percent share. These exemptions are applied when the court considers equal distribution unfair to one of the partners. To some these safeguards resembled hedged bets. The Matrimonial Property Act disappointed those women who had worked so hard for the principle of deferred sharing, which would have automatically provided 50-50 splits, with the option to appeal to the courts for a larger share.

In retrospect, the end result of the 1973 Supreme Court of Canada majority ruling might be viewed as an illustration of the Law of Unintended Consequences. The four Justices who applied existing law inadvertently accelerated the matrimonial property reform movement.

The most unfortunate outcome of the Irene Murdoch case was the effect the publicity had on her personally. Although she fought tenaciously on her own for her share of the matrimonial property, she chose not to join the ranks of those fighting publicly for matrimonial property reform. The problem was that Murdoch became the high profile case-in-point. There is considerable evidence that she was upset by media contacts and the ensuing published interpretations of her lifestyle and views. The most notable one was probably her reaction to the March 1983 *Chatelaine* article "Farm Wives Ten Years After Murdoch." Here the author, Suzanne Zwarun, used a human interest approach to her subjects, describing these women's lifestyles and including their comments. The article opens with this vivid precis of the Murdoch case:

> It was after her husband, Alex, broke her jaw and locked her out of their farmhouse in 1968 that it occurred to Irene Murdoch that she shouldn't be driven penniless from the Alberta cattle ranch that the couple had bought 15 years after their marriage and which she helped to build. Murdoch took her case to court, where she discovered she had about as many rights as the abandoned stray dogs that farmers are always driving off their property.[25]

The author later describes intimately Irene Murdoch's reaction to unsolicited inquiries, "Murdoch answers the phone with the wariness of someone resigned to being ferreted out yet again and paraded in the merciless glare of publicity." Then notes, "She won't talk to the press. 'The less said, the sooner forgotten. There's already been too much heartache for everyone.'" As might be anticipated from these insights, a problem did develop with regard to some quotes Zwarun attributed to Irene Murdoch which the latter felt were taken out of context. The situation upset Irene Murdoch to the point that she asked *Chatelaine* to publish her objections. A copy of that letter is in the LCW files. *Chatelaine* reprinted the contentious passages under "Last Word" in its May 1983 issue. Doing so allowed Irene to clarify three points. The first was that she did not find Calgary a real downer; she just preferred country living. The second point raised was that she didn't want the case resurrected because now it would do more harm than good. The final misinterpretation probably proved most upsetting because Irene Murdoch had an unmarried son. The quote attributed to her predicted that greedy young brides in future divorce settlements could grasp half the husband's land. Irene Murdoch totally disclaimed the idea.

The concluding paragraph confirms that she neither cherished the memory of her legal struggle nor viewed it as worthwhile. "Since my divorce, what I have said over and over again is that I want to forget those eight miserable years that led up to it. I have a new life now and I want to forget the old." Other women didn't.

Part Three

Life Member
Autobiographies

Honorary Life Members Group, 1967, includes **Mrs. A.C. (Millie) Luft** *(seated, far right),* **Mrs. A.A. (Flo) Frawley** *(standing, far left),* **Mrs. C.R. (Beth) Hoar** *(standing, 6th from left), and* **Mrs. Oscar (Grace) Stonewall** *(standing, far right). (courtesy of Glenbow Archives).*

Mrs. John (Ruth) Gorman, O.C.
Calgary Local Council
Convenor of Laws

Mrs. H.K. (Frances) Roessingh
Local Council Natural Resources
Committee Chairperson and Alberta
Provincial Council President

Mrs. Stanley (Marjorie) Norris
Local Council President (1972-73)

Mrs. H.A. (Margaret) Buckmaster
Local Council Environment Committee

Mrs. Trevor (Dorothy) Groves
Local Council Vice-President

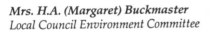

Mrs. L.A. (Gwen) Thorssen
Local Council President (1975-77)

Mrs. Urban (Mary) Guichon
Local Coun cil President (1980-81)

Mrs. K.L. (Donalda) Vine
Local Council President (1981-85)

Chapter 15

Eleven Ladies Plus One

∞ ∞ ∞ ∞

Ruth Gorman, BA, LLB, LLD, OC

I am a native Calgarian who grew up in a Mount Royal home. My father was M.B. Peacock, a prominent partner in R.B. Bennett's law firm, my mother was a concert pianist, and I was their only child. You might say I grew up in a world of privilege, but I was also expected to follow in the family tradition and become a lawyer.

Upon graduating in law from the University of Alberta in 1940, and while taking my articles in my father's law firm in Calgary, I was asked to be the Local Council's Convenor of Laws. I was the first such convenor for Local Council who was actually a lawyer willing to take on an unpaid, time-consuming job which entailed a long-term commitment. There were, of course, very few woman lawyers around. As I recall, only one other woman practised law in Calgary when I did.

When I told my mother about my intention to accept, she recommended against it. To my further amazement, she announced that years before, for a very brief time, she had been a Local Council Convener of Laws. This absolutely amazed me. My mother had a university degree, but it was in the field of music and her knowledge of law was almost nil. She was loaded with charm and great common sense, but I couldn't see how she could advise other women on their needs in the field of legal rights. Her explanation was simple. She said, "I just came home and asked your father and he told me what to do." Since my father was an able lawyer, the system worked fine. But in earlier days, that was actually how LCW worked. Women who had been denied experience in the world of government leaned on the advice of supportive husbands to achieve their reforms.

I was to stay on as Convenor for another twenty-three years, part of that time serving also as the National Council of Women's Honorary Convenor of Laws. They were very rewarding years indeed, not only because of the fine women I met and worked with, but for what we were able to achieve.

There were exciting women on Local Council. Some were young women concerned for the future of their sons and daughters. Our Council membership consisted of two elected or appointed members from each of our affiliated clubs, so they were already concerned women prepared to be active in their communities. Later, when I became the chairman of the Nominating Committee, we inaugurated the policy of inviting women from the community who had special interests and training in the fields of health, education, etc. to serve on our various study committees. Often they became so interested in Council's achievements that they would join as an individual member, and so we were able to expand and enlarge our interests in women's problems even beyond that of our affiliated clubs' specific interest.

The procedure followed when my Laws Committee or a club proposed the endorsement of a reform was that we would first study it in the Laws Committee to determine if the proposal was possible, compatible with Council's purpose and likely to be supported by a majority of the affiliates. Since there were strong differences among church groups themselves, as well as within political groups, it was a sensitive and time-consuming job, but worth it. When a resolution received the support of Local Council's membership, it meant that it was backed by a very vocal proportion of Calgary women. Calgary's City Council respected us so much that we were allowed to hold meetings without charge in City Hall's council chambers when they were not being used by the aldermen. My experience was that politicians on all levels of government gave careful consideration to our well-analyzed and thoroughly backed demands when I presented them on behalf of LCW.

The legal reforms we considered and backed were, I am afraid, never carefully recorded by me except in our minutes, and LCW's minutes have blanks in them. This was due to the fact that we had no club house, and executive members, including secretaries, changed frequently, as changes occurred in affiliate membership. Fires, moves, death and illness also caused breaks in a permanent and continuous record being handed on. For my part, I never had extra time to allocate to keeping a personal account of my experiences. Local Council always had many and varied legal projects going on at the same time. So it was a relief to be done with one project, whether we succeeded or failed, because there were always others we would have to deal with immediately in various stages of study, passage or implementation. Taking the required time to record the sequence was not a prime object. We were all volunteers and all women serving not just in one field but in several. I must now apologize for any omissions due to my own imperfect memory of past events.

By the time I became the first trained lawyer who reviewed and recommended legal changes for the Local Council of Women, the nature of Calgary had changed. We were now a large city, beginning to gain both population and financial growth through the petroleum industry's growth. The whole nature of government had changed. Local Council had never really been a money-raising organization, and we found the mothering role, through which we had improved our community for so many, was now largely under government control. If we wished reforms in these fields, we were referred to the various departments of health, welfare and education at the appropriate provincial or national level. These departments were manned by civil servants who would alter or consider our proposal but not too often act on our recommendations, preferring instead that they come only from their own departments. The fact that we represented a healthy portion of voters was of little interest to them.

Women's roles in our communities had begun to change, especially after World War II. More women were full-time workers and therefore less able to be active in club activities. Also, more women held either advisory or elected positions. True, we now had new societies like the business and professional women's auxiliaries, auxiliaries to unions (the Women's Typographical Union), and fewer private church groups or charitable organizations. The women's auxiliaries to the political parties were often busy establishing themselves in an effort to obtain representation on their party's own executive and stand for elected office.

However, despite these changes, the CLCW found many times they could still serve the communities well. Often the male-dominated political parties turned a deaf ear to their own women members. As an alternative, these women could then unite with other women from political parties affiliated with Local Council to lobby for desired improvements, working through Council to goad governments in areas where reform was felt to be needed.

My own very first effort at legal reform as their Convenor of Laws, I think, was what converted me for the next twenty years to work with Local Council. Council members and other Alberta women had been instrumental in passing the province's Dower Act, an act which recognizes the wife's right to a voice in the disposal of the family's home, and requires the spouse's consent by affidavit before the home can be sold out from under the other person. As the law then read, if the husband sold without the wife's consent, her only recovery was against her own husband. This claim was all too frequently useless, as he had left the country, and thus the wife found herself and her children penniless and on the street. The law could be amended so the wife could recover her share from the purchaser, who had often, in connivance with the husband, just paid the money over to him. I had watched a case in the courts like this, so as their Convenor of Laws, I persuaded Local Council to ask the provincial government for a change in law. Mr. Aberhart had been newly elected to government by a tremendous landslide, so I, inexperienced as I was, took it upon myself, once I had the LCW affiliates' backing, to visit him personally and recommend this change. I emphasized that all persons who had no monetary intent for prosecuting their wife would approve of its passage. To my amazement, he personally agreed to present it at the Legislature, and to my consternation, he even suggested I become his attorney-general as he was having some difficulty finding one! I explained that I really had a husband and small baby to care for, but I remember realizing how powerful was LCW and how valuable to the community and women of Calgary, and for the next twenty years I gladly served as their Laws chairman. As a result the Dower Act was later amended, and today women have an enforceable legal right in their own home.

However, in my first years with Local Council we nearly did part company, and this was over the matter of us being determined that the City should provide public toilets. The resolution had found its way into LCW from farm women's groups who came to the city to shop. Each year LCW would endorse this resolution, and as Convenor of Laws, I was sent before our City Council to request it. My appearances were always met with some raunchy jokes, and invariably the resolution was turned down. The City was not going to get into the business of financing public toilets. I finally told LCW I just couldn't waste my time or theirs on more appearances promoting this. However, despite our failure in this issue, as a result of the publicity we gave the matter, department stores eventually saw it expedient to put in more public toilets. Putting a slightly different complexion on the matter, a law was passed saying wherever women were employed in the same building with men, separate toilets should be available for them, so I guess it wasn't a total loss.

In my time, especially at the local level, many resolutions we passed had to be presented to boards, and I usually fell into the job. It was our president, Mrs. Alberta Clark, and I who had to appear before the Public Utilities Board to argue for skim milk for Calgary. The unions, the dairy industry and the dairy men all appeared with the high-priced, most able lawyers in town opposing it, but our plea that skim milk was as nutritious but lower in price and should be available for growing children won our point. This is just another recollection of our ongoing efforts in presenting resolutions and preparing written briefs which I presented to government advisory boards and commissions for the protection of the public at large.

In the field of crime law, we became concerned over the different treatment of women from men. We agitated for and got one-way vision mirrors to enable women to identify their attackers without fear of reprisal. Women were added to the police force too. We took note of the poorer treatment that women received in jails in comparison to men. Two of our presidents, Jessie Hutchinson and Grace Johnson, made a personal inspection of the jails and reported on the conditions they saw. Women prisoners' complaints were often negated by the women authorities, and the women prisoners were afraid to testify. We therefore took tape recorded evidence from them and presented that to the government on their behalf.

LCW was certainly outstanding in its promotion of tolerance in this city. We had all political parties as members, and we had the majority of different religious denominations. Furthermore, we had as executive members at various times, a Native woman, Daisey Crowchild, representing native Indian school children, and from a Baptist church a very fine African-Canadian woman, Mrs. Stella King, who was honored with a life membership in LCW, and the Jewish women's clubs had at that time a representative at our meetings. In a practical way, we practised tolerance, and we knew it worked. As is explained in Lilian MacLennan's detailed history, we had participated in 1951 in the first promoting of the brotherhood banquets. Before I came on the scene, that great friend of the Indians, John Laurie, could count on LCW to endorse the Indians' requests for improvements to their conditions, and such requests were sent frequently to Ottawa. When I became the Indian Association of Alberta's volunteer lawyer, CLCW was most active in backing up my three-year Hobbema legal trial which allowed treaty Indians to remain on their reserves. When I went to Ottawa, I carried the great support of not only Calgary's LCW but of local councils across Canada in my request for the removal of the compulsory Franchise section from the Indian Act. Such removal would then allow our Indians to vote without losing their homes and treaty status as Indians.

It was LCW with its community conscience which worked for the establishment of much-needed centres for two disadvantaged groups in Calgary. Along with their affiliates, Local Council persevered in establishing the Indian Friendship Centre, and it was a vice- president, Grace Johnson, who devoted the last years of her life to running it for them until it eventually moved from renting an old house to the fine centre we have now. The LCW also promoted understanding and tolerance for the physically disabled citizens of Calgary and were of unbelievable assistance in helping me to get the first centre for this group. Later, with their backing again, I appeared before the school board and demanded we create a form of public schooling for disabled children, children limited to schooling by correspondence because of their crippled bodies, not their minds.

The women seemed to be very understanding of injustices to such groups, no doubt remembering their earlier battles to obtain fairness in law and status themselves.

Grace Stonewall

Among the present honorary life members, my Local Council connection seems to go back the farthest. My mother, Dorothy Little, joined the Calgary Local Council of Women in the 1930s. It was she who encouraged me to attend one of the meetings. I did so in 1949.

Let me begin by saying that I am a native Calgarian, born in 1922 at the Holy Cross Hospital, the seventh and last child of Methodist parents, Mr.

and Mrs. David Little. My heritage was British – a English mother and a Scottish father with a few drops of Irish blood in his veins. As a young man "with sand in his shoes" he left the old country to seek his fortune in America. After a brief stay in Philadelphia, he travelled to the far West, to Washington State. While there he sent for his British sweetheart, Dorothy Dixon, and my parents began married life in the United States. A few years and one child later, they decided that Canada's British values were better suited to raising a family, so they moved north in 1907 to take up land near Rimbey, Alberta. After a time farming, they moved to Calgary, where father went into the draying and real estate business, then bought out the Crown Coal Company, changing its name to the David Little Coal Co. Mother was his office manager and bookkeeper until his death, then stayed on to help my brother, Andrew, who took over the business.

While faithfully carrying out her family and business obligations, my mother made time for church and lodge work, community service, women's lobby organizations, and campaign work for the Conservative Association, which she joined immediately after women got the federal vote in 1918. She became my role model.

Mother was a woman with a strong social conscience who began her philanthropic work with the Ladies' Orange Benevolent Association (LOBA) in 1916. There she gave decades of dedicated service. Soon after joining she organized and supervised Lodge tag days, which raised funds for a motherless children's home at Olds run by the Reverend George Woods and his wife, Annie. This old country couple – practicing Christians they truly were – gave most of their limited personal resources to provide a loving, decent home atmosphere for children rendered motherless by death, illness or abandonment at a time when the fathers were fighting World War I. When the Woods Home relocated to the western edge of Calgary in the former Bethel Sanatorium at Bowness, my mother became the first woman Board member and through that association became a close friend of Mrs. Annie Woods. She served on the Board until her death.

My mother's first contact with the Calgary Local Council of Women was probably through her friend and President at the time, Mrs. F.G. Grevette, who thought the work would interest her. It did. Mother served on committees (Immigration being one) and held the office of vice-president. Later on, when I was married with a young family of three girls (now, by the way, all graduates of the University of Calgary), she suggested that the CLCW would probably interest me because I already belonged to an affiliate, the Crystal Chapter LOBA. My earliest recollection of a Local Council meeting, which I likely attended in 1949, was that it was held in the old YWCA and John Laurie was the guest speaker. He had been one of my favorite teachers at Crescent Heights High School and was on that day speaking about his work as Secretary of the Alberta

Indian Association. Thus began my 40-year membership in the Local Council.

When I first joined the Calgary Council of Women as an individual member, the organization was flagging. The President, Mrs. Lillian Clarke, realized that a reorganization was required, so she scheduled a "George Washington Tea" at Central United Church in the hope that others would undertake executive roles. Among those who came was another Mrs. Clark – Mrs. Russell Clark – who had come to Calgary from Regina, where she had been a leading Local Council of Women officer. Alberta Clark proved to be the organization's revitalizing force, able to energize others. When she was president, the first Calgary branch of the Council of Christians and Jews formed, and the Council of Women sponsored the celebratory banquet that was judged such a success that it was declared an annual event. Alberta served as our president for four years, from 1951 until 1955, and in 1960 was elected a vice-president of the National Council of Women of Canada, one of the very few Calgary women to be so recognized nationally. A few years later, in 1959, during the presidency of Jessie Hutchinson, ten new associations affiliated, bringing the total to 25. One of these, The Friends of the Indians Society, with professional advice from our Convenor of Laws, Dr. Ruth Gorman (herself a lawyer), undertook a special study of the Indian Act. Their particular concern was that when an Indian voted, certain restrictive clauses in the Indian Act, if applied, would result in the loss of that person's home on the reserve. A resolution requesting the removal of the appropriate restrictive clauses was prepared for circulation to our affiliates. I also supported Dr. Gorman in her campaigns to establish a native Indian rest and information center and to save the cupola from Calgary's first high school, James Short. Probably my longest commitment, though, was to the acquisition of land for Nose Hill Park. For many years I represented the Calgary Local Council of Women there, working on committees to ensure that what is now Canada's largest urban park would remain in its natural state.

I became an affiliate representative to Local Council through active participation in politics. In the post World War II period of the late 1940s, I worked on a campaign to send Conservative candidate Colonel Douglas Harkness to Ottawa. Partly through our friendship, I spent many active years in the Calgary Women's Progressive Conservative Association. After I was designated the Association's representative to the Council of Women, I became so interested in Local Council's work that I went on to serve as its president for four years (from 1959 to 1963) during a period of growth and extensive involvement with the community and various levels of government. We started the custom of inviting the mayor's wife to serve as our honorary president. In this capacity, Mrs. Don Mackay, Mrs. Harry Hays and Mrs. Jack Leslie graciously hosted our annual teas in their homes. Jean Leslie had also been one of our Local Council vice-presidents before her husband became mayor. I remember Mrs. Grant MacEwan presented me with my honorary life membership in the National Council of Women during her husband's mayorship. In retrospect, our community profile was particularly high in those years. As a long-time member it seems to me that this organization moves in cycles. It flourishes and fades but manages to survive.

My other community service included two terms as a member of the first University of Calgary Senate, the presidency of the Mount Royal College Auxiliary, and five years on the City of Calgary Library Board. My lifetime church affiliation has been Rosedale United.

My husband, Oscar, always gave me full support because he felt women could do anything if given the opportunity. Now that he has retired from the position of Credit Manager of the *Calgary Herald*, I share his athletic interests – the Calgary Outdoor Hiking and Skiing Club, the Calgary Senior Skaters, and Canadian and American Elderhostels.

Flo Frawley

I was born of United Empire Loyalist stock during a 1914 February blizzard which swirled around our homestead near Quill Lake, Saskatchewan. Two unusual facts related to my arrival. My father delivered me because the storm was so severe that help could not get through, and my birth was not officially registered until November.

My schooling began in the nearby town of Wadena. Then, when I was nine, my family moved to Prince Albert. Because we could not afford another year of high school, I left Prince Albert Collegiate at the end of grade 11. Bookkeeping was the only course I didn't take when enrolling that summer at the McPherson Secretarial School, but oddly enough, it was the reason I got my first job offer within a few weeks. The Texas Company of Canada hired me as a bookkeeper because it was company policy to train employees in their own system. Texaco sent a man from Saskatoon to instruct me.

I learned first of all to play an organ when I was so small that my feet couldn't touch the pedals. Then, when we got a piano, my mother, who was a music teacher, gave me lessons. As I progressed through the piano grades we would travel to Saskatoon for my adjudication by McGill University examiners. As a young woman, I played second violin with Prince Albert's Haydn Symphony and popular tunes on the piano in the Moonlight Reveller dance band. Later, when I came to live in Calgary, I played in Renelle Carey's Orchestra. It was an all-girl group, and in order to get hired, I learned to play the tenor saxophone.

I joined the Conservative party as a young woman and worked during elections. Although we were not always on the winning side, there were happy outcomes. One happened in my Prince Albert days during the 1934 provincial election when I had my first serious date with Albert Andrew

Frawley, the man destined to become my husband. We both worked during that June 19th election – he as a CCF scrutineer and I as a poll clerk. When a mutual friend invited us to her Liberal victory party so that we could "drown our sorrows" we accepted and "drowned" them with Coca-Cola. Not long afterwards, in the depth of the Depression, we married when Bert got a job in Alberta at Vegreville, then we moved to Calgary when he was hired as a linotype operator by the *Morning Albertan* (now the *Calgary Sun*).

When World War II came along, Bert joined the Royal Canadian Ordinance Corps and spent four years overseas attached to its printing department. I didn't go to work when Bert was in the Army because we both agreed it was more important for me to keep the home fires burning for our children, who now had only one parent to care for them. Ten years after the War had ended, when our children were older, I worked as a cashier and bookkeeper for Heintzman Piano Company and also for various printing firms as a linotype operator. I had a six-year apprenticeship in printing. I became a member of the International Typographical Union (ITU) at a time when I was the only non-union employee in the firm and they needed my support to qualify for union status.

My early commitment to politics never ceased. I served as president of the Calgary North Women's Conservative Association, whose members worked so successfully to elect Doug Harkness to Ottawa that he once told me, "With your Calgary North Women's Conservative Association behind me we didn't have to count the ballots – we weighed them." That compliment filled me with pride, but my proudest moment came when, as an official delegate to the 1957 Conservative Leadership Convention in Ottawa, I helped elect John Diefenbaker to lead us. The next year he carried our party to victory. I had known the Diefenbakers personally since my Prince Albert days, and I did feel my advice was respected especially when, on behalf of the Calgary North Conservative Association, I contacted our new Prime Minister to endorse John Laurie's sponsorship of Alberta's James Gladstone of the Blood Indian Reserve as Canada's first native senator. I sensed that John was very happy to have that distinction go to the West.

I left the Conservative Party towards the end of the '60s over the issue of bilingualism. After writing letters to the editor to explain my stand, I received enough enquiries to convince me that what this country needed was a new political party dedicated to maintaining Canada's traditional values. The Dominion of Canada Party (DOC) was founded in January of 1969, and its motto became "One Official Language – One Canada." The initials "DOC" are used as a symbol meaning "to cure the ailments of this country." That same year I was elected National leader by a mail-in ballot in which over 95 percent of the membership chose me. There were, however, three write-in candidates – the nominees being former Manitoba Premier Duff Roblin, Alberta's Ernest Manning and John Diefenbaker. I notified each one of his nomination and received replies from two. John Diefenbaker's response was, "I will die a Conservative."

During the first nine years of DOC, we worked to build up our membership before holding our first national conference in 1977 here in Alberta at Botha on Labor Day weekend; however, DOC never received official party status. We applied to the Chief Electoral Officer in November of 1977 but were refused on the grounds that our name – Dominion of Canada Party – could be confused with those of political parties already registered. The word "Dominion" was very important to us because the Fathers of Confederation, recognizing that Canada was a Christian country, adopted the word from Psalm 72:8, "He shall have dominion also from sea to sea." The similarity of name ruling seemed unfair. At that time there were two Communist parties with remarkably similar names – the Communist Party of Canada and the Communist Party of Canada (Marxist-Leninist). Furthermore, the word "Dominion" did not appear in the name of any of the other 17 parties. They were the Liberals, the Conservatives, NDP, Social Credit, Nude Garden Party, Rhinoceros Party, Canada Party, Modernization Party, Québec Libre Party, Parti Nouvelle France, Libertarian Party of Canada, United Provincials National Party of Canada, Canadian Union Party, Canadian Political Party, Canadian Alternative Party, American Party of Canada and the United Free Enterprise Party. After our application was refused, we asked our members to support instead DOC members who ran as Independent candidates and Conservative candidates willing to state their opposition to mandatory bilingualism. We did at one time enjoy a large lobby membership, particularly in New Brunswick. Over the years our numbers have dwindled, due in part to our initial older membership and in part to the rise of the Reform Party, which also supports traditional values. Now, at 80 years of age, I still prepare our newsletter, which is mailed to our membership, to federal cabinet ministers, to premiers, and some newspapers across Canada. My closing signature was and is "I'm a fighter – I am." By that I mean a fighter for our British heritage, our Christian values and for the will of the majority.

Besides being active in politics I belonged to quite a few other organizations over the years. I particularly valued the training I received in public speaking as a member of the Fraternal Order of Eagles, the Rebekahs and the Ladies' Auxiliary Patriarchs Militant. For several years I served on the executive of Calgary and the Provincial Business and Professional Women's Clubs. A highlight for me was being named an official delegate to the 1970 National B. & P. Convention in Halifax. When I was active in the Local Council of Women, in the very early '60s, I served on the provincial executive as well. My affiliate was the Calgary Women's Conservative Association. The projects I remember best during those times were our successful efforts to save the James Short cupola, to have a police dog added to the Calgary force, and to have one-way glass installed to protect witnesses who were asked to identify police suspects in lineups.

Our children had turned out well. Our daughter and my namesake is Secretary of the United Church in Stettler and our son, Frank, who now lives in Victoria, is a specialist in book binding. I now have seven grand-children and nine great-grandchildren. I lost my husband of 57 years and loyal supporter of our Dominion's heritage in 1991.

Church and religion have always meant a great deal in my life. As a young girl I accepted Christ as my Savior while attending a Friday afternoon Scripture reading given in a rural school by a devout teacher. Years later, when we lived in Calgary, my son Frank and my daughter Flo and I all taught Sunday school in the same church, Parkdale United. I believe in God, in the Ten Commandments, in the power of Faith. Faith gives meaning to life.

Frances Roessingh (Fennigje Kerkhoven)

I was born in 1919 in Bandung on West Java, the main island of Indonesia. My parents ran a tea plantation which my grandfather had pioneered in 1873 on land granted to him as a 75-year lease. I was educated by a governess until Grade VII, when I went on to a Christian school in Bandung after passing my plus eleven exams. From there I attended lycée in Holland and finishing schools in Switzerland and England. My formal education culminated with a BA degree in geology at the University of Leyden, in Holland.

I met my future husband, Hank, during my first year. We university students lived in turbulent times then because World War II was immin-ent. When a group of Dutch students in Utrecht burned the university records in protest against Nazi policies, the Germans in reprisal picked up 5000 students across Holland. Hank was one of those marched off to be taken by train to a concentration camp elsewhere in Holland. We girls were locked in a room during their removal so that we could not see where they went. Later, a sympathetic railman who walked the railroad secretly passed their destination on to me. It was unsigned and written upon a piece of toilet paper. To our great relief the churches which were still powerful in Holland put pressure on the authorities and the students were freed. Hank was very lucky that the Germans never found out that he worked for the underground.

After Hank and I married in the December of 1943, living in Holland was still not safe for him, so he arranged to leave the country in February of 1944, when I was pregnant with our first child. His "flight" was to a Swiss concentration camp which was actually a work camp. He left there when Shell Lumina paid for his student fees at a polytechnical school in Zurich. When Paris was liberated in late August of 1944, the Dutch army in London called him up to finish his officer's training. Meanwhile I wrote him letters through the Red Cross and received a few. As a safety subterfuge we corresponded as cousins (we were in fact distant cousins) instead of as husband and wife. I managed to "pass on" as gossip the news that we had a son.

Holland was liberated in April of 1945, and Hank came home in May to meet, as a stranger, our son who was now nearly a year old. After several different postings in the Dutch Cavalry, Hank left to finish his Master's degree. He was hired right away by Standard Oil. Following a brief orientation course in the United States, he went to Indonesia as a field geologist, and despite the waiting lists, I soon followed with our two children. We stayed four years. The company provided a school and hospital for its employees and their families.

After we returned home to Holland in 1952, we soon sensed that we needed to emigrate. Our first prospect was the United States, where we had a sponsor in California, but in August of 1954 we actually came to Calgary, where we had friends in the oil patch. We arrived with our five children.

The need to earn extra household money attracted me to my first job – a flyer-boy supervisor at $30.00 per month – in 1955. My involvement with kindergarten started because our five-year-old daughter, who didn't speak English well, needed help with the language before entering grade one. What pre-schools there were at that time were private. They were few and far between and in no way able to meet the number of postwar babies. (One hundred children lived on our city block alone.) After a few months' wait, I registered her in a class conducted in a small basement room by a qualified kindergarten teacher. The next year, with me as manager, we moved the kindergarten into a larger, temporary facility in my home. In that first year, I remember, we had 46 children in the school, and the fees of $7.00 per month included milk and cookies. In the second year, the classes were moved into a newly-built church, Saint Phillip's Anglican, then to Riverview United Church. Eventually, we were operating 22 classes with over 600 children. I remained as manager until the government introduced Early Childhood Services in 1973 and we turned over our whole system to the Calgary School Board in 1975 after operating for two years under ECS.

In those years, we made several attempts to persuade the Social Credit government to include kindergartens in the school system but without success. We were supported by the Calgary Kindergarten Teachers' Association, but the government had a "better" solution: they suggested that nurses and social workers from the Department of Social Services would take over the kindergartens and would evaluate the teachers' qualifications and the program. There was a virtual revolt by the teachers.

That is when I went to a meeting of the LCW to ask for help in our struggle. I became an individual member and later represented the Women's Liberal Club. Under the chairmanship of a very professional, enlightened teacher, Jean Mekitiak, Local Council of Women renewed interest in education. Both the LCW and the Women's Liberal Club sent resolutions to the government regarding kindergarten education.

Due in no small way to a far-sighted President, Mary Winspear, our Council of Women also launched a strong lobby for land conservation and reclamation. The news of a coal slide in the Crowsnest area in which two men died motivated her to initiate a public protest meeting at the Calgary Power auditorium. Over 100 people came and Bill Kerr was elected president of the organization which formed that night.

After the sudden death of Ethel M. Johnson in 1966, I was invited – delegated that is – by Mary Winspear to "temporarily" take over her leadership of the Alberta Provincial Council of Women. My term of office lasted until 1969. In 1967, we organized the 50-year women's franchise celebration with a luncheon in Red Deer, attended by 136 prominent women. Red Deer LCW was the host, but Laura McCullough and I looked after the preparations, including arranging a $1000 grant from the government. Our National president, Mrs. H. Steen, was the main speaker. Mrs. S. Ruemper from Edmonton took over the Alberta presidency in 1969.

I served on various committees of the Calgary Local Council for ten years, from 1963 to 1973. One of these was the Natural Resources Committee, which was of particular interest to me because in 1960 my family had started a summer camp for children. This, in time, developed into Silver Creek Ranch, Water Valley, an outdoor education centre operating year round, mainly for grade six students, but also widely used for workshops and retreats. It had a capacity of over 100 guests, a large theatre, log cabins in remote areas, and many miles of riding and ski trails. The buildings were all of our own design, intended to fit in the natural environment of the Ranch. When the year-round work got too heavy for us, we sold the Ranch in 1985, but it is still operating around the year, making its contribution to education in and about the out-of-doors.

We were active members of the Alberta Camping Association, of which I was president in 1966. Both my husband and I served on several provincial and national committees, participating in federal student exchange programs, which resulted in many years of bilingual music camps. In 1985 we were awarded Honorary Life Memberships of the Alberta Camping Association.

In 1982 I received an honorary National Council of Women life membership from five LCW members as a token of friendship and support, which was very much appreciated.

Beth Hoar

I was born Catherine Elizabeth Hewson on November 9, 1918, in the Faulkner farmhouse a mile north of Delia. It was at the time of the 1918 influenza epidemic, and the doctor felt there was a danger of infection in the Delia hospital. I grew up on the family farm ten miles northwest of Delia, where I have fond childhood memories of playing with my pets. In winter my dog, Jiggs, pulled me on a toboggan, and I just lay back flat as Jiggs followed a rabbit path under the barbed wire fences! I had a long-suffering cat that I would dress up as a baby and wheel around in a doll's carriage. To this day, I am still fond of cats.

For my primary grades I attended Sentinel Hill School, just one and a half miles northeast of home. This country school had opened some years earlier with my brother Marshall in grade one and my mother as the first teacher. She had received her training in Ontario and taught there before coming west. Out here on the prairie she had to teach all grades in one room. Like other children, most of the time I rode a horse to school.

I went to high school in Delia except for my grade 11 year, 1935-36, when I went to Alberta College in Edmonton, where my brother Cecil taught and was Assistant Dean of Boys. My future husband, Dick, was also attending there, and one afternoon, as captain of a "pick up" softball team, I picked Dick for my team. He was not a very good ball player, and I had no idea I was picking a mate for life! We celebrated our 50th anniversary in 1991.

I took nursing at the University Hospital in Edmonton for one year, 1937-38, and decided that was not for me. So the next year I enrolled in the Normal School in Edmonton. The following year, 1939, the year that World War II broke out, I taught at Ant Hill School near Rowley. Like my mother, I also taught in a one-room school. I boarded with a farm family, sharing a bed with one of the daughters. We slept upstairs, and I can remember on some winter mornings finding snow which had drifted in through cracks in the walls onto my pillow. The next year, 1940-41, I taught closer to home at Farrell Lake School, just 17 miles north of Delia, and lived by myself in the teacherage.

On Friday, the 18th of July, Dick received his posting to Toronto, and five days later, on Wednesday, July 23, 1941, we were married at the United Church in Delia. The father of a friend of Dick's was the CPR station agent in Calgary, so to help us newlyweds he arranged to change Dick's first-class voucher for one into a coach-class ticket for two!

Our first home was in a house that had been built by one of the Massey family in Toronto. We rented a large room that had been set up for rental in the attic. I'll never forget one arrangement – an eight-foot long cast iron, four-legged bath tub, tucked in behind the kitchen cupboard! Dick attended a six-week course to become an aircraft inspector for the Commonwealth Air Training plan. Although that six weeks was our wartime honeymoon, one consolation was that we were not separated during the war. We lived in Edmonton and Calgary before being posted to Boundary Bay, where you might say Dick was an officer in the RCAF at Boundary

Bay, British Columbia, but we actually lived at Boundary Bay, USA. The customs was not open when Dick left for work, so each evening he drove part-way across an unmarked gravelled area, lined up on the boundary markers in the distance, and left the car approximately in Canada. When the signals came at Boundary Bay, USA, one November night in 1944 that our daughter, Joanne, was about to arrive, we drove 45 miles to the Vancouver hospital, since the ferry on the short route did not run at night. Anyway, she was not born in the USA. Our son Alan's arrival in January of 1947 in Calgary was not nearly so exciting, thank goodness.

Like many other Alberta farmers, my parents supported Social Credit in the founding years of the movement. Because of their interest in the problems of the Depression and its effect upon people's lives, I think I always felt that support of the concerns of the community was deserving of my time and effort. This seemed to go hand in hand with responsibility to my family. I think we should all have a hand in shaping the world which we leave to them. While our children were in school I served the Home and School Associations at King George, Crescent Heights, and on the Calgary Home and School Council, and was for a time president at King George.

At Pleasant Heights United Church I worked with the Explorers and taught Sunday school. One of my special projects with the young people included, along with Ellen Mayo, putting on a delightful operetta, *Johnny Appleseed*.

It was my work with the Explorers that led me into the United Nations International Children's Emergency Fund. In fact I, along with one or two others, may have been responsible for introducing UNICEF to Calgary. I was Alberta chairman for a number of years. I represented the organization on the Calgary and District International Development Society. It was in that capacity that I, with Dick's help, had a major part in the Miles for Millions walks in the early seventies.

I was honored when the Calgary Local Council of Women welcomed me in the early 1960s as a representative of UNICEF, and I appreciated their wide support in the Hallowe'en canvasses. I served as chairman of the International Affairs Committee of the Council. Among many notable events, one that stands out is when the Council held a standing room only gala summer coffee party in the home of Dr. and Mrs. Thorssen to welcome Dr. Truman, Canadian Executive Officer of UNICEF.

I worked as a docent (guide) with the Glenbow Museum for over 14 years, specializing in the native Indian section. Meeting Cynthia Havergal, a great niece of Col. Macleod, on a trip to England sparked my interest in Macleod's place in the history of the West. Cynthia sent me an account her mother had written which told of "Uncle Jim" coming to Ontario and telling of his experiences in the West with the North West Mounted Police. This account is now in the Glenbow Archives.

When Confederation Park was being considered for dedication in Canada's centennial year, 1967, I served on the Park Committee and was responsible for organizing public contributions, mostly for trees. I remember one hot summer afternoon, with Dick's help, looking over the park area for possible skiing and tobogganing areas and marking these slopes on the plans "No Trees." Now we both smile on bright winter days as we watch the children tobogganing on these treeless slopes.

Dick and I enjoyed camping, trailering, hiking, downhill and cross-country skiing. A memorable week was with the Skyline Hikers of the Canadian Rockies at Owl Lake. Another great week was at the Lodge in Assiniboine Provincial Park. Our daughter, Joanne, expanded one camping experience in Idaho into a great tale at our 50th anniversary. "A fly on the wall of a tent could tell a lot about a family," she said.

Dick and I still live in Calgary, and while we are no longer very active in community work, we look back with some pleasure, and some concern, on how the world is developing. We hope it will give our two grandsons, and two granddaughters a good place to live and develop their respective talents.

Millie Luft

I was born after my parents, Adam and Mary Georlitz, came to Canada from Saratov, Russia, with their sons to take up homestead land near Dewinton. The land had first to be cleared, and I remember being told by my brothers that it was so hard to clear the brush that they hired the Indians to help them. I went to public school at Dewinton and attended Cresent Heights High School in Calgary. To earn my keep I worked for my board and room with Mr. and Mrs. Chesney (of Chesney's Hardware) taking care of their two boys, Art and Doug, and babysitting their sister Wynn, who was very young at the time. A while after leaving high school I decided to become a hairdresser and took a course. There were only two training schools then.

As a young girl I always enjoyed athletics, especially softball. I played third base, "the hot corner," for the Paramounts, one of the first girls' teams in the city. When Pete Eagon, the theatre man, took our team over, girls' baseball came to the fore in the city. Everybody wanted to play. We won the city championship and finally the provincial.

I met my husband, Sandy, on the baseball diamond when he came to watch us girls play. When he was through playing on his team we would walk home together, and that is how our courtship started. We married during the Depression in 1933. Times were hard and I took part-time hairdressing work whenever I could. After receiving more training I was later able to open my own parlor in the old Legion Hall near the York Hotel. My first and best customers were my lady ball player friends. They gave me my start, and I enjoyed running my own business, Millie's Hairstyling, so much that it became my career and I established a second shop later. I was able to work because I had a wonderful lady who was like a mother to our two boys, Barry and Murray. Our boys have turned out well. Barry is now a Counselor at Viscount Bennett School, and in 1993 Murray returned from Bolivia, where he had been working for CANSAVE.

Although I didn't have much spare time, I did join the North Hill Business and Professional Women's Club. I enjoyed the Club and its members so much that I went on to become president. Our Club was an affiliate of the Calgary Local Council of Women, and that is how I came into the Council. At first I served on committees, then, in 1969, when it seemed time for a newer member to take over the Presidency in order to get other new members involved, I was asked and I accepted. When my term as president was over, I continued to be involved and served as Social Convenor because I always believed it was very important for women to enjoy each others' company while working together. In appreciation of my work with the Council, I was given an Honorary Life Membership. My one regret was that because I had both a business and a family to manage, I could not give it all the time I wanted to.

Both my husband and I are long-time members of the Crescent Heights Baptist Church. Although we live in a different part of the city we still attend because we have long-time friends there.

Marjorie Norris

My roots are British. My paternal grandparents, William and Louisa Parsons, who were both born in England, emigrated with their children in the early 1880s to take up farmland in western Canada near Oak Lake, Manitoba. My mother, Jessie Barron, was born near Carberry, Manitoba, the eldest daughter of Ontario Scots, John Gerrie and Ellen Hope Barron, whose families had originally come from Aberdeenshire. As a young woman my mother travelled to Alberta to train at the Calgary General Hospital, then later became a World War I nursing sister overseas.

I was the unexpected extra who arrived in February of 1923, 20 minutes after a daughter, Louise, was born to Oliver and Jessie Parsons at their farm home near Oak Lake, Manitoba. By the time we were school age, our family had left the unremitting cold of Manitoba winters to reside in the legendary Chinook belt south of Calgary at Nanton.

My school years were the dry years of the Great Depression when people shared what little they had with their own neighbors in tougher circumstances. A series of spinster schoolteachers, well aware that minor neglect of the 3Rs could mean dismissal, kept full control of the classroom. Lack of intellectual rigor and lapses in self-control provided equally sound excuses for the strap or after-school detention. To them I owe my lifelong fear of not learning well. Outside of school hours, the dominant United Church and informative neighbors mentored my morals. Beyond that I enjoyed myself completely with my choice of pets, a pony in the summer and a "best" friend.

I noticed as I grew older that my parents' religious and political persuasions differed. Father was Anglican and Conservative while mother was Presbyterian and Liberal. They seemed to have reached an accommodation, however. Our family attended the United Church, and mother rarely mentioned that her father had stood for Liberal member of parliament. Nonetheless, political discussions did take precedence over religion in our home. Optimists in our windblown country town believed that hard times would end if the spring rains fell next year, or if the grasshoppers didn't hatch, or if Alberta elected the Social Crediters. Father counted more on nature.

After completing high school, I went on to the World War II atmosphere of the University of Alberta, where servicemen received intensive technical training in short crash courses offered by the Faculty of Engineering. The sailors were billeted in St. Joseph's College, where I took my education courses. Strictly by serendipity, I chose my future husband during a dance for such sailors sponsored by the Co Ed Club, of which I happened to be the president. As the lights dimmed for a ladies' choice waltz, I scanned the line for "a nice, polite-looking sailor." Stanley Norris of Cornwall, Ontario, also became my lifetime choice when we were married a year and a half later in Knox United Church, Calgary, in August of 1945.

In the spring of 1944, I graduated with a Bachelor of Education degree, and I probably owed my first teaching position, vice-principal at Rocky Mountain House, to the wartime shortage of men. After our marriage I spent the fall substitute teaching in Halifax schools, quite taken aback to find that women were paid less than men. We returned to Alberta after Stan was demobbed because I could get a better position in the province where I had trained. He attended DVA school in Calgary and University in Edmonton.

The initial reason for my joining clubs was spousal – it was expected of me. When we moved south to Stan's first teaching position in the town of Stavely, I supported the Home and School Association there as the new vice-principal's wife. Then, after an initial favorable assessment as to personal compatability, I was sponsored for membership in a lodge. In my case it was the Rebekahs, the ladies' counterpart of the Odd Fellows. I found lodge work fascinating: each member's respect for the proper conduct of meetings, each officer's precise memorization of her charge of office and devoted practice to perfect the degree team's marching patterns.

It was while Stan was principal at Cayley that his high school inspector suggested that he study for a post-graduate degree at Stanford University in California. Laine and Margaret, our two daughters, were six and four by then. The end result was that I took over the principalship of the Cayley school for a year while he obtained his Master's, then our family moved to Calgary, where Stan had been appointed an Assistant Professor of Science Education at the young University of Alberta, Calgary Branch. For several years afterwards our family moved back and forth to Stanford while Stan completed his doctorate.

It was in 1956 that I attended the founding meeting of the Women's Faculty Club, a social association of women faculty members and staff spouses. Six years afterwards, the president, Mary Winspear, persuaded us that our organization should affiliate with the Calgary Local Council of Women. Once federated we became part of Local Council's resolution-vetting process. Stimulating ideas emerged during the very enthusiastic debates because our Faculty Club was made up of women of very diverse backgrounds who had come from other parts of Canada, the US and overseas. A new horizon dawned for me there. After my WFC presidency, I became an LCW delegate in 1970, moving on to its executive committee, then to the presidency in 1972, where I served only one term because our family travelled overseas in the summer of 1973 to Leeds University, where Stan had accepted a visiting professorship. Upon our return I became Local Council's citizenship chairman. The duties I most enjoyed were monitoring City Council meetings and some of the 1975 Calgary Convention Centre judicial inquiry, described in the *Albertan* as, "The biggest and most mysterious business deal in 90 years of local politics." My lasting recollection of that is how some of those called to testify were not gifted with long memories.

After that most interesting citizenship term, I developed a desire to try for municipal politics myself. Not on Calgary's grand stage, but on something more my size. After chairing Local Council's host committee arrangements for the 1978 National convention at the Banff Springs Hotel, I felt I had given my all, and turned to the prospect of seeking elected municipal office.

When our cottage subdivision on the western shore of Sylvan Lake petitioned for summer village status, I won election to its first council after visiting cottagers to explain Sylvan Lake's relevant Management Plan issues. Our Half Moon Bay Council subsequently appointed me its representative to the Red Deer Regional Planning Commission, a learning opportunity I truly wanted. Even though at first there were times when I was the only woman in attendance, I was always treated with eminent fairness during those nine years. I chaired the 1985 municipal study of Sylvan Lake access issues, the 1986 Sylvan Lake Management Plan, and served on the Commission's Board of Directors for three years. Within a short time after becoming a Half Moon Bay councillor, I was elected to the Board of Directors of the Alberta Association of Summer Villages. During my four-year presidency there I proposed, then headed the first province-wide survey of summer village council concerns and their proposed solutions. The Association voted me an honorary life member in 1987. In retrospect, I enjoyed my eleven years in municipal politics most of all.

Over the years my Council of Women services have been generously remembered. In 1977 the NCW awarded me the Queen Elizabeth Jubilee medal, and in 1994 a group of Local Council friends honored me with a Life Membership in the National Council of Women of Canada, a companion to my earlier Local Council Honorary Life Membership. My greatest personal reward, however, was working with some of Calgary's incomparable women who served during the '70s – those watershed years of environmental issues and status of women concerns.

Our close-knit family has grown to include three grandchildren, and I'm still with my lifetime choice. Lest anyone think otherwise, our 50 year partnership has never been a silent one. Stan always maintains, "If two people agree, one isn't thinking."

Margaret R. Buckmaster

I was born in Richmond Hill, Ontario, an only child and sixth generation Canadian. Before coming to Calgary in 1963 I lived in Vancouver and London, England. It was only after I married Dr. Harvey Buckmaster, a physics professor at the University of Calgary, that I had the luxury of not having to support myself and could undertake volunteer commitments. After working on several program committees at the YWCA and participating in their fund-raising for a new building, I represented the "Y" on Calgary Local Council of Women, starting in 1972. I continued to be associated with the YWCA and chaired and co-chaired the YWCA Alumni from 1990 to 1992. In 1993 I was made an Honorary Life Member.

It was because of my experience in environmental issues that I was asked in 1972 to chair Local Council's Environment Committee. Thus began my several years of total involvement in environmental issues. In July of that year I presented a brief on behalf of LCW at Calgary City Council requesting that Nose Hill be set aside as future park in the North West Sector Plan then under consideration by City Council. Marjorie Norris, as LCW President, attended that meeting with me. This was the beginning of a twenty-year fight to create a 2900 acre park on Nose Hill. Then, a month later, in August of 1972, I was approached by one of the community association presidents, Rosa Gorill, who wanted the Fish Creek area saved for a park. I became a member of the steering committee comprised of representatives from community associations and special interest groups. We were successful in having Fish Creek made a 2500-acre park by the Government of Alberta in 1973. Frances Roessingh replaced me on the steering committee when the Calgary Local Council of Women named me to the Provincial Environmental Conservation Authority (ECA) Public Advisory Committee in October of 1972.

On the Public Advisory Committee (PAC) I served as a member and Chairman of the Non-Renewable Resource Committee, as well as Chairman of the Resolutions Committee and member of the Public Advisory Co-ordinating Committee from 1972 to 1976. I authored a paper entitled "Slow Growth, Alpine, Sub-Alpine Areas, Eastern Slopes, Alberta," which was presented to the ECA Public Hearing on the Eastern Slopes. I also co-authored an invited paper entitled "Fish Creek and Nose Hill Parks, A Case Study In Contrasting Forms of Public Participation" which was presented at the 1977 Canadian Conference on Public Participation in Banff, Alberta. In late 1976 I resigned from the ECA, Public Advisory Committee, when the Government of Alberta chose to emasculate this organization and replace it with a government-controlled Environment Council of Alberta. The original ECA was so successful in empowering the citizens of Alberta concerning environmental issues that it became a Canadian model and threatened those in political power who had other agendas on these issues.

While serving on the executive of the Calgary Local Council of Women I wrote environmental resolutions on land-use policy for Canada and for the transition from a consumer to a conserver society for the National Council of Women of Canada. The Calgary Local Council voted me an honorary life member in 1975.

At the community level, I was the treasurer, secretary and member of the Bankview Community executive. For five years, from 1980-85, I worked in consultation with residents and city planners to create and implement an Area Redevelopment Plan for our district. From 1978-85 I also worked on committees lobbying to save inner city schools. My husband and I were honored by having an inner city park named "Buckmaster Park" in 1991 in recognition of our contributions to community and park planning.

I have always been a strong supporter of the arts and served on the Pumphouse Theatre board for five years during the 1970s and 80s. I was also on the board of New Works Calgary (classical music) for four years as their secretary-treasurer. During this time, I prepared successful grant applications to civic, provincial and national funding agencies.

Last, but certainly not least, for a period of six years during the 1980s a city alderman and I presented very well-received lobbying workshops. After being personally involved in volunteer activities for many years, I appreciated how inadequate most people were in the lobbying process.

In June of 1993 my husband and I moved from Calgary to Victoria. Due to a congenital back problem I am prevented from making the ongoing contributions to society that I once could.

Dorothy Helen Groves

I was born in Nova Scotia, where for at least five generations my roots were a combination of British and Nova Scotian forebears who had married back and forth over the ocean. Some of them lived a very long time. I was indeed blessed to have a remarkably independent great-grandmother who lived until I was in my 20s. Granny was a farmer who drove by horse and buggy five miles in to the market each Friday until she was 85, giving up the farm only when the government seconded the land for the Naval Air Base at Shearwater.

After matriculating from Halifax County Academy, I took a secretarial course at Maritime Business College, then worked for two years during World War II as a Royal Canadian Ordinance Corps stenographer. From 1943 until 1947, I trained as a nurse at the Victoria General Hospital in Halifax. After nursing briefly in Nova Scotia, I moved to Quebec, where I became a staff nurse at the Montreal General Hospital. Because I wanted to work with both students and patients, in 1949 I enrolled in the one-year post-graduate diploma course in teaching in schools of nursing which was offered at McGill.

It was inevitable, it seems to me, that I, too, would marry someone from over the ocean. I've never been sure whether this was because no one here would have me or whether I was looking for adventure, but my husband, Trevor, was born in India, the son of an English soldier who married a Belgian. We met as students at McGill when we appeared in Ibsen's *Ghosts* for the McGill University Players. Life has been a play ever since. (Somewhat Shakespearian, I think.) We married in 1950 and have six children, all born before 1969. For those who don't know, that is when we Canadian women were allowed access to birth control. On second thought, maybe I would have had six children anyway, but certainly not the first five in a six-year period.

Trevor went to work for the Defense Research Board after university, and in 1957 we left Ottawa to come west to the Suffield Experimental Station. In 1963, after almost seven years there, Trevor decided to return to take his PhD in Mechanical Engineering, and we travelled back east. By "we" I mean the six children, my mother, Trevor and me in a station wagon. We returned to Alberta in the spring of 1966, when Trevor was appointed Associate Professor of Mechanical Engineering at the University of Calgary.

One of my mother's brothers, Jack Lloyd, was a Liberal member of Parliament, and I have been extremely interested and active in politics from the age of 15. Since coming to Calgary I have worked on election campaigns at the three levels of government, being enough of a committed Liberal and optimist to accept the party's Calgary North Hill candidacy in three provincial contests.

I also have been a delegate to many provincial and federal conferences and have especially enjoyed working on panels dealing with politics, women's issues and health topics. From 1978 to 1981, I was appointed by Order-in-Council to serve as southern Alberta's representative on the Canadian Advisory Council on the Status of Women. Doris Anderson was chairperson then, and it was a very important time in the women's movement. Whenever there was a release of a position paper, a meeting that was open to the press and public was held at the same time as the Minister received the document. We also began the preparation of what became a ten-year follow-up report on the progress made towards implementation of the 167 recommendations incorporated in the Status of Women report. Most of our meetings were held in Ottawa, but we did meet with women's groups elsewhere around the country. The latter provided an invaluable exchange of viewpoints. Then, in 1984, I received a different kind of federal appointment, a three-year term as chairperson of the Unemployment Insurance Commission's Board of Referees, Alberta Regional Division. We dealt with appeals. Since 1989 I have served on the Calgary Board of Health, and in 1992 I was elected by that Board to membership on the Health Unit Association of Alberta. In December of 1993, I was elected the association's first vice-chair.

My voluntary association memberships have included UNICEF, the Calgary Birth Control Association, and Planned Parenthood, Alberta. In 1983 the Calgary Local Council of Women nominated me for the YWCA's Woman of the Year award.

It was as past president of the Women's Faculty Club of the University of Calgary that I got my introduction to the Calgary Local Council of Women. By 1974 it had become a tradition that I was pleased to continue. I first served as publicity convenor, then recording secretary, then vice-president from 1978 until 1981, when I was made an Honorary Life Member. At the provincial level, I was chairperson of the Status of Women Committee.

What I value and cherish most about the Council of Women was working with a wonderful group of women who were able to focus on important issues but always ready for the healthy diversion of a good laugh. When I look back on my active years with the Calgary Local Council I remember things like working hard to spread a pro-choice stand for women; bringing forward to Council Irene Murdoch's case, which was of particular importance in enhancing matrimonial reform for the Province; representing the Calgary Local Council of Women on the steering committee for a proposed Alberta Council of Women's Affairs. In this last regard, I still regret that we were not able to convince the Province that arm's length autonomy was important. Unlike the federal Status of Women Council, Alberta chose not to allow its Council to go public with its research and resolutions at the same time that the Minister was informed. I think this is why the provincial Council has not been more effective in writing and presenting briefs.

I am 71 this year and so pleased to still be active on three boards and to be a senior who receives invitations to speak on panels. My life has been rich indeed – four of our children live in Calgary, one in Ottawa, and one in Vancouver. We have six grandchildren to date and are expecting another one soon. Since he retired from the University of Calgary, my husband has been busy as an inventor, and I act as his secretary, typing papers and letters. Despite the scorn some women feel about typing, I have to say I still believe that being able to type is of value in any revolution – certainly I have found it a plus in all my endeavors. My only regret is that it took me until 1986 to be able to access a computer.

Gwen Thorssen

I first became a fortunate Calgary citizen and third-generation Canadian during the last year of World War I. This timing shielded me from the Great War's fallout and consequences, allowing me an innocent, happy childhood in a family of two parents, two sisters and one brother. Life was simple in the Calgary I remember when it was a city of 60 000. My world revolved around home, church, school, good friends and play activities all located within a safe walking distance from home, which was in the Beltline district not far from the house where suffragette Nellie McClung once lived. My father, Robert Weir, served as a city alderman for 14 years.

In my own loving, balanced family, I was happy and carefree, despite the required household chores and discipline of continuing lessons in piano, cello, singing and elocution. This quite idyllic beginning climaxed in graduation from Normal School with a first class Teacher's Certificate and my working days in the profession of my choice began.

A green city girl, I spend my first three years in country schools, where I taught grades one through twelve in one room and organized much-appreciated community activities in any spare time. In my fourth and final year, I returned to Calgary to teach at Wood's Christian Homes, and for the first six months there undertook the added onerous role of housemother to 60 resident orphans. From these varied teaching and community responsibilities I gained a wealth of real life experiences early on.

Around this time my best friend's brother, Leroy (Chick) Thorssen, became my best beau, and in September of 1941, we were married in traditional style in Grace Presbyterian Church, which my father had helped found many years before. As newlyweds we settled in Edmonton, where Chick was assigned by the Wartime Bureau of Technical Personnel to teach the University of Alberta engineers for the Armed Services, and our first four children (three sons and a daughter) were born and started school there. Mothering duties were my priority, but they were enjoyably shared with faculty affairs, Red Cross work, and a 25 year commitment to church school teaching in a close-knit community bonded by rationing and the pervasive war effort. In 1952 we left Edmonton's academic life and returned to the business world of our home town, Calgary, where our fourth son was born.

I was always fortunate enough to have reliable home help and a supportive husband who encouraged me to pursue my volunteer interests. In the '60s different social needs were developing, and I was privileged to work on the initiation and first board of directors of Meals-on-Wheels. My teaching background was utilized in religious education work as chair of North Hill United's Christian Education Committee and the (Ecumenical) Calgary Lay School of Theology. When religious teaching in the public schools became an issue in the late 1960s, a two-year Advisory Committee on Religion in Education was struck, comprising teachers, clergy and the laity. I represented the United Church. Our resultant brief to the Board of Education was accepted and became stated policy. Our consensus view was that teachers should be permitted and encouraged to explore religious topics, values and ethics, as these arise naturally in any subject of study. Within a public school system that serves a pluralistic society, we acknowledged the importance of education in our own and other religions, without proselytizing, and keeping the matter of faith and prayer a private responsibility.

As a native Calgarian raised with a sense of social conscience, I also welcomed the opportunity to give three years of service on the Calgary City Council Social Services Committee and nine years on the Provincial Welfare Appeal Board. Both experiences provided me with insights into the special problems of disadvantaged and struggling citizens and how government levels address their needs.

Throughout the 1970s, the Calgary Local Council of Women became my main focus after I joined as a representative from the United Church Women's Presbyterial. I soon progressed from there to the executive and a two-year presidency. It was at this time that the new women's movement began to attract politically-minded young women to its ranks, and I was particularly concerned that their energizing potential would be lost to our own Local Council membership. Alienation could be avoided if our Council of Women acted like a mother with an independent daughter and counselled her wisely. As Local Council's Status of Women Committee chairperson at the time, I helped found Calgary's Status of Women Action Committee (SWAC), which quickly became a strong organization in its own right. In 1975 our two committees drew other women's groups together in a landmark celebration of the first International Women's Day, which was held in the old YWCA. Then, in concert with the Junior League, Hadassah and the University Women's Club, on October 29th we held a gala International Women's Year Wrap-Up, which I chaired, highlighted by a public meeting where the Honorable Marc Lalonde, Federal Minister for the Status of Women, explained his government's policy and responded to audience questions. These occasions renewed public recognition of our Local Council's co-ordinating role among women's groups.

In response to other issues, our Calgary Council forwarded a brief on highway and city traffic recommendations to the provincial government. A Calgary resolution submitted to the National Council of Women of Canada urged a uniform age nationally for young offenders. Closer to home, we played an influential part in the 1975 lobby for an alternate site for the Max Bell Arena, away from the banks of the Bow River. Instead of being built on 18 acres near the Pumphouse Theatre, the sports complex was erected between Memorial Drive and Barlow Trail.

After finishing my Calgary presidency, I accepted the leadership of Alberta's Provincial Council of Women, where our extension efforts culminated in a newly organized Lethbridge Council of Women joining our provincial body. Briefs to the Alberta Government on the issues of accessible day care, opposition to the proposed transfer of divorce jurisdiction to the provinces, and equal rights for women evidenced our responses to contemporary issues. The protracted 1980s campaign to ensure Sunday store closing was an unsuccessful but worthwhile fight. We believed that families especially needed one day a week which was not a working day for either parent.

I have always believed the best way that women can bring about changes in government policy – and that is where change has to occur – is through working together. Public and elected representatives should know what women think and care about in their society. Our Council of Women petitions were not all successful by any means, but they did raise awareness of those concerns which we agreed were important. You might say our role was consciousness-raising.

Now, I am enjoying the senior plateau, keeping links with our YWCA, co-editing a pictorial history of our Local Council for Calgary's Centennial, and just concentrating on family and friends, thankfully in good health, and with the same loving, supportive partner with whom I started the adventure.

Mary Guichon

I was born at the Holy Cross Hospital on December 30, 1924, an extremely cold day, but my birth was not registered until the following March. The three months between were tragic for my father. My ailing mother, Mary Louise McGannon McCormick, who had fuelled the great happiness of his life, died on January 21, 1925 from spinal meningitis. The second great blow came when it was discovered that I had absorbed the toxins in my mother's system when I was taken to her to be nursed, and it was thought that his new baby daughter would not live.

My mother was a member of a large, historic Canadian family who had settled in Prescott and Brockville, Ontario. She was educated in the convent of Notre Dame at Kingston, where she learned the womanly arts of needlework, painting and music. Mother had a great talent for friendship, and her home was always open to my parents' friends, who provided a strong support for my father in the difficult years without her.

My father's family of seafarers came from the island of Barra in the outer Hebrides and migrated to County Antrim in Northern Ireland. When he was a boy the English had decreed that Irish children were not to be educated. So they learned in secret, hidden behind the hedges, where they used a simple rock slate as the tool for writing and doing arithmetic in what were appropriately called "hedge schools." Being a short boy, my father was able to learn more than most before his head appeared above the hedges and he had to "graduate." He loved learning but believed that the first thing a student must learn was that he could learn all his life provided he could read and do mathematics. At the age of 14, my father came alone to Canada, where he first apprenticed himself as a saddlemaker in Hastings, Ontario, then worked his way westward as a journeyman until he arrived in New Westminster, BC, as a master of his trade.

I finally arrived home in the sixth month of my life, after having been taken from the hospital to be cared for by an infant's nurse in a private house. Our home was a busy place, now in the charge of a remarkable new housekeeper, Mrs. Cassidy, who had been educated at Boston College. She did not like nursery rhymes, so she read to us from Thoreau and Thackeray. That was our light reading. Being a very proud Yankee, she also read Benjamin Franklin's federalist papers, and later my older brother, Michael, read law to us.

Mrs. Cassidy stayed, but our new immigrant maids came and went like people going through a revolving door. To ease their pain of loss and separation, they played the balalaikas and guitars given to them as parting gifts. We learned a little Russian, German, Czechslovakian, Polish and Yugoslavian and a great deal about how fortunate we were to have a dedicated father, a warm home with lots of food, and a government we could elect for ourselves, one that was guaranteed not to invade our households as we slept. These 18 and 19-year-olds, who came from childhoods dwarfed by World War I, were the spearheads for their families. Their loneliness sent the girls in search of young mates on their Sundays and Thursdays off. When they located the right man, they married with only dreams in their pockets and brought back tiny new babies to show us that they now had something to build for.

Dad believed anyone could do anything, and he did – he ran his two-storey leather business, formed a company that drilled for oil in Turner Valley, began a radio station in his house, and was a founding member of the Knights of Columbus and the downtown Rotary Club.

Politically he was a Laurier Liberal, but he felt an affection for R.B. Bennett. Although they did not agree on policy, my father admired his fine mind.

Our house was alive with people when Dad became an alderman. I remember Mrs. Harold Riley arriving at eight in the morning with a sheaf of papers to support her crusade for children's rights and protection. I remember, too, when Nellie McClung arrived at our house on the 19th of October, 1929, in the company of two other women. She was wearing what I, as a child, judged to be her ceremonial hat, for it was much larger than the small capped ones then in fashion. It framed her exultant face as she stood in the sunlight of the doorway at 4:30 that afternoon and asked my father if she could broadcast her great news. I had just come part way down the stairs after my nap and was standing on the steps at the same level as her eyes. They were dancing with joy. When one of her friends remarked that I was a very pretty little girl, Nellie took my chin in her hands and said, "You can be as pretty as you wish, Mary, but never forget women." Then she sailed into the broadcast area of the house. They warmed up the set, and she told the world that women could now become members of the Federal Senate. As a result of the suit brought by the magnificent five Alberta women, the Privy Council of England had declared that women were persons before the law.

As she was broadcasting this good news, the conversation in the den was hushed. Those there had a different concern – the falling stock market. Nellie came out of her euphoric state when she went into the den to meet the men and women she knew well. But even her wonderful news could not change their mood, and she must have felt like ice had been dropped down her back. She left in search of happy people to share her victory with, and I'm certain she found them.

On June 30, 1930, Dad married Mary Veronica Curley of Sudbury, Ontario. He had known her since she was a child because he had apprenticed himself as a journeyman to her father. The marriage was a good one. They did everything together, and his life changed totally. Now he was no longer alone with his responsibilities. My stepmother had been trained as a social worker after World War I. When she came to Calgary she brought her skills to the new board of the Community Chest and to the YWCA. She also worked for the Catholic Women's League and the Scarboro Community Association.

My stepmother was a great friend to me in my adolescent years, when I was dancing the Second World War away with the young navigators of the Australian Air Force who were training in Calgary as part of the Commonwealth Air Training Program. We had parties in our home and danced at the YWCA under the watchful eyes of chaperones.

As a child I was taught by Ursuline Nuns and lay teachers at Sacred Heart School and after that by the Sisters of the Faithful Companions of

Jesus at Saint Mary's Girls' School in Calgary before I went east to university. I received my Bachelor of Arts at the University of Western Ontario in London and my Bachelor of Social Work at the University of Toronto.

I married Urban Guichon from Quilchena, British Columbia, on September 26, 1950, after a brief courtship. Urban, who had been born on a large family ranch near Merritt, went to war after having earned his degree in agriculture. After Urban retired from being District Agriculturalist in Kamloops, we lived on the Alkali Lake ranch. We came to Calgary to help my father, who was not well. We took over his business of Riley and McCormick, which Urban, the former rancher, built up to thirty-five stores in western Canada.

In 1981 the banks called in our loans that were being paid currently, because they had lost confidence in the West due to falling oil prices. We filed for bankruptcy, but with a western heritage, Urban and three of our children, Gregory, Carolyn and Brian (all under 31 at the time), raised money, bought some of the assets and started to rebuild a company begun in 1901. The memory which nourished me during this period was of my own father when his business burned in June of 1929 and his oil well brought in water. After viewing what was left of the store on the morning after the fire – a large, hot and steaming safe and an empty hole in the ground – my Dad picked up my brother Michael's little-boy hand, looked at him sadly, and said, "Oh Michael! this is a great country, a man can always start again." He did – and we did. Courage is contagious.

Although my husband always put his family first, he also served the city he enjoyed. He loved the opera and served on its board. He was a president of the Red Cross Society, and the Downtown Rotary was a joy in his life. When he died on October 9, 1993, the city lost a great supporter and we lost more than words can express.

In addition to working alongside my husband as secretary-treasurer and a director in Riley and McCormick, I always tried to give service to my church, my community and the Liberal Party. In the 1950s I became a member of the Catholic Women's League and a member of the Founding Board of the Catholic Family Service Association. Then, a decade later, I served on the Building Board of Providence Crèche, and after that on the Inter-faith Lacombe Building Foundation. During the 14 years when our five children – Gregory, Anne, Carolyn, Julie and Brian – were in different schools, I belonged to their Home and School Associations.

Here in Calgary I continued my University of Toronto affiliation serving as the Calgary president of its Alumni Association for four years. That University later honored me with the Sesquicentennial Award, which is accorded to a U. of T. alumnus who has served her community with distinction.

I was elected to the Senate of the University of Calgary in 1978, where I later chaired the Concerns and Enquiry Committee. During this same period, 1978-81, I was also a member of the Calgary General Hospital Board, of which I became vice-chairperson in 1980.

Conversations in our home often centred on politics, and the Liberal Party in particular, so those interests came naturally to me. Beginning in 1969 I served a four-year term as president of the Calgary Women's Liberal Association, then in 1972 I ran as Federal Liberal candidate in the Palliser Constituency. Earlier that same year I was appointed Alberta representative on the Liberal Commission mandated to advise on equal opportunity requirements of women within the party. After that I became a member of two different International Women's Year consultative committees whose function was to advise government concerning women's expectations for the International Women's Year program. By 1977 I had acquired a good background in women's issues. That year I was the Canadian guest of Mrs. Lyndon Baines Johnson on the occasion of the relocation of her husband's office from the White House to Austin, Texas, an American tradition which honors former Presidents.

I attended the Calgary Local Council of Women as the representative of the Women's Liberal Association and moved from convenor of the Health and Welfare Committee to vice-president to president in 1980.

My years of activity in the community ended with the problems of 1981. After that I gave myself exclusively to the needs of our family and the business.

Each phase has been a challenge and each change has been a great opportunity – a great gift from the country of my birth, the family into which I was born and the one I chose. I was fortunate to be born in 1924. We developed the mindset of a time full of optimism, with a "can do" approach to life. All lights were green for us on the paths of our lives. May they continue to be so with God's unending assistance.

Donalda Vine

My parents, Donald and Susan Mills, were brought up on farms in Ontario and Manitoba with six and seven siblings. In 1926 they moved to Edmonton, where I was born, then came to Calgary a year later and my sister was born. My parents named her "Armis" because she arrived on Armistice Day, November 11, at the 11th hour.

I graduated in nursing from the Calgary General Hospital in 1948 and a few months later travelled overseas to Cardiff, Wales, to enroll in the diploma course offered at the Prince of Wales Orthopaedic Hospital. The reason for my distant choice was family-related. My uncle, Mr. A.O. Parker, was the Hospital's chief of staff. After my return to Calgary, I nursed at the old Children's Hospital. In 1950 I married Kenneth Vine, a World War II veteran who had served overseas as a Lieutenant in the

Winnipeg Dragoons. We stayed in Calgary and our family grew to three children, our daughter being the middle child.

My introduction to the Young Women's Christian Association occurred after I had returned from Britain when I joined the YW Kappa Gamma Club, a young working women's service group within the YWCA. From there I went on YW committees and the Board of Directors in 1963. It was at the YW board level that I became a delegate to the Local Council of Women's general meetings, which were held once a month in City Council chambers. As their representative I eventually reported back to the YW social issues committee. I continued in that role, off and on, for almost 20 years. Within my own affiliate, the YWCA, I served on the selection committee for the YW Women of Distinction for 1981-82 and am now a past co-chair of the YWCA Alumni.

Within the Local Council of Women I chaired the Arts and Letters Committee, the Social Committee, and held the office of treasurer for several years, then served as LCW's president from 1981-85. Those were the years when Local Council's leadership recognized new issues espoused by the women's movement as well as carrying on customary obligations. As LCW's president, I represented the Local Council at numerous affairs, from feminist protest marches for pro choice Calgary Birth Control Association and the Alberta Status of Women Action Committee to the Soroptimists International Convention held here, where I was the guest speaker. LCW was also an active participant in what started as Save Our Sundays lobby and became the Quality of Life Committee. I was also treasurer of a group which proposed the Provincial Council on Women's Affairs. It later became the Alberta Women's Advisory Commission.

These varied commitments to women's organizations acknowledged, the one precedent I did set I owe to my husband, who had belonged to Calgary's Downtown Kiwanis Club for 33 years when he died. After his death, I was invited to join in his stead. At first I declined, then, realizing that my membership would set a timely precedent for the admission of other women, I accepted.

For many years Council of Women meetings were held in prestigious locations. We held our executive meetings in the boardroom of the *Calgary Herald* building at Seventh Avenue and First Street Southwest. When the *Herald* moved to its new site east of the Deerfoot Trail, they invited us again, but the distance was a deterrent. We started meeting in our own homes or business board rooms. We continued our regular meetings in City Council chambers until the new City Hall was built. Because there was no longer an equivalent facility there available to us, we moved to my church, Grace Presbyterian, and continued to meet there until the spring of 1994.

When Calgary hosted the National Council of Women Annual Meeting in Banff in 1978, I was on the organizing committee. 1982 was the Seventieth Anniversary of our LCW, and we celebrated in the auditorium of Alberta Historical Resources Foundation on Tuesday evening, October 26th, with old friends, special guests, spouses and family. While I was the Calgary Council's president I attended the NCW Annual Meeting in St. John, New Brunswick, in 1981 and the 1982 Annual Meeting in Saskatoon. More recently, as a National Life Member I have attended two NCW annual meetings – the 99th, held in Surrey, BC, in 1992, and the 101st, which was held this year in Vancouver. In my opinion, the processing of fewer resolutions has made NCW conferences appear more efficient.

From my long participation in our own Local Council, I have seen its character change within the last decade or so. During a low point in the 1980s when we functioned without a nominating committee, the problem of too few LCW committee chairpersons arose. The executive, while trying to keep its committee of officers up to strength, accepted into membership all those who applied for affiliation without the customary vetting. Consequently, individual members and groups not in harmony with NCW slipped into our Local membership. The YWCA and I as their representative left the LCW in 1992 because of a mutual feeling that our purposes were not in harmony with the existing Council.

Recognitions of my volunteer efforts include the CHQR Citizenship Award, given in September of 1980 to commemorate Alberta's Seventy-fifth Anniversary, and a 500-hour St. John's Ambulance brigade award. I am now nearing 20 years of driver service for Meals on Wheels, and I still co-ordinate the Time Out program for Grace Presbyterian Church, an undertaking I began in 1979.

I have been privileged to meet many outstanding women in Calgary and nationally who have worked for the betterment of women and the family in Canada and to call them friends. Thank you.

What do we live for if not to make the world less difficult for each other?
George Eliot

Calgary Local Council of Women Presidents

෨ ෨ ෨ ෨

Madame Charles Rouleau	1895-98
Mrs. R.R. Jamieson	1912-16
Mrs. George Kerby	1917
Mrs. Charles Fenkell	1918-19
Mrs. P.S. Woodhall	1920-21
Mrs. H.G.H. Glass	1922-23
Mrs. W.A. Geddes	1924-25
Mrs. A. MacWilliams	1926-27
Mrs. H.J. Akitt	1929-29
Mrs. H. J. Robbie	1930
Mrs. Guy Johnson	1931-32
Mrs. F.G. Grevette	1933-34
Mrs. R.L. Freeman	1935
Mrs. A. Blight	1936-37
Mrs. F.G. Grevette	1938
Mrs. Ervin Hirst	1939-41
Mrs. F.S. Ditto	1942-43
Mrs. Wallace Neale	1944-45
Mrs. L.G. Fisher	1946-47
Mrs. H.F. Clarke	1949-50
Mrs. Russel Clark	1951-55
Miss Una MacLean	1955/58
Mrs. A. Russell Hutchinson	1958-59
Mrs. O. Stonewall	1959-63
Mrs. K.F. MacLennan	1963-65
Mrs. A.D. Winspear	1965-67
Mrs. H.G. McCullough	1967-68
Mrs. A.C. Luft	1968-69
Mrs. Barbara Langridge	1970-71
Mrs. Marjorie Norris	1972-73
Mrs. Joni Chorny	1973-74
Mrs. Gwen Thorssen	1975-77

Mrs. Betty Shifflett	1977-79
Mrs. Dode Chapman	1979-80
Mrs. Mary Guichon	1980-81
Mrs. Donalda Vine	1981-85
Mrs. Sheila Scott	1985-87
Mrs. Jean Mekitiak	1987-88
Mrs. Lynn Arling	1988-89
Mrs. Jackie Elliot	1990-92
Mrs. Carol Tholenaer	1993-94
Mrs. Peggy Anderson	1994

Selected Bibliography

ೲ ೲ ೲ ೲ

Shaw, Rosa L. (1957). *Proud Heritage: A History of the National Council of Women of Canada*. Toronto: Ryerson Press.

Griffiths, N.E.S. (1993). *The Splendid Vision: Centennial History of the National Council of Women of Canada 1893-1993*. Ottawa: Carleton University Press.

Gray, James H. (1973). *Red Lights on the Prairies*. Scarborough, ON: The New American Library of Canada.

MacEwan, Grant. (1957). *Eye Opener Bob*. Edmonton, AB: The Institute of Applied Art.

Foran, Max & Jameson, Sheilagh S., eds. (1987). *Citymakers, Calgarians After the Frontier*. Calgary, AB: Historical Society of Alberta, Chinook Country Chapter.

Hacker, Carlotta. (1974). *The Indomitable Lady Doctors*. Toronto: Clarke, Irwin & Co.

Duley, Margot L. (1993). *Where Once Our Mothers Stood We Stand*. Charlottetown, PEI: Gynergy Books.

Strong-Boag, Veronica Jane. (1975). *The Parliament of Women: The National Council of Women of Canada 1893-1929*. PhD. Dissertation, University of Toronto.

Sheehan, Nancy M. (1980). *Temperance, the WCTU and Education in Alberta, 1905-1930*. PhD. Dissertation, University of Alberta, Edmonton.

Johnston, Sheila Moore. (1987). *Giving Freely of Her Time and Energy, Calgary Public Women, 1910*. MA Thesis, University of Calgary.

Nicholson, Barbara Jean. (1970). *Feminism in the Prairie Provinces to 1916*. MA Thesis, University of Calgary.

Foran, Maxwell Lawrence. (1981). *The Civic Corporation and Urban Growth: Calgary 1884-1930*. PhD. Dissertation, University of Calgary.

Notes

ဢ ဢ ဢ ဢ

Chapter 1

1. Mrs. Willoughby Cummings, "The National Council," *Woman's Century*, Special Number, September, 1918, p. 25.
2. Griffiths, N.E.S. *The Splendid Vision, Centennial History of the National Council of Women of Canada 1893-1993*. Ottawa: Carleton University Press, 1993. p. 9.
3. Saywell, John T., ed., *The Canadian Journal of Lady Aberdeen* (Toronto: Champlain Society, 1960), p. 24. Referred to hereafter as *Cdn. Journal*.
4. *Cdn. Journal*, Introduction, p. xxiv.
5. During a two-week period in August of 1894, Lady Aberdeen personally mentored the formation of the first three eastern Canadian councils: St. John, Halifax and Yarmouth.
6. The suffrage cause had been pressed without success in Ontario for 27 years, but in 1890 the Legislature did at least give serious discussion to a women's enfranchisement bill before shelving it to await the day (a frosty Friday, no doubt) when women themselves reached unanimity on the issue.
7. *Cdn. Journal*, p. 89.
8. "President's Address," *Women Workers of Canada, Proceedings of the [1894] First Annual Meeting and Conference of the National Council of Women of Canada* (Ottawa: April 1894), p. 22. Referred to hereafter as *Yearbook*.
9. Ibid., p. 11.
10. *We Twa, Reminiscences of Lord and Lady Aberdeen*, Vol 1. Ch. XX, p. 272. Referred to hereafter as *We Twa*.
11. That 1889 bout with exhaustion prompted her concerned doctor to advise a restorative autumn trip to a country where they would be unknown. They chose Canada.
12. Cited in *Cdn. Journal*, Introduction, p. xxv.
13. Voluntary work with the Society for the Prevention of Cruelty to Children, the Associated Workers' League, the Strand Rescue Mission, the Women's Industrial Council in London and the Women's Protective and Provident League in Glasgow attested to the conventional Victorial commitment to mothering. Her support for women's suffrage organizations – the Society for Promoting the Return (election) of Women to all Local Governing Bodies, the Women's Franchise League, and her presidencies of the Women's Liberal Federation of Scotland (Lady Aberdeen was its founder) and the English counterpart (she succeeded Mrs. Gladstone) – revealed a less conventional, feminist experience. One of the most idealistic of these groups was the Associated Workers' League. Begun by Edinburgh students, it remained a small religious organization which attracted politically and socially influential members who personally strove to "make their lives more fruitful to others." (*We Twa*, Vol. 1, Ch. XV, p. 207-08). In the couple's memoirs, Lady

Aberdeen credited her presidencies of the London Women's Industrial Council and the Glasgow Women's Protective and Provident League with ". . . much valuable though painful education regarding the conditions under which so many women workers earned their living." (*We Twa*, Vol. 1, Ch. XX, p. 276.)

14. *We Twa*, Vol. 1, Ch. XV, p. 198.
15. *We Twa*, Vol. 1, Ch. XX, p. 275.
16. *Encyclopedia Britannica*, 14th ed., Vol. 23, p. 711.
17. "Frontier Town Calgary," a lecture given by historian Max Foran on January 19, 1994.
18. "Monday Aug. 5th, Edmonton," *Cdn. Journal*, p. 262-63.
19. "Friday Oct. 13th [12th], Calgary," *Ibid.*, p. 132.
20. Lady Aberdeen launched the idea for the society in Winnipeg during her "restorative" trip to Canada in 1889. Fourteen hundred people attended a Winnipeg meeting chaired by Lady Taylor, and by the time the Aberdeens returned to Canada in 1891, that branch was well-established. The idea eventually spread to Halifax, Ottawa, Toronto, Vancouver and ultimately to 18 centres. Volunteers who packed parcels of reading materials were expected to correspond twice a year with the families to whom the parcels were addressed. This contact helped to determine the preferences and needs of the recipients. (*We Twa*, Vol. 1, Ch. XXI, p. 297.)
21. *Cdn. Journal*, p. 134.
22. Because there were very few societies in Edmonton at that time, certain ladies who belonged to more distant churches represented those churches: ". . . the Roman Catholic ladies gave an account of the convent work going on, both at Edmonton and St. Albert. . . ." *Women Workers of Canada, Proceedings of the Second Annual Meeting and Conference of the National Council of Women of Canada*, p. 56. Referred to hereafter as *Yearbook, 1895*.
23. "Edmonton Local Council," *Ibid.*, p. 55.
24. "A Royal Reception," *Alberta Tribune*, November 30, 1895, p. 4.
25. "The Hospital Ball," *Calgary Daily Herald*, November 29, 1895, p. 1.
26. *Alberta Tribune*, November 30, 1895, p. 4 item.
27. *Ibid.* item.

Chapter 2

1. *Yearbook*, 1896, p. 572.
2. *Ibid.*, p. 22.
3. Untitled item, *Calgary Daily Herald*, December 13, 1895, p. 4.
4. Item, *Calgary Daily Herald*, January 20, 1896.
5. "Countess Aberdeen Addresses The National Council Of Women," *Calgary Daily Herald*, December 11, 1896, p. 1.
6. *Yearbook, 1897*, p. 60.
7. Untitled item, *Calgary Daily Herald*, November 29, 1895, p. 4.
8. "The Famine In India," *Alberta Tribune*, February 6, 1897, p. 1.
9. The Indian Famine Fund did, however, prove a phenomenal success on a national scale. It was estimated by *The Montreal Star*, which received the subscriptions, that the $50 000 donated came from upwards of 200 000 persons, 100 000 school children, almost 100 000 church members of all faiths,

and thousands of private citizens. In Calgary the April 10, 1897 edition of the *Alberta Tribune* considered the participation showed Canadians' "real interest in the whole Empire" in philanthropy and patriotism.

10. A classical allusion to Greek mythology. Terpsichore was the muse of dancing.
11. "The Panopticon," *Alberta Tribune*, September 14, 1895, p. 3.
12. Social and Personal column, *Alberta Tribune*, January 25, 1896, p. 5.
13. Mrs. Selby Walker, "How Hospitals Are Born."
14. Lady Aberdeen fought diligently against prolonged and powerful opposition from the medical profession to establish the concept of the Victorian Order of Home Helpers. While her own efforts were not successful, the notion succeeded elsewhere. It evolved into the Victorian Order of Nurses (VON), established by Royal Charter on May 18, 1898, as a memorial to Queen Victoria's Diamond Jubilee.
15. Calgary's was not the only short-lived Council. Edmonton's Local Council, formed a year earlier in October of 1894 under less impressive circumstances, lasted only a year and a half. By the time of the 1896 NCWC Annual Conference, the Edmonton Local Council had decided,"for local reasons, to discontinue active work for a time." They did, however, express their hope to reorganize.
16. *Cdn. Journal*, Introduction, p. xxvi.
17. Aberdeen, Countess Ishbel, "The National Council of Women of Canada: What It Means and What It Does," reprinted from the *Canadian Woman's Handbook*, p. 14. See pages 6-13 for quoted tributes from Canadian prime ministers, Sir John Thompson and Sir Wilfrid Laurier, federal cabinet ministers, provincial premiers and church leaders.
18. *Ibid.*
19. *Yearbook 1896*, p. vi. Beginning in 1894, men holding high office – among them the Governor-General, lieutenant governors and senators – did become patrons.
20. "Fifty I.C.W. Delegates Pay City a Flying Visit," *Calgary Daily Herald*, July 8, 1909, p. 1.

Chapter 3

1. "Suffragettes In Calgary Are Very Successful In Debate," *Morning Albertan*, April 16, 1912, p. 4.
2. "Votes For Women Result Of Debate Anti's Subdued," *Calgary News-Telegram*, April 18, 1912, p. 11.
3. "Women Shouldn't Be Given Franchise – R.B. Bennett," *Calgary News-Telegram*, April 1912, p. 25.
4. "The Suffragette Outrages May Become Common In Canada," *Calgary News-Telegram*, December 16, 1912, p. 4. The public lecture referred to here may have taken place on November 20th, when Dr. Amelia Yeomans delivered what reporters from the three daily papers described as a witty, interesting address to the Woman's Canadian Club. Dr. Yeomans was, however, no longer a Winnipeg resident, having lived in Calgary for six years by this time. She was vice-president of the Dominion WCTU and honorary vice-president of the Ottawa Equal Suffrage Association as well as of the Calgary WCTU.
5. "The Other Half," *Calgary News-Telegram*, April 10, 1912, p. 9.

6. "Work Of The Associated Charities Hinges On Intemperance," *Morning Albertan*, July 18, 1912, p. 4.

7. "Wheels Of Justice In Calgary Move Slowly," *Morning Albertan*, August 30, 1912, p. 4.

8. "Distressing Conditions Said to Exist in the Pest House; Patient Alleges Barbaric Indifference," *Calgary News-Telegram*, April 13, 1912, p. 14.

9. "Officials Roundly Condemned," *Calgary Daily Herald*, July 8, 1912, p. 1.

10. "Quoth The Raven: 'Nevermore,'" *Morning Albertan*, July 19, 1912, p. 1.

11. The idea of canvassing these 1600 women voters had already been discussed by the WCTU in March of 1912. They considered this undertaking in the aftermath of the rather narrow support for a city bylaw allowing the production of malt in Calgary. ("Do Enfranchised Women Vote?" *Calgary Daily Herald*, March 6, 1912, p.12)

12. "Calgary Women Purpose Forming A Civic League," *Morning Albertan*, August 1, 1912, p. 4.

13. "Women Discuss Civic League," *Calgary News-Telegram*, September 14, 1912, p. 24.

14. "Organization of Civic League For Women Deferred," *Calgary Daily Herald*, September 13, 1912, p. 23.

15. "Committee Of Three Will Not Submit Resolution," *Morning Albertan*, October 9, 1912, p. 4.

16. Another critique of the local council option in the pages of the *Calgary News-Telegram* raised specific doubts. Could such a general organization do justice to a civic league's special plans and work? Would not National Council of Women fees – purported to range from $5 to $100 – prove to be a financial barrier to the ordinary woman voter? Would not the influence of a civic league be diluted within the voting structure of a local council where each member was allocated two votes? The view was that there was room for both.

17. "Mrs. O. Edwards Addresses Women's Canadian Club," *Calgary News-Telegram*, October 26, 1912, p. 26.

18. "Mrs. Edwards Will Address W.C.C.," *Calgary Daily Herald*, October 5, 1912, p. 20.

19. "Civic Workers Will Organize Under Local Council Of Women," *Morning Albertan*, November 6, 1912, p. 4.

20. *Ibid.*

21. "Will Not Organize A Civic League," *Calgary Daily Herald*, November 6, 1912, p. 14.

22. It was anticipated that Mrs. Newhall, Jamieson and Lampard would become LCW's standing Civic Committee, but this didn't happen. The interim executive appointed a four-member standing Committee on Civic Work. Mrs. Newhall (convenor), Mrs. C.A. Stuart (acting convenor), Mrs. Cuddy and Mrs. Clark were to "look into" the work to be done by the civic committee. The group also had the authority to add to their membership when necessary. Although not explicitly stated, the real purpose must have been to set up the proposed civic committee, which it did.

23. "Sixteen Women Bar Reporters Of Local Newspapers," *Morning Albertan*, November 26, 1912.

24. "The Women Electors," *Morning Albertan*, December 7, 1912, p. 3.

25. These questions, condensed, formed the six-point "Women's Platform," which was published the following day by the *Morning Albertan* in the form of a notice at the beginning of an information section prepared for the instruction of women voters.

26. An editorial item in the *Albertan* of September 28, 1967, was titled "Wanted: Another 'Tappy'" and called for another alderman like him who would personally check out the calibre of city work to see that citizens received full value for tax dollars spent.

27. "Reform Laws Projected In Calgary," *Calgary News-Telegram*, December 13, 1912, p. 4.

28. "Women and the Municipal Franchise," *Morning Albertan*, January 4, 1913, p. 6.

Chapter 4

1. "Miss Boulton of Toronto Speaks To Calgary I.O.D.E.," *Calgary Daily Herald*, June 2, 1913, p. 20.
2. "Clubs and Societies," *Calgary Daily Herald*, March 28, 1912, p. 16.
3. "Almost 100 Members Of New American Club," *Morning Albertan*, April 5, 1912, p. 4.
4. "No Militant Methods Necessary For Vote In Canada," *Morning Albertan*, February 28, 1913, p. 44 (Anniversary Number).
5. *Calgary Daily Herald*, December 18, 1886, p. 3. Telegraphic.
6. "A.W.C. in Sympathy With Local Council," *Calgary Daily Herald*, November 8, 1912, p. 12.
7. "Calgary Women's Press Club," *The Western Standard*, June 12, 1913. Opportunity Number, n.p.
8. "Y.W.C.A. Shames Y.M.C.A. In Their Yearly Report," *Morning Albertan*, May 13, 1913, p. 4.
9. "Menace Of Picture Shows To Be Discussed By Calgary Mothers," *Morning Albertan*, November 20, 1912, p. 4.
10. "Business Girls' Club Is Organized In City," *Calgary News-Telegram*, December 16, 1912, p. 14.
11. "Women's Council To Present Petition To Premier," *Morning Albertan*, March 31, 1913, p. 4.
12. "Business Women Will Ask For Bylaw From Calgary City Council To Reform Conditions," *Morning Albertan*, June 21, 1913, p. 1.
13. This estimate is derived from a listing of Sunday Services in Calgary which appeared in the *Calgary News-Telegram* on November 2, 1912, p. 27.
14. "Just Among Ourselves," *Calgary Standard*, January 25, 1913, p. 3.
15. "Council Of Women Would Have Calgary In Cent Belt," *Morning Albertan*, January 27, 1913, p. 1.
16. In the interim, at least two of the smaller affiliates increased their delegate allocation to four, indicating prompt conformity to the NCWC ruling. The Naomi Mothers' Society appointed three more delegates to the Local Council at its February 19th meeting, and the Calgary Businesswomen's Club did the same at its March 11th meeting.
17. "Discuss Reforms In Local Council," *Calgary News-Telegram*, January 28, 1913, p. 14.

18. "Was Mrs. Harold Riley Double-Crossed By Canadian Club?" *Morning Albertan*, January 31, 1913, p. 4.

19. Mrs. Riley seems to have left the club executive at this juncture. She is not named as a Local Council delegate at the May eighth meeting, nor is she listed on the Canadian Club executive for 1914. Her name is not mentioned in the well-publicized debates over widening the membership – and Mrs. Riley was a debater. Her charges against Mrs. Stuart must have had repercussions elsewhere, since the two women were executive members of other organizations.

20. "Calgary Ladies Institute A Very Strong Chapter," *Morning Albertan*, October 21, 1909, p. 1.

21. McGregor, *Calgary Club Woman's Blue Book*, 1915, p. 16.

22. *Ibid.*, p. 52.

23. The second of its kind held in Canada, it was led by a newcomer, the wife of the manager of the Northern Crown Bank, Mrs. Baldwin Hutton, who had initiated the "Made in London" show two years earlier while living in Ontario. Calgary's show, from April 23-26, 1913, realized approximately $1500, at least $300 of which was distributed to other charitable organizations. It received the wholehearted support of the Calgary Industrial Bureau.

24. "Startling Speech Is Made In Council By Alderman Frost," *Morning Albertan*, January 14, 1913, p. 1.

25. "L.C.W. To Send Bill To The Legislature for Detention Home," *Calgary Daily Herald*, March 8, 1913, p. 18.

26. "Girls' Detention Home Is Discussed By The Council Of Women," *Morning Albertan*, March 8, 1913, p. 4.

27. "Women Interview Premier," *Calgary Daily Herald*, April 5, 1913, p. 18.

28. "Old Proposals Renewed," *Morning Albertan*, May 15, 1913, p. 4.

29. The issue was resolved by the Club in June in reaction to a tactless intrusion into IODE policy by Miss Doulton, President of the Woman's Canadian Club in Toronto. In an address to Calgary IODE members entitled "Daughters Of The Empire Must Go After Lowly," she urged the IODE to reach "'the men and women on the street – the lower classes' and make of them good citizens," but she exempted her own Canadian Club, whose members should be "None but naturalized Canadians." A reporter in the *Morning Albertan* of May 31, 1913 (p. 5) noted that the exclusion of foreigners from membership opened ". . . an old and still rankling sore among all nationalities in Calgary" and predicted that the matter would have repercussions in the next Canadian Club meeting. It did.

30. "Woman's Canadian Club Extends Welcome To Foreign-Born Citizens," *Morning Albertan*, June 27, 1913, p. 4.

31. Mrs. A.M. Scott was a leading member in the other patriotic societies, serving as first vice-regent of the Colonel Macleod Chapter of the IODE in 1911. An executive member of the Alberta Woman's Association from the time of its formation in October of 1911, she was elected its second vice-president in May of 1913.

32. "Mrs. R.R. Jamieson, Police Magistrate," *Woman's Century*, April 1917, p. 8.

33. A social item in the *Calgary Daily Herald* of March 1, 1912, records Mrs. Riley's hosting of "a little tea" for Mrs. Murphy at the King George Hotel. Mrs. C.A.

Stuart, president of the Woman's Canadian Club, Mrs. Cruikshank, Mrs. Spence, Mrs. McDonald and Mrs. Wolley-Dodd completed the party.

Chapter 5

1. "Agenda From LCW Makes Trouble In Club," *Calgary Daily Herald,* April 13, 1914, p. 12. The actual wording of the contentious clause was preserved in the 1914 minute book of the Women's Canadian Club, now held in the Glenbow Archives. It reads: "That nothin short of castration be sufficient for such moral perverts and that, if such punishment is not allowed by law we request the National Council of Women to petition the federal government to have the same enacted."
2. "Social Problems Shock Women," *Calgary News-Telegram,* April 14, 1914, p. 13.
3. *Ibid.*
4. "Watch For the Agenda," *Calgary Eye Opener,* April 25, 1914, p. 1.
5. "Agenda From Women's Council Passed By Overwhelming Majority Yesterday." *Morning Albertan,* May 16, 1914, p. 4.
6. *Eye Opener,* May 23, 1914, p. 1.
7. "Note and Comment," *Calgary Herald,* December 14, 1920, p. 12.
8. "Today's Comment," *Albertan,* December 15, 1920, p. 4.
9. "A Defense Of The Curfew Bell," *Calgary Daily Herald,* July 25, 1921, p. 8.
10. "Legal worries sideline curfew bylaw proposal," *Calgary Herald,* May 4, 1994, p. B4.
11. "No Coppers For H.B. Co. Woman's Council Frame Petition," *Morning Albertan,* January 30, 1913, p. 4.
12. "L.C. of Women Will Frame Petition," *Calgary Daily Herald,* January 30, 1913, p. 16.
13. "Retail Grocer Explains Reliable Business Methods In That Line To Consumers," *Morning Albertan,* November 29, 1913, p. 11.
14. "Council of Women Discuss Franchise Restriction," *Morning Albertan,* July 31, 1913, p. 4.
15. "Knox W.M.S. Donate $125 to Robertson College," *Morning Albertan,* September 25, 1913, p. 4.
16. "Stricter Enforcement of Regulations Necessary Among Ruthenians," *Morning Albertan,* December 18, 1913, p. 4.
17. The 1925 *Yearbook* of the Local Council of Women contains a special summary of petitions asked for since 1912. There is no reference to the Ruthenian girls' school request.
18. Ruthenian men were disenfranchised in 1917 during World War I. The removal of this citizenship right seemed rough justice to Alberta's many loyal Ruthenians whose sons were fighting for Canada, but they suffered much less than those suspected of disloyalty. Along with other immigrants from eastern Europe, many were imprisoned in the Rockies west of Calgary in work camps, where they endured harsh treatment, deprivation and exploitation. Other eastern Europeans not sent to the camps were required to carry identification papers and report to police. It was the "Canadian way" in wartime. See "The Prisoners of Castle Mountain, Dark Times," *Calgary Daily Herald,* May 22, 1994, p. A4.

19. "What The Women Of Alberta Are Doing And Saying," Nellie McClung, *Woman's Century*, December, 1917, p. 17.
20. "Women Heckle Men Who Would Serve Calgary In The High Places," *Morning Albertan*, December 6, 1913, p. 1.
21. The petition now asked "that the franchise be extended to women on the same basis as to men. We feel the time has come when we must have power to back our requests to the legislature." See "Equal Suffrage Urged," *Western Standard*, January 25, 1914, p. 4.
22. "Council Of Women Out For Franchise: Past Year Saw Important Work Done," *Morning Albertan*, January 24, 1914, p. 9.
23. *Ibid.*
24. Because the Daughters of the Empire and both the Canadian and American Women's Clubs forbade political discussion of any sort, they could not endorse the petition; however, their members could sign if they belonged to other affiliates.
25. Calgary's delegation comprised Mrs. Jamieson and Mrs. Kerby (from the Local Council), Mrs. Langford of the WCTU, and Mr. Calhoun and Mr. Price of the Trades and Labour Council.
26. "Suffrage Cannot Come Before Present Edmonton Session," *News-Telegram*, October 14, 1914, p. 8.
27. "Premier Encourages Equal Suffrage Delegates," *Morning Albertan*, October 12, 1914, p. 4.
28. "Woman Suffrage Is Ever With Us," *Western Standard*, March 6, 1915, p. 4.
29. "Women To Canvass City For Prohibition Signatures," *Morning Albertan*, June 22, 1915, p. 4.
30. "Out of 12,000 Votes 7,565 Are Polled For The Prohibition Act," *Calgary News-Telegram*, July 22, 1915, p. 3.
31. "Alberta First Province To Give Full Franchise Rights To Its Women," *Calgary Daily Herald*, July 16, 1921, p. 13.
32. *Ibid.*
33. "Alberta Women Hear Reading Of The Woman's Suffrage Bill," *Calgary News-Telegram*, March 2, 1916, p. 3.
34. "Lively Session Of Alberta Legislature Ends In Second Reading of Franchise Bill," *Calgary News-Telegram*, March 2, 1916, p. 1.
35. "Provincial Committee On Laws For Women Formed," *Calgary Daily Herald*, March 16, 1916. p. 4.
36. McCormack, John, "A Week At The Capital," *Calgary News-Telegram*, March 9, 1916, p. 4.
37. "Dominion Franchise Not For Women Voter Under The Federal Act," *Calgary Daily Herald*, March 1, 1917, p. 1.
38. "Mr. Bennett Favors Federal Franchise for Canadian Women," *Calgary Daily Herald*, April 26, 1917, p. 11.
39. That supportive April 13th meeting promptly crafted and passed an "alien enemy birth" resolution. It read, "... recognizing the detriment to the country of a large vote of 'alien enemy birth,' the franchise be withheld from all men coming in that class for the duration of the war and for five years afterwards, and that in granting the franchise to women, the same restrictions apply to them as to the men." *Ibid.*

40. Dr. Naomi Griffiths has noted that the 1912 first NCW platform "centered upon control of prostitution and the rights of women as parents." (*The Splendid Vision*, p. 114)
41. "Notes on the Annual Meeting," *Woman's Century*, July-August, 1920, p. 12.

Chapter 6

1. "Alberta," *Woman's Century*, November, 1919, p. 49.
2. "28th Meeting Of The National Council," *Woman's Century*, June & July, 1921, p. 11.
3. Formed in June of 1916 by "50 bright young servant girls," the purpose of the Housekeepers' Association was to be both a "self-improvement society" and a trades union. These "housekeepers," as they wished to be called, were to have training in domestic science, to conduct themselves properly and perform their duties professionally. In turn, employers were to abide by fixed working hours and respect the housekeepers' right to proper board and lodging. "An Experiment in Calgary," *Woman's Century*, November 1916, p. 16-17.
4. "Calgary Greets Canada's Woman's Parliament," *Calgary Daily Herald*, June 11, 1921, p. 9.
5. "Parents Should Know Pictures Children See," *Calgary Daily Herald*, May 21, 1921, p. 10.
6. "Favorable Reports Of Women's Work In All Parts Of Canada Are Presented At The National Council Convention," *Morning Albertan*, June 14, 1921, p. 2.
7. "Women, Through the Vote, Can Enforce Many of Vital Principles, Says Speaker," *Calgary Daily Herald*, June 16, 1921, p. 6.
8. The premier was likely alluding to a 1920 request by the Alberta Provincial Council of Women asking for a detention home for immoral women. He told the deputation, which also included representatives of the provincial WCTU and Women's Institutes, that enabling legislation could only be passed by the Dominion government because crime was a federal matter.
9. In the husbanding of the civic reception account, the Local Council acquired memorabilia in the form of dishes and cutlery. An explanation of the account owing for the Lougheed reception included a charge for chipped dishes. Mrs. Nelson was asked to inquire if the chipped dishes could not be retained as the property of the Local Council. The Council already had purchased spoons for the reception at a cost of $9. Total convention expenses amounted to around $1000. When all bills were paid and special allocations made, $60 remained.
10. "Mrs. McClung's Inspiring Words To National Council Delegates," *Morning Albertan*, June 11, 1921, p. 7.
11. The prairie activist and prohibitionist preferred the WCTU. One source, Veronica Strong Boag's *The Parliament of Women*, (p. 158), quotes Nellie McClung's assessment of the NCW: ". . . it is unwieldy, vague and diffuse, and cannot be brought to bear on any issue."
12. "Inspiring Talks Before National Women's Council," *Herald*, June 15, 1921, p. 14.
13. Dr. Gullen's reference to women's small brain size was reported differently in the *Albertan* (page 12, June 16) as: "Of late years the appalling discovery

has been made that the size of the brain had nothing to do with the matter; . . ."

14. Mrs. Clement, who served on the nine-member Board of Welfare responsible for supervising all of Manitoba's welfare institutions, reported that the Board had now asked for a Department of Public Welfare to be headed by a cabinet minister.
15. The Provincial Council of Women's Hearst embargo request certainly fell in line with the Ontario Legislature's earlier resolution asking the Canadian government to ban all Hearst publications, including newspapers, magazines and wire services. However, the Ontario Legislature was likely more influenced by the powerful Canadian National Newspaper and Periodicals' Association lobby, which wanted to stop readership revenue flowing across the border.
16. "Women In Convention Discuss Important National Matters," *Morning Albertan*, June 15, 1921, p. 7.
17. "28th Meeting Of The National Council," *Woman's Century*, June & July, 1921, p. 12.
18. *Ibid.*
19. *Ibid.*, p. 11.
20. "Education In Canada Is Under Discussion At Women's Convention," *Morning Albertan*, June 16, 1921, p. 7.
21. Although the granting of divorce fell within the jurisdiction of most provinces, this was not the case in Canada's two most-populated provinces, Ontario and Quebec.
22. "Alberta. Shall We Abolish The Senate?" Constance Lynd, *Woman's Century*, December, 1919, p. 55.
23. "Local Labour League Objects to Women Entering Politics," *Calgary Daily Herald*, January 21, 1921, p. 18.
24. *Woman's Century*, April, 1921, p. 27.
25. "Women And The Senate," *Morning Albertan*, June 17, 1921, p. 4.
26. "28th Meeting Of The National Council," *Woman's Century*, June & July, 1921, p. 12.
27. "Will Alberta Woman Be First To Enter As Member Of The Canadian Senate?" *Morning Albertan*, November 10, 1920, p. 5.
28. "Council Looked To In Fight For Needy Mothers," *Calgary Daily Herald*, June 17, 1921, p. 28.
29. *Ibid.*
30. "Women's Right In The Senate Being Tested," *Herald*, March 14, 1928, p. 1.
31. Charles Bishop, of the *Herald*'s Ottawa bureau wrote an excellent background summary of the person's case under the caption "Senate List Expands For Government Choice." It appeared on the front page of the *Calgary Daily Herald* on October 18, 1929.
32. "Mrs. Murphy Says Decision Helps National Unity," *Calgary Daily Herald*, October 18, 1929, p. 1.
33. "First Woman Senator Chosen," *Albertan*, February 17, 1930, p. 1.
34. According to an article in *The Calgary Herald* of June 24, 1994, entitled "Campaign Urges More Women In Senate," Margaret Ritchie, President of the Human Rights Institute, was considering lodging a complaint with the

United Nations in order to ensure that the number of women appointed to the Senate by the prime minister will become more equitable. That agency has a clause in its convention on the Political Rights of Women which reads as follows: "Women shall be entitled to hold public office and to exercise all public functions, established by national law, on equal terms with men, without any discrimination." As commendable as the move seems, eons could pass ere equality theories become practice.

Chapter 7

1. "National Council Of Women Needs New Focus," *The Calgary Herald*, May 20, 1978, p. A7.
2. "Women's Group Given New Approach," *The Calgary Herald*, May 18, 1978.
3. "National Council Of Women Needs New Focus," *The Calgary Herald*, May 20, 1978, p. 7.
4. Calgary's Council of Women had weathered a few storms during the watershed years, which began as early as the 1971 Annual Meeting. Although contentious debate seemed to be the order of that day, one purpose of the meeting was to process resolutions and amendments. When votes were cast, the support was there. *Calgary Herald* reporter Doris Milke noted "heated opposition" to a majority of the nine resolutions, which dealt with issues as diverse as native funding for Friendship Centres, continuing the ban on commercial supersonic flights over Canadian territory, the preservation of a green belt around Calgary, equal employment and training opportunities for women, and prohibition of sex and marital status discrimination in employment and training. On the advice of Mary Guichon, who drew upon her background with the Children's Aid Society, and Captain Marguerite Lloyd of the Salvation Army Children's Village, the battered child resolution passed only after the removal of the clause making it an offense to maliciously or falsely report child mistreatment. Milke noted another tension: the "two hour heated debate" between "the old guard and the young activists" over constitutional changes "intended to make the council, which purports to a voice for all women's organizations in the community, a viable force for social action groups. . . ." Most were approved. ("Council Of Women Shows Many Concerns," *The Calgary Herald*, April 29, 1971, p. 61).
5. "In the period under consideration [1970-80], membership in the National Council of Women of Canada fell; it was accorded less publicity by the media; and the federal government gradually paid it less attention. At the same time the National Action Committee developed and flourished, gained important recognition as a powerful voice for women's views, was accorded a growing importance by bureaucrats and politicians at both the federal and provincial levels, and obtained significant federal funding. . . ." (*The Splendid Vision*, p. 325).
6. *The Splendid Vision* includes a particularly insightful assessment of the rise of the NAC and its impact on the National Council.
7. Mrs. Hinkley knew that the National Council's annual meeting with the federal cabinet was already in jeopardy. Careful subsequent fence-mending on her part saved National's privilege for a while, but only until 1987.
8. The banquet grant had been confirmed very much at the last minute, and one of my follow-up reports to NCW, dated September 6, 1978, contains this bit

of memorabilia: "Our Alberta Government has approved our Banquet grant allowing $10 for every delegate and spouse plus the unforgettable MLA, John Kushner. I am not going to query his being placed in the allocation category of a delegate or spouse. This grant caused me a great deal of work. I had to totally re-submit the application on a new form as the Government changed the guidelines in effect in the middle of our conference. The cheque still has not arrived. . . ." (GAI-LCW files).

9. A Calgary politician of heroic aspiration, to this very day his political record goes unchallenged. Before Kushner's career was over, this Calgary Public School Board locksmith's devoted voters had anointed him for all three levels of government, and at one period he served the citizenry simultaneously in two capacities, as an alderman and as a public school trustee.

Chapter 8

1. "Male Claims Sex A Factor," *Calgary Herald,* October 26, 1992, p. B2.
2. Calgary Charter. Ordinance 33 of 1893 of the North-West Territories. "The persons qualified to be elected Mayor or Alderman of the City of Calgary, are such persons as reside or have their chief place of business within the City, and are natural born or naturalized British subjects, males of the full age of twenty-one years, and who are not disqualified under this ordinance, and own at the time of their election Real Estate rated in their own names on the last revised assessment roll of the City, to at least the value of one thousand dollars [or personal real estate rated in their own names on the last revised assessment roll of the city to at least the value of two thousand dollars] over and above the amount of all encumbrances thereon." No. 33, 1893. *An Ordinance to Incorporate the City of Calgary* [assented to Sept., 1893].
3. "No Demand For Ministers In Council, Says Ross; Garden Would Like Some Women Aldermen," *Morning Albertan,* May 15, 1913, p. 1.
4. "Abolishment of Ward System And Votes For Women Recommended," *News-Telegram,* May 15, 1913, p. 11.
5. *Op. Cit.*
6. "Legislative Committee Would Extend Franchise To Women Tenants And To Men Paying Poll Tax," *Morning Albertan,* May 15, 1913, p. 1.
7. "A Civic Authority On Kitchens," *Calgary News-Telegram,* May 16, 1913, p. 4.
8. Indeed, the number of women voters could make a difference, since that spring the municipal franchise was also extended to include a woman assessed as a tenant of her husband's property. According to one estimate, 6000 women would now be eligible to vote. The actual number was 4531.
9. The LCW also requested a poll tax for self-supporting women because this levy would enable them to vote on all matters except money bylaws. It was tabled, partly because the City Council realized its existing poll tax on males was not collected in a satisfactory manner. (City of Calgary Archives, Clerk's papers)
10. "Ladies Seek Election On The School Board," *Calgary News-Telegram,* June 20, 1913, p. 4.
11. "Council Of Women To Present Candidate," *The Morning Albertan,* November 13, 1913, p. 4.
12. "Eye Openers," *Calgary Eye Opener,* December 6, 1913, p. 2.

13. "Candidate, Miss A. Foote, Issues A Manifesto," *Calgary News-Telegram,* December 8, 1913, p. 15.
14. "A Notable Success For A Calgary Woman," *Calgary News-Telegram,* December 9, 1913, p. 4.
15. "Miss Foote Attributes Her Success To Efforts Of Women On Her Behalf," *Calgary Daily Herald,* December 9, 1913, p. 1.
16. "Heading the Poll," *Calgary Daily Herald,* December 10, 1913, p. 6.
17. "Miss Foote Holds Out For Economy," *Calgary News-Telegram,* January 8, 1914, p. 4.
18. "Some Reasons Why We Should Vote For Miss Foote," *Morning Albertan,* December 6, 1913, p. 4.
19. "Estimates Are Passed At Lively Meeting Of The School Board," *Calgary Daily Herald,* February 4, 1914, p. 11.
20. "The Appointment Of A School Board Chairman," *Calgary News-Telegram,* February 4, 1914, p. 4.
21. A pre-determined intent to pass school medical inspection over to the city may explain why the estimates for medical health officers and school nurses were missing from the school budget estimates. Meanwhile, the dismissal of the two health doctors was held in abeyance.
22. "Eye Openers," *Calgary Eye Opener,* November 21, 1914, p. 3.
23. *Ibid.*
24. The announcement of Kerby's candidacy received general approbation. Principal of Mount Royal College for four years and pastor of Central Methodist Church for eight years before that, he had travelled and studied education systems in Canada and the United States. The Reverend Dr. Kerby stood second in the School Board polls, and in January of 1916, he was elected Chairman. He retired from the Board in 1917, at the same time as Annie Foote.
25. The medical inspection service was essentially the one proposed by Trustee Macdonald. The expenditures included $4000 to equip a room as a dental clinic; $1000 to equip another for eye, ear, nose and throat inspections; $2000 per annum to hire a full-time doctor to inspect all public school pupils and $500 for a part-time consulting physician; and $3750 to pay five full-time nurses $75 monthly for the ten-month school term. Specialists were expected to donate part of their service and needy children would not be charged.
26. Some citizens concurred, and in February of 1915, Local Council's executive was approached with a request to oppose it. At first the executive considered calling a public meeting, until they realized that such action implied a lack of confidence in a duly elected Board. A supportive Mrs. Marion Carson identified the expenditure as being the start on "a much needed free dispensary" and urged "... if ten thousand dollars will mean free nurses, free dental and free medical inspection, the council should endorse the action instead of questioning it." ("Women of City Endorse Medical Inspection," *Morning Albertan,* February 20, 1915, p. 4.) The executive passed a resolution endorsing the School Board's decision – unanimously.
27. "Eye Openers," *Calgary Eye Opener,* December 11, 1915, p. 1.
28. "The Importance Of Women's Municipal Vote Is Explained," *Calgary News-Telegram,* December 6, 1915, p. 6.
29. "School Board's Final Meeting For The Year 1917," *Morning Albertan,* December 12, 1917, p. 8.

30. "Reverend Council Candidate," *Calgary News-Telegram*, November 29, 1916, p. 4.

Chapter 9

1. "Mrs. Gale, President Women Ratepayers Association," *Calgary Daily Herald*, April 13, 1917, p. 10.
2. A history of this High School For Girls describes it as one of the most successful educational establishments in the Midland Counties. In November of 1880 a group of middle-class men started a limited company selling shares at five pounds each – the amount which would allow one girl to attend. It began with 39 pupils and soon attained a high reputation. Admissions were by nominations of shareholders, and examinations were conducted by the College of Preceptors and the Cambridge Local Examination Board. When Annie Rolinson attended, there were probably about 100 pupils. (Ref. Dudley Libraries, Archives and Local History Service, Coseley, Dudley.)
3. Women were admitted to the lectures of the University in the year 1880, to its examinations in 1884, and to degrees in 1920.
4. An excerpt from Henry Gale's May 1971 letter to the Glenbow states that in 1913 the Gales built a four room bungalow and had to undertake a $1600, three-year mortgage at 8 percent. He recalls, "My mother cried bitterly over being forced, by miscalculation of the costs of the house, to borrow this sum and needless to say, nothing else was bought except essential necessities until this was paid off in 1916."
5. Glenbow Archives, Annie Gale Typescript, p. 1. Referred to hereafter as *GAI-AG*.
6. The Consumers' League's campaign for a revitalized municipal market owed its origin to the Home Economics Committee of the Calgary Local Council of Women, at a time before Annie Gale was directly involved as a committee member.
7. "Women Heckle Men Who Would Serve Calgary In The High Places," *Morning Albertan*, December 6, 1913, p. 1.
8. Gale, Mrs. W.J., "Canada's First Woman Alderman," *Maclean's*, September 1919, p. 95.
9. *Ibid.*
10. Interest in cultivating the lots waned after the war. By the summer of 1921, many abandoned former garden plots posed a serious weed threat. Civic officials undertook cleanup measures and added the cost to the negligent owner's taxes. ("Abandoned Vacant Lots Are A Problem," *Morning Albertan*, July 16, 1921, p. 3.)
11. The success of two rather ingenious and related projects was attributed to Board member Annie Gale. In September of 1914, a flower auction with R.B. Bennett as auctioneer and Annie as clerk raised over $700 for the Patriotic Fund. In 1917, when Calgary had more than 6000 lots in potatoes alone, Annie, then the Club's honorary president, arranged a potato luncheon which showcased this locally grown quality product.
12. "Calgary Women Don't Want To Enter The Political Field Yet," *Calgary Herald*, May 16, 1917, p. 8.
13. "Ratepayers' Ass'n Nominates Adshead For The Mayoralty," *Calgary News-Telegram*, October 31, 1917, p. 10.

14. "Costello is Still Silent Anent The Mayoralty Race," *Calgary News-Telegram*, November 12, 1917, p. 8.
15. "Local Council to Send Circular To All Women Voters," *Calgary Daily Herald*, November 27, 1917, p. 12.
16. "L.C. Would Retain Present Municipal Governing Bodies," *Calgary News-Telegram*, October 26, 1917, p. 8.
17. "Straight Fight for Principal Civic Offices," *Calgary Daily Herald*, December 3, 1917, p. 5.
18. "Eye-Openers," *Calgary Eye Opener*, December 8, 1917, p. 3.
19. "Who's Who On Municipal Slate," *Calgary News-Telegram*, December 8, 1917, p. 4.
20. *Maclean's*, September 1919, p. 94.
21. "Graves Has Had No Free Hand To Run Municipal Market," *Calgary Daily Herald*, December 6, 1917, p. 7.
22. Archival records of City Council business do not contain a record of William Gale's departure. When she was on Council there was a newspaper reference to Alderwoman Gale as being her employee husband's boss. Furthermore, the privately published history *Alderman Annie Gale*, by Lishman, tells of his forced resignation from the city engineering department in 1923.
23. "Civic Office Candidates Discuss Municipal Issues," *Calgary News-Telegram*, December 6, 1917, p. 3.
24. That year Calgary inaugurated a complex preferential ballot with the result being that many ballots were spoiled. Instead of using the former "X" mark, voters had to place a "1" in the square in front of the preferred candidate's name. After that, voting was strictly optional. Second-, third-, fourth-, etc., choice candidates were supported by the corresponding numbers "2," "3," "4" placed in the appropriate square. In the 1917 election, a candidate had to receive over 520 first choice votes to be declared elected on the first count. Annie Gale got 334.
25. On November 8th, soon after nominating Annie Gale, the Women Ratepayers' Association was invited to amalgamate with the South Calgary Men's Association. They declined to merge when the men's general membership would not grant approval for women to serve on the new executive. ("Women Ratepayers Will Remain A Separate Assn.," *Morning Albertan*, November 9, 1917, p. 4.)
26. Editorial, *Woman's Century*, March 1918, p. 10.
27. "Women In Public Life," *Morning Albertan*, November 29, 1919, p. 6.
28. "Eye Openers," *Calgary Eye Opener*, September 13, 1919, p. 4.
29. "Citizens Would Stir Up Interest In City Contest," *Calgary Daily Herald*, December 2, 1919, p. 11.
30. "Women Alleged To Have Formed A Civic Cabal," *Calgary Daily Herald*, December 4, 1919, p. 1.
31. "Women Listen To Civic Candidates Give Platforms," *Calgary Daily Herald*, December 9, 1919, p. 16.
32. "Ladies Withdraw Names From List," *Morning Albertan*, December 4, 1919, p. 6.
33. "Women's Labor Council Plans To Investigate Children's Nourishment," *Morning Albertan*, November 21, 1919, p. 6.

34. "Money Rights Against The Human Rights," *Morning Albertan*, December 8, 1919, p. 5.
35. By 1921 Mrs. Mary Ellen Smith's B.C. legislative credits included the Deserted Wives' Maintenance Act, the Equal Guardianship of children, and the House Minimum Wage Bill. She was now Minister without Portfolio, having in January declined the speakership of the B.C. Legislature because accepting that office would exclude her from assembly debates and, thus, the advocacy of women's concerns.
36. "Stewart Gov't. Has Given The Province Very Best Of Laws," *Morning Albertan*, July 16, 1921, p. 6.
37. *Ibid.*
38. "Mrs. Gale Claims She Will Go Over The Top July 18," *Calgary Daily Herald*, July 15, 1921, p. 18.
39. "Mrs. Gale For Prohibition And More City Power," *Morning Albertan*, July 9, 1921, p. 6.
40. "Mrs. Gale Did Not Claim Any Endorsation," *Morning Albertan*, July 12, 1921, p. 6.
41. "Direct Appeal To Women Voters in Calgary Riding," *Morning Albertan*, July 11, 1921, p. 4.
42. "The Provincial Campaign," *Western Farmer* and *Weekly Albertan*, July 13, 1921, p. 6.
43. "Women Express Their Opinions On The Election," *Morning Albertan*, July 19, 1921, p. 5.
44. "Women Accept Their Defeat In Good Spirit," *Calgary Daily Herald*, July 19, 1921, p. 5.
45. *Op cit.*
46. "Ill-Advised Action," *Calgary Daily Herald*, December 13, 1921, p. 11.
47. "Civic Candidates Make Last Appeal To The Electors," *Calgary Daily Herald*, December 14, 1921, p. 90.
48. Named for the alderman who proposed a direct tax on single and married men, based upon income.
49. "Group Government," *Morning Albertan*, December 14, 1921, p. 4.
50. "Much the Largest Municipal Vote Ever Polled in Calgary; How the Votes Were Shifted for Aldermen," *Morning Albertan*, December 16, 1921, p. 12.
51. This reference cannot be confirmed in the 1923 city of Calgary records, but Chapman was the city engineer at that time.
52. Lishman, p. 50.
53. LCW Minutes, 1919 - 1924, pp. 117-118.
54. "The Women's Position," *Calgary Daily Herald*, December 10, 1923, p. 8.
55. "Candidates in Farewell Speeches in Municipal Election Campaign," *Morning Albertan*, December 12, 1923, p. 3.
56. "4,240 Women Cast Civic Votes on Wednesday," *Calgary Daily Herald*, December 14, 1923, p. 17.
57. "Independents Needed," *Albertan*, December 4, 1923, p. 4.
58. "The Women's Position," *Calgary Daily Herald*, December 10, 1923, p. 8.
59. When Mrs. McKillop spoke to a September 1992 LCW general meeting in defense of the present Board structure, Mrs. Jamieson, Mrs. Kerby and Mrs. Stavert, among others, agreed that the present management was efficient and

economic. To many, the McKillops were above reproach. Before the meeting closed, a motion protesting any change in the Public Welfare board carried.
60. "Alderman Gale and Church Taxation," *Calgary Daily Herald*, Nov. 10, 1919, p. 14.
61. "Club Women Bid Farewell to Mrs. A. Gale," *Albertan*, May 20, 1925, p. 6.

Chapter 10

1. In 1908 the federal government passed the Juvenile Offenders Act, which permitted the establishment of juvenile courts when so desired by a provincial government. The object of these courts was,"... to exclude that publicity which the common courts afforded to delinquents, and to avoid as far as possible branding young persons of each sex with the ignominy of conviction. Prevention was intended to characterize the administration of this court, and protection from contact with criminals both in the lock-up and the jail was to predominate." (*News-Telegram*, February 2, 1914). It was hoped that by 1913 the Dominion Delinquents Act would come into force in Alberta, because this legislation would allow courts to fine and imprison adults who contributed to the delinquency of a child.
2. "The Children's Aid Has Many Cases," *Morning Albertan*, December 17, 1913, p. 4.
3. A 1910 amendment to the Children's Protection Act required centres with a population of 10 000 or more to provide and staff these shelters.
4. "The Children's Aid Has Many Cases," *Morning Albertan*, December 17, 1913, p. 4.
5. *Ibid.*
6. "Woman Magistrate At Juvenile Court," *Morning Albertan*, January 31, 1914, p. 9.
7. "A Lady Magistrate Appointed For Calgary," *News-Telegram*, February 2, 1914, p. 4.
8. "A Judge," *Everywoman's World*, June 1914, p. 6.
9. "Work of Calgary Women Well Known," reprinted from *Women's Century* in *News-Telegram*, April 20, 1914, p. 15.
10. "Was This A Miscarriage Of Justice?," *News-Telegram*, November 14, 1913, p. 4.
11. "Eye-Openers," *Calgary Eye Opener*, November 22, 1913, p. 1.
12. *Ibid.*
13. *Ibid.*
14. "Petition For Franchise As Protection For Girls." *Morning Albertan*, November 29, 1913, p. 4.
15. "Swat All The Moral Lepers, Says Head Of Children's Aid," *Morning Albertan*, May 15, 1914, p. 7.
16. *Calgary Eye Opener*, April 25, 1914, p. 3.
17. "Women Endorse Appointment of Mrs. Jamieson," *News-Telegram*, May 8, 1914, p. 16.
18. *Ibid.*
19. "Deplores There Is No Woman Judge For Juvenile Court," *Morning Albertan*, December 11, 1914, p. 5.
20. O.C. 1444/16, Salary was $100 per month.

21. "Appointment To Juvenile Court Made During Week," *Western Standard*, January 16, 1915, p. 1.
22. "Children's Aid is Great Asset," *News-Telegram*, December 17, 1915, p. 10.
23. "1304 Dependent Children Cared For In Alberta," *Calgary Daily Herald*, June 13, 1919, p. 6. The large number of neglected children (1304) stemmed from ". . . the siege of epidemic influenze that swept over the province during the early fall months of last year, and the sudden death of one or both parents, leaving many children absolutely helpless. In a great many instances near relatives were discovered who were easily persuaded to take charge of these children. In many cases where no relatives were to be found, they were treated as other neglected or dependent children and placed in foster homes. During the year, 182 were adopted and 267 placed in private homes under temporary agreements."
24. Superintendent Chadwick did not live to hear his innovation vindicated. He died in the spring of 1915, shortly after Mrs. Jamieson and Mrs. Langford were officially appointed.
25. "Alberta Women We Should Know," *Calgary Daily Herald*, October 1, 1932, p. 27.
26. "Calgary Has First Woman Magistrate In The World In Mrs. Alice Jamieson," *Calgary Daily Herald*, March 13, 1920, p. 16.
27. *Ibid.*
28. "Counsel Disputes Right Of Woman Magistrate To Sit," *Calgary Daily Herald*, May 18, 1917, p. 9.
29. "Calgary Has First Woman Magistrate In The World in Mrs. Alice Jamieson," *Calgary Daily Herald*, March 13, 1920, p. 16.
30. *Ibid.*
31. "Woman Vagrant Is Sent To Jail For 4 Months," *Calgary News-Telegram*, December 10, 1917, p. 3.
32. Although strong and able, Bertha refused to work when sent to jobs by the Associated Charities. When charged, she was living in a condemned vacant house, "and was cooking a goose on this stove that she had picked out of a garbage box, which was almost too awful to take to the incinerator."
33. "Position Of Women Magistrates On Bench Is Secure," *Calgary Albertan*, December 1, 1924, p. 7.
34. "Mrs. Jamieson Gives Up Presidency of Local Council," *Morning Albertan*, January 16, 1917, p. 4.

Chapter 11

1. *News-Telegram*, editorial, "The Introduction Of Women As Police Officers," March 14, 1913, p. 4.
2. "Outrages On Little Foreign Girl By First St. West Chinaman; Revelation to Local Council," *Morning Albertan*, July 31, 1913, p. 4.
3. During the second annual conference of NCWC (1895), a Mrs. Parker, recording secretary for the Winnipeg Local Council, reported efforts there to have "a female officer in charge of females" appointed for the police station. A later report indicates no progress. Women police (an idea proposed by the 18th century British prison reformer, John Howard), took almost 20 years to find even limited acceptance in Canada by the 20th century. But the WCTU's movement for appointment of police matrons, which originated in the

United States, did meet with more success in Canada. By 1895 the cities of Toronto, London, and Montreal had police matrons employed at the police stations. (*1895 Yearbook*, p. 313.)

4. "When Women Are On The Police Force," *Morning Albertan*, September 9, 1913, p. 4.

5. "Shall There Be Women Police On Calgary Force? Women Ask For It But Chief Cuddy Is Much Opposed," *Morning Albertan*, October 17, 1913, p. 8.

6. By the fall of 1913, Cuddy's staff numbered 100 men, and morale and efficiency were high. The rank and file wore smart modern uniforms and worked shifts more suited to their needs. The city had four new substations, two of them ranked as the most up-to-date in the Dominion.

7. "Dangerous Dances Will Be Prohibited By Head Of Police," *News-Telegram*, November 8, 1912, p. 11.

8. Early in 1914, the tango attracted special attention when a professional dance duo from Buenos Aires, Mr. and Mrs. A. Roes, came to Calgary to demonstrate the intricacies of the Argentinean and Parisian tangos. Whether it was a bit of press mischief or not is not known, but in the first week of February the *Albertan* informed readers that Chief Cuddy was one of a distinguished three-member civic jury (Alderman Frost and Reverend D.A. McKillop being the other two) selected to preview the tango and judge its effect upon "the moral and spiritual welfare of its citizens." In Bob Edwards' style, the reporter fantasized the outcome of a favorable verdict: ". . . within the course of the next few days, Calgary's babies will be tangoing on their mothers' knees, Calgary's business men will tango on their way down to the office, and Calgary's women will tango themselves into forgetfulness of their household duties – a situation that promises well from a newspaper point of view." ("Chief Cuddy To Pass Upon The Tango," *Morning Albertan*, February 6, 1914, p. 9.)

9. Albert Cuddy resigned four years later, on July 31, 1919, to help organize the newly formed Alberta Provincial Police.

10. "Wanted Position As Policewoman," *Morning Albertan*, December 8, 1913, p. 16.

11. "Eye Openers," *Calgary Eye Opener*, December 6, 1913, p. 1.

12. "Crime Is Now On The Decrease In City Of Calgary," *Calgary Daily Herald*, January 6, 1914, p. 15.

13. Irish-born, Dublin-trained nurse, Mrs. Effie Bagnall, began her duties as a woman probation officer on November 11, 1912, shortly after arriving from Scotland, where she had been matron of a children's home.

14. "Policewoman Not Likely To Be Appointed," *News-Telegram*, April 22, 1914, p. 14.

15. *Ibid.*

16. "Policewomen Are Still Necessary, Say Women," *Morning Albertan*, April 24, 1914, p. 4.

17. "Alderman Frost In Reply To Critics," *Morning Albertan*, April 25, 1914, p. 1.

18. "Council Votes For A 'Lady Detective,'" *Morning Albertan*, April 28, 1914, p. 7.

19. "Woman Will Be Placed On Police Force," *News-Telegram*, April 28, 1914, p. 9.

20. "Members of National Council of Women Score T.A.P. Frost," *Calgary News-Telegram*, April 29, 1914, p. 13.
21. "Will Not Attempt To Retire Alderman To Private Pursuits," *Morning Albertan*, April 30, 1914, p. 5.
22. "Poem By Chief Cuddy," *Herald*, April 29, 1914, p. 6.
23. "Will Not Attempt To Retire Alderman To Private Pursuits," *Morning Albertan*, April 30, 1914, p. 5.
24. *Ibid.*
25. "Alderman Frost In Reply To Critics," *Morning Albertan*, April 25, 1914, p. 8.
26. "Appointment Of A Woman Constable Promises To Be The Cause of Civic Discord," *Calgary Daily Herald*, April 28, 1914, p. 5.
27. *Albertan*, April 30, 1914, p. 7.
28. Surplis, Herb. Ed., "At Your Service, Part Two," *Women Police*, p. 239, Century Calgary, 1975.

Chapter 12

1. "New Market Is Badly Needed," *News-Telegram*, May 8, 1913, p. 14.
2. By the first week of May the Home Economics Committee had three petitions ready for discussion. The first proposed a wholesale market, the second a better location for the underused city market, and the third requested city officials to publish the exact price of wholesale market items, not a range.
3. "Tribute To Late Mrs. G. Newhall," *Calgary Daily Herald*, November 19, 1932, p. 17.
4. "Organization Completed," *News-Telegram*, May 30, 1913, p. 14.
5. "Organization of Consumers' League Attracts Widespread Attention – Is First In Canada," *Morning Albertan*, May 29, 1913, p. 1.
6. "Tregillus Market Plan Meets With Approval," *Morning Albertan*, June 7, 1913, p. 1.
7. "Petition of Consumers' League Is Only Partially Acceded To By Aldermen," *Morning Albertan*, June 24, 1913, p. 8.
8. "Dull Council Meeting Is Enlivened By Discussion Over Market Appointment," *Morning Albertan*, October 14, 1913, p. 1.
9. "Consumers' League Adopts Constitution; Makes Ready To War On The High Cost Of Living," *Morning Albertan*, May 22, 1913, p. 4.
10. "Consumers' League Explains Position," *Calgary News-Telegram*, June 21, 1913, p. 26.
11. "Butchers' Licenses Reduced to $1 A Year; Vote Taken Under The Eyes of Women Advocates," *Morning Albertan*, November 25, 1913, p. 8.
12. "Consumers' League Favors Wholesale Market For City," *Morning Albertan*, April 24, 1914, p. 7.
13. "Consumers' League," *Calgary Daily Herald*, April 29, 1916, p. 6.
14. "Market Master Did Erase Names From Market Book," *Morning Albertan*, December 2, 1916, p. 6.
15. "Appeals To Women To Stand Behind The Public Market," *Morning Albertan*, December 9, 1920, p. 7.
16. "The Market Investigation," *Morning Albertan*, December 4, 1916, p. 3.
17. This did not happen, even though by the spring of 1914 Calgary's League membership had grown to over 1000 and Regina was reported to have

formed a League modeled on the Calgary plan (its Local Council ran the market there). Closer to home, Edmonton also established a very successful Consumers' League, but it concentrated on consumer education and a made-in-Edmonton campaign and left the city to manage its own poorly located public market.

18. Calgary agreed to adopt its more conservative objectives but retained its own name.
19. With the exception of the endorsement of importation and manufacture of oleo margarine, its record of accomplishments did not seem contentious — fish, poultry, and produce sales.
20. *1919 Annual Report,* National Council of Women of Canada, p.106–107. Newhall declined office in 1920.
21. "Tribute to Late Mrs. G. Newhall," *Calgary Daily Herald,* November 19, 1932, p.17.

Chapter 13

1. "The River Front," *Morning Albertan,* December 16, 1912, p. 3.
2. LCW Brief To November 1965 City Council Public Hearing On Zoning By-law, p.1 . GAI-LCW archives.
3. "$35 Million Face-Lift For Calgary Revealed," *Calgary Herald,* April 5, 1963, p. 1.
4. "River Beautification Speed-Up Forecast," *Calgary Herald,* April 6, 1963, p. 27.
5. The write-up underneath, "Your slip is showing Mr. Mayor," clarified that not all was being revealed, "Is there more to come? Bottom portion of map in mayor's office showing CP downtown plans was tucked in at area depicting city's southside. Mayor Harry Hays, left, rushed to cover up as hidden portion suddenly unrolled. His haste to hide the slip led to speculation of new developments in southeast Calgary. CP Vice-President Ian Sinclair laughs at confusion caused by unscheduled unveiling."
6. LCW minutes, general meeting, May 22nd, 1963, p. 1, GAI-LCW archives.
7. City of Calgary – CPR Development Proposals, p. 3, GAI-LCW archives.
8. Report on the Proposed Central Area Redevelopment Project, City of Calgary, van Ginkel Associates, June 24, 1963, p. 1-4.
9. "This Is Text Of Draft Agreement," *Albertan,* January 23, 1964, p. 2.
10. "Calgary Group Asks Commission To Study Scheme," *Albertan,* March 5, 1964, p. 3.
11. "The City's Performance," *Albertan,* March 7, 1964, p. 19.
12. "Solicitor's Charge Jars CP Hearing," *Calgary Herald,* March 6, 1964, p. 1.
13. "CPR Plan Seems Doomed," *North Hill News,* March 12, 1964, p. 1.
14. Letter to Mrs. Kay [sic] MacLennan, GAI-LCW archives, March 19, 1964.
15. "Mayor, Alderman Booed, Hissed At Noisy City-CP Project Forum," *Calgary Herald,* March 10, 1964, p. 19.
16. According to one source, the word used could have been "untruths." The mint word "disinformation" had yet to be coined.
17. "Solicitor To Stay With City: Mayor," *Calgary Herald,* March 10, 1964, p. 1.
18. "Mrs. Ruth Gorman Attacks CP Plan," *Albertan,* March 12, 1964, p. 11.

19. "Listening To Calgary Council Suggested As Murder Penalty," *Calgary Herald*, June 16, 1964, p. 21.
20. "Cost of CP Project Hiked By $5 Million," *Calgary Herald*, June 9, 1964, p. 19.
21. "Council To Eye Probe Proposal After 'Political Morality' Meet," *Calgary Herald*, June 9, 1964. p. 19.
22. "Death Blow," *Calgary Herald*, June 23, 1964, p. 4.
23. "A Revelation," *Albertan*, June 24, 1964, p. 4.
24. "LCW Sets Fall Date On Probe," *Calgary Herald*, June 27, 1964, p. 25
25. LCW executive minutes, October 8, 1964, Glenbow Archives.
26. "Former Mayors Gather To Celebrate Civic Centennial," *Calgary Herald*, April 30, 1994, p. B9.

Chapter 14

1. "Ranch Wife Denied Claim," *Rockyview News*, October 9, 1973, p. 1.
2. "No Evidence Of Partnership," *Calgary Herald*, July 15, 1974, p. 8.
3. "Plea For Half Husband's Ranch Fails," *Calgary Herald*, October 3, 1973, p. 45.
4. "Irene Murdoch Fund Initiation To Local Council Of Women," Patricia Krasinski Manuscripts, GAI Archives, March, 1974, p. 4.
5. *Ibid.*, p. 2.
6. *Ibid.*, p. 3.
7. "Council To Press For Halving Assets," *Calgary Herald*, April 29, 1972, p. 62.
8. "Fund Started to Pay Woman's Legal Fees," *Calgary Herald*, April 10, 1972, p. 22.
9. "Women Are On The March," *Albertan*, April 17, 1974, p. 10.
10. "Farm Wives Succeed In Equality Bids," *Albertan*, April 11, 1974, p. 2.
11. "Court Reserves Decision On Murdoch Divorce Battle," *Albertan*, September 30, 1976, p. 23. The estimate was used. During the September divorce proceedings, George Leslie testified on Irene Murdoch's behalf that he appraised Murdoch's land and associated ranching property at approximately $240 000.
12. GAI-LCW Archives.
13. "Report Of Meeting With Irene Murdoch," GAI-LCW Archives, February 19, 1975. Krasinski also reported Irene Murdoch's personal plight. She had suffered continually with her wired and broken jaw. It was not uncommon for her to be kept waiting in her lawyer's office hours beyond her appointment time or even "asked to come back the following day." Krasinski's comment: "This has been going on for six years. What other woman would have such patience and perseverance?"
14. GAI-LCW Files.
15. GAI-LCW Files.
16. GAI-LCW Files.
17. "Property Division 'Needs' Reform," *Albertan*, April 25, 1974, p. 5.
18. "Options Still Open For Mrs. Murdoch," *Calgary Herald*, May 17, 1974, p. 36.
19. GAI-Patricia Krasinski manuscripts, incomplete press release to the *Albertan* dated, May 21, 1974.
20. "Campaign Became Hysterical," *Calgary Herald*, July 15, 1974, p. 8.

21. "Mr. Murdoch Will Collect," *Calgary Herald,* July 16, 1974, p. 19.
22. "Schmidt's Language 'Abusive,'" *Calgary Herald,* July 24, 1974, p. 6.
23. GAI-LCW Archives, Letter dated July 30, 1974.
24. "Marriage Equality," *Calgary Herald,* March 12, 1975, p. 6.
25. "Farm Wives Ten Years After Murdoch," *Chatelaine,* March 1983, p. 59.